DOUBLE FEATURE

By The Same Author

Stamp Album

Coming Attractions

TERENCE STAMP

DOUBLE FEATURE

for the lovely
Lynn
from

Terence
Stamp

BLOOMSBURY

First published 1989
Copyright © 1989 by Terence Stamp

British Library Cataloguing Publication Data

Stamp, Terence
Double feature
1. Acting. Stamp, Terence – Biographies
I. Title
792'028'0924

ISBN 0 7475 0393 1

10   9   8   7   6   5   4   3   2   1

Photoset by Rowland Phototypesetting Ltd,
Bury St Edmunds, Suffolk
Printed in Great Britain by Butler & Tanner Ltd, Frome and London

'You take away the breath I was keeping for sunrise.'

Pete Townshend, 1967

PICTURE CREDITS

CONTENTS

IT BEGINS

1

I was once told that the Cherokee Indian believes the centre of the Universe is where he is, at any given moment. I wasn't familiar with the philosophy when my big break came, although I frequently experienced something akin to it. But then I was on such an ego trip it took a while to realise the Sixties weren't only happening to me.

They had barely drawn breath when I won the coveted title role in Peter Ustinov's film of *Billy Budd*, Ustinov's wife, Suzanne Cloutier, having no small hand in the choice. The day after the screen test I had been invited to their suite at the Connaught and while Peter took a transatlantic call in the bedroom, she told me that my presence on film had reminded her of Gérard Philipe, one of the three great loves of her life. She was quite forthcoming, considering we'd only just met, but then she was sophisticated and foreign, the first French woman I'd met, not counting the international table-tennis team who spoke no English. I stood by the fireplace – all the best hotels in London had them, I'd heard – and rested my arm on the mantelpiece in an attempt to look casual. Suzanne paced around me as though inspecting a bargain item.

'He's determined to take you,' she said, 'but you will have to be patient: it is not easy to convince the studio to take an unknown, especially an English. It may take time.'

'ABC?' I said.

'No, the Americans – Allied Artists is putting up the *monnaie*. Peter is clever: he will get what he wants, but *you* must sit still and be quiet.'

'Eh?'

'Not say anything to anybody until we tell you.'

'Ah!'

'Zees play that you are in, is this a problem?'

'Well, if it runs.'

'Will it? You think it's good?'

'Yeah, could. It's unusual. Lionel Bart's a talented writer. Could do.'

'We worry when the time comes. I'm telling you because Peter won't, he doesn't want to build your . . . '

'Hopes?'

'Yes, but I don't care, you will do this part.'

Peter came back into the room, doing his head-of-major-studio impersonation.

The play *Why the Chicken* was over and forgotten by the time the call came. We had opened at Wimbledon (the Ustinovs came and enjoyed it) and then taken it on the road, where Lionel tried everything he knew to prevent it being his first flop, even writing in a part for Mike Caine as my big brother, Honky, to lift the ending a bit. Mike was terrific as the slightly deranged heavy. When I'd given up hope of ever hearing, Ustinov rang, apologised for keeping me waiting so long and told me I was to play the part. He would send me the script to study prior to our departure for Spain in June, but I should keep the news to myself as he planned a surprise launch a few weeks before we were to begin shooting. It was our secret.

Mike and I had the flat at Ennismore Garden Mews to ourselves now, but Doug Sheldon called by most days. I couldn't keep this from them, so amidst much swearing to secrecy I broke the great news.

Mike said it called for a celebration, but as we were boracic it looked like instant coffee all round. Then there was a tooting outside and Doug, who was standing by the window, spotted Penny from over the road. She frequently parked the gun-metal Karman Ghia with its personalised registration plate in the mews opposite Number 12 and it hadn't taken her long to realise how hard-up her neighbours were. We often came home to find a steak from Harrods, or Rods, as she called it, pushed through our letter box. Doug opened the window and started dialoguing her.

Mike said to me, 'Go and cool him down, he'll be falling out the window.'

I went over and, when it became clear she didn't have anywhere in particular to go to, we invited her up for a drink. Being Penny, she nipped back home and brought us a bottle of champagne, Krüg. Mike thought it a good omen. He wasn't superstitious but he did have a thing about champagne. Every New Year's Eve he would go to great lengths to secure a bottle, raising his glass full of the fizz that ensured a well-heeled twelve months.

My promise of fame didn't weaken our team at all: Mike and Doug contributed with everything they had as though my success was theirs too. Doug placed himself and his car at my disposal, selflessly driving and waiting as my schedule became hectic. Mike went through the text with me every day and, when I decided to do it with a Bristol accent, he taught me a song, which I had to sing in dialect: 'My father is the Keeper of the Eddystone Light, He slept with a mermaid one fine night . . . ' I was cajoled into singing it everywhere. Sometimes, whilst walking in crowded streets, he'd start me off and, if I was too embarrassed, he would bellow it raucously until I joined in.

'If you can sing in a dialect, it makes speaking it a doddle,' he assured me. He didn't say, 'Not many people know that,' in those days, only raised a blond eyebrow in such a way that you knew it wasn't just hearsay but a theory tried and tested in the field.

'There's a lot of pressure up there in front of cameras, believe me. I've seen good actors, old troupers with years of experience on the boards, fall apart when the lights go on and it's all down to them. Stage actors who've never tried think it's a piece of cake! "Oh, there's always another take, luv!" But there ain't, it's not like that, the first take is always the last. When you get up there, see what a lot of manpower it entails, you realise that they're all waiting, watching to see how you perform – if you can deliver! It ain't slow, heavy, spread-out pressure like a first-night, it's sharp, hypodermic pressure. And lonely. And here's a funny thing, you have to resist playing to the crew. The camera is your lady, never forget it. Right, here endeth the first gospel; now: "My father is the Keeper of the Eddystone Light, He slept with a mermaid one fine night, From that union there came three, A kipper and a porpoise and the other was me."'

That was the only verse he knew, and we sang it over and over until I could do a West Country burr as good as the guy on the telly who'd written a book about cheese.

Early days as a blond.

I could never repay old Mike for the help he gave at the beginning and, when he decided I was cramping his style and went his own way, I didn't feel dumped. He'd spent a long time honing his dream, and who was I to question his realising it to perfection? I'm not sure I could have realised mine without a big hand from him.

It was Robert Krasker's notion to make me a blond. As he was one of the greatest cameramen of the day – *The Third Man*, to name a few – I wasn't in any position to argue; it was the only way to conform to the light-artist's vision of what was to be his last black and white film. I agreed to sacrifice my black mop, which was to be bleached white and then tinted ash-blond. The barnet had other ideas, however, finally succumbing after eight hours of peroxide. I did feel a bit silly sitting in Robert Fielding of Knightsbridge; crimpers hadn't yet become aristocrats and unisex salons were a thing of the future, but I had to admit that even allowing for the bleach burns on my scalp it looked better than I'd expected.

Two sisters had come my way and, although taken by the younger, it was the elder who scoured London with me searching for a jacket to fit my new look. Bike jackets were two a penny but I'd set my heart on a three-button roll-to-two like Mr Grant had worn in *North By Northwest*, only in black leather. One eventually surfaced in Westbourne Grove and, although it wasn't the softest skin, I thought I looked like the dog's dinner or, as my dad remarked later, 'Blimey! You look like not long I'll wait in that.' Things really hotted up once I'd had the dye job. I started to believe that perhaps blonds did have more fun.

My agent, Jimmy Fraser, had negotiated the deal with Bob Lennard. He'd secured me £900 for the film linked to an exclusive seven-year ABC contract. I was pretty green at the time; Ustinov was not around and Lennard had convinced Jimmy Fraser a deal with ABC would make it easier for Peter to sell me to the Americans. As I trusted Jimmy implicitly, I agreed, on two provisos: the salary would be doubled, on a sliding scale starting at £40 a week instead of £20 – and the screenplay for *You Must Be Joking*, which Mike and I had written, could be made into a film outside the deal. ABC agreed and I had no reason not to sign. I didn't actually feel good about it, although Mike said the regular readies would more than come in handy. As it turned out, the £900 was all I received contractually but ABC did buy me a suit, made-to-measure in a week, by Cyril Castle. It wasn't Savile Row, but as near enough as made no difference.

This bespoke charcoal-grey flannel was due to be finished, with only one fitting, on the morning of my big launch. In fact, Mr Castle had done precisely as briefed and completed the day before, just time enough for me to swan around in it a bit and shake out any little oversights, as he put it, which could then be corrected in good time if necessary. That was the plan, anyway. Barry Norman (not the star of stage, screen and radio cab he is today) somehow sniffed out who was to be Ustinov's new player and broke the story a day early on the front page of the *Daily Mail*.

Our phone, which was next to Mike's bed, rang at seven-fifteen a.m. He picked it up, gave me a shout and, like Byron, I awoke and was famous. It was Bob Webb, ABC's intrepid publicist from Elstree. The *Mail* had leaked the story. He'd had a quick powwow with Ustinov and in the tradition of great studio PRs was planning to turn mishap into miracle: the press launch was being brought forward a day. The Savoy's River Room had been secured. Showbiz scribes were being contacted as we spoke. All I had to do was pick up my new whistle and flute from Sackville Street, wear it with a clean shirt and meet him at the Strand entrance of the hotel at three-thirty p.m. Bob intended to authorise a studio car to run me around, but I assured him I didn't need it. I knew Doug would give his eye teeth rather than miss the action, and what action it was.

Mr Castle was as proud as could be with his single-breasted creation, which was considerably sleeker than my previous made-to-measure from Brick Lane. It was minus the gangster shoulders, for a start. This suit had a soft natural line and it succeeded in making me look pencil slim. The matt black horn buttons – I'd never come across horn before – were apparently the berries. Doug giggled in the corner of the curtained fitting-room at my efforts to give the impression that this was an everyday occurrence.

Mr Castle said finally, 'Well, what do you think?'

'Not bad,' I said. I was still trying to get used to the silk purse that was emerging in the full-length mirror. My hair wasn't yet the ash that Krasker had demanded as the dude at the salon had done it 'baby-blond' which, in his considered opinion, was less common. 'Bona omee,' he'd remarked when he'd finished combing me out, a moment almost as traumatic as if I'd undergone cosmetic surgery.

'Not bad,' scoffed Mr Castle, jerking me back to reality. 'Not bad?'

'Oh Tel,' said Doug, 'don't be poultry.'

'Poultry?' said Mr Castle, lifting a Tyrone Power eyebrow and glancing from me to Doug and back again, as though he'd suddenly discovered two escapees from bedlam in his shop. Now I come to think about it, the tailor did bear more than a passing resemblance to Mr Power, my hero from *The Razor's Edge*, but then again, maybe it was only me seeing the bright side of everything that day.

'He means paltry, I think.' I pointed at Doug, who was grinning ear to ear and hopping from one foot to the other as though in urgent need of seeing a man about a dog.

'He's excited because he'll get to wear his own gear for a change.' Doug gave me a thumbs-up.

'It's splendid, Mr Castle. Perfect. I don't think I'll ever feel the way I do now about a suit.'

It was the master tailor's turn to be embarrassed. He shrugged his shoulders and adjusted the jacket on mine, even though a brain surgeon would've had difficulty easing a scalpel between the coat and my shirt collar. The tailor might have thought I was giving him a bit of flannel, but at the time I had a sense that I would never experience anything quite like this moment again. I hadn't even heard of the old Greek from Ephesus, let alone his theory about never stepping in the same river twice, but that day in St James's with the white Sprite outside ready to take me anywhere, I knew my words to be true.

Mr Castle was taking no chances on me ruining his suit's debut by wearing a tie that was out of keeping. He surmounted this problem by selecting one from his stock and giving it to me as a present.

'Gratis,' he said, 'for luck,' as he escorted Doug and me out of Number 10, wincing as I clambered over the car door and slid into the bucket seat clutching the garment still on its bespoke hanger. His choice of tie was interesting: silk, of course, but almost heavy enough to be a madder, its blend of muted colours saved from being too conservative by the glow they gave off.

Doug and Mike watched me get dressed like two proud fathers.

I had borrowed a decent shirt from Lionel Bart's *Great Gatsby* collection and had pulled a knot into the tie even my dad would have approved of. The shoes were the problem. I knew you could always tell the measure of a dresser by the look of his feet so it was safe to assume the doyens of Fleet Street would be equally well informed. The Clark's deserts wouldn't cut the mustard on this outing. I did possess a hand-benched pair of full brogues that had once belonged to a relative of Marie Devereux. She'd contributed them to our audition outfit. Caine couldn't get into them and they'd fallen to me, but they were a weathered tan and, whilst today I'd ease into them without a second thought, that afternoon I wasn't loose enough to match brown shoes with dark grey. It would have to be the black side-lace-ups I'd sprung for from John Michael's first shop, when I was at Webber D. They'd looked unusual in the King's Road window but from the moment I left the establishment I wasn't happy with them. They didn't suit my Levi's and I wound up wearing them when only black would do, like today. As I already had Li's shirt on, Doug offered to give them a brush. I breathed a sigh of relief when he located a tin of Cherry Blossom that still contained a rind of polish. We congregated in the kitchen, Mike and I having a last Disque Bleu while Doug beavered away, squatting on the marbled pink rubber tiles that were almost black with grime. Mike regarded the short laces let diagonally into the side of the shoe with scepticism.

'You do have some quaint ideas about gear, my old Tel,' he said. I didn't comment.

Doug said from the floor, 'Do you think those socks make it, Tel?' nodding to the shocking puce cotton novelties I was standing in.

'They make it because I can get my shoes on over them,' I said. 'When I get my hands on some bread, I'm gonna buy socks every colour of the bloody rainbow, so I can forget about it.' It seemed I'd been concerned with socks for most of my life. Early on, my gran had taught me how to darn the big holes – spuds we called them – with the help of an egg cup, and here I was on the threshold of stardom with only two undarned pairs to my name.

Mike had meandered over to the stable window which was open and looked out on to the last cottage on the other side of the mews. It was shaped like a wedge of cheese, the thinnest end being only two feet thick. I'd once said you'd need to be a razor blade to live in the place, and ever since then the unknown resident had been referred to as Wilkinson, or sword. Mike turned in to face us, leaning on the bottom half of what I suppose was once the opening through which the hay was delivered.

'I'd like to play a character in a film who never wears anything that matches,' he said profoundly. Doug got up, proudly rubbing his corduroy sleeve across the toecaps of the shoes.

'Why's that, Mike?' he asked.

'I dunno,' replied Mike, 'it's just something I'd like to do.'

Doug drove me to the Savoy. I'd just climbed out of the car and Doug was wishing me luck, when Bob Webb swung through the revolving doors, his face red.

'Oh boy, I'm glad you're here,' he said, 'over thirty people have turned up.'

'That's good, isn't it?' I said.

'Terrific, but I'll have to drag you off at five-thirty. We've got a spot on the six o'clock news. Live from the Aldwych.'

I heard Doug say, 'Strewth-t.' His voice sounded distant. 'You mean going out on the telly at six?' He wrinkled his forehead like Hardy Kruger.

'Yeah – great, isn't it? Bit of luck,' Bob beamed across at Doug.

'I'll have to get a message to my mum and dad,' I said, 'can't have them miss that. Christ, what's the Hobbses' number?'

'We've got to get you into the River Room, son,' Bob reminded me.

Doug said, 'Don't worry about it, Tel. I'll take care of it, you worry about that lot upstairs. Hobbs, was it?'

'Yeah, 13 Egham Road, Albert Dock number. Just ask 'em to please let me mum know.' Doug put the car into gear, spun it around and took off. At the Savoy Grill corner he gave a Montgomery Clift wave, without looking back.

2

I'd never met any of the press before, had yet to experience them on the turn. I strolled into the River Room feeling as cool as freshly peeled cucumber. I could have spared myself the concern about the black lace-ups.

The large room, which looked out over the Thames, was filled with people drinking and nibbling at bits from the tables. I wondered where my dad's tug, the *Rodeo*, was this afternoon: the tide looked high. Bob and I stood by the door not knowing quite what to do, while twenty feet away everyone near Peter was laughing, including a giant of a man I recognised as the usually sombre Robert Ryan. I needn't have come, I thought. Bob held up his hand and for a dreadful second I thought he was going to announce me, but instead he greeted a chap who came over.

Bob said, 'This is the man you're here to meet, let me introduce Terence Stamp.'

'I'm from the *Mirror*,' the man said.

'I've been reading Jane for years,' I countered.

'Is that right?' he said, scribbling shorthand into a little pad. I didn't feel the need to answer.

'Your folks real cockneys?' He looked up and winked at me.

'Yep.'

'Where do you come from, Terry? You don't mind if I call you Terry?'

'No,' I said, 'it's my name.' I knew that most people, unfamiliar with the East End, would have heard only of the notorious Cable Street. Also, Bob had told me that he figured the rags to riches angle would secure the most column inches.

'Cable Street,' I said, 'born in Cable Street.'

The biro flashed more symbols across the paper.

'Ole man still work the tugs, does he, your dad, I mean?'

The intrepid Bob Webb.

'Man and boy, fourteen years. Probably out there now.'

'You don't say.' He beckoned to someone. 'Like to get a few snaps, Terry, if you don't mind.'

'It's what I'm here for,' I said, returning his wink.

Bob introduced me to other people. They worked in pairs: one asked me questions while the other snapped away with a camera and they all seemed fascinated by the fact that Dad drove a tug. Thank God he'd been promoted and I didn't have to tell them he was a stoker. Nobody asked what experience I'd had or how I came by the part. I think everyone assumed Ustinov had bumped into me on Petticoat Lane. I probably wouldn't have been so flash if I'd known I was being transformed into Tugboat Terry, a name that would cling like a hair in my mouth. The photographer from the *Daily Mirror* took me out on to the river bank, bought me an ice-cream and photographed me eating it. When I was duly returned, Bob and I headed off to the TV station, arriving by taxi although the journey was only a few hundred yards. I was whisked into a minute studio, introduced to the newscaster and seated in a chair opposite him. The camera behind him looked me over as a red bulb above the lens was pointed out.

'When that lights up, we're on.'

I nodded. The light glowed, the interviewer shifted in his seat and the questionnaire on his lap slipped to the floor. I watched his hand groping for it as he continued to look my way. I thought: This guy's more rattled than I am, I'll stay put. I smiled encouragement. His fingers eventually retrieved the notes and he started asking me about myself. Unexpectedly, I felt at home in the little pressure-cooker although it was only when the red light dimmed and I'd shaken hands with my interviewer that I realised how painless it had been. I rejoined Bob Webb who'd watched me on a monitor.

'You did great,' he said.

'Are you sure?'

'Yeah, why d'you ask?'

'It wasn't slow? Didn't sound gormless?'

'No, on the contrary, smooth and deliberate is how I'd describe your essential style, to use a mountaineering term. Your suit looked terrific, too.'

We walked back to the Savoy, but the River Room was empty except for a few die-hards who were putting an end to the Scotch.

One of the best cornets I ever had.

'Where would you like to go? I'll drop you off,' Bob said.

'I'm fine. I think I'll just stroll for a bit.'

'That's right. You enjoy your anonymity – it may be the last chance you'll have.'

I looked at him, not fully taking in what he said. He grinned, showing wolfish teeth, all up-front trying to get a look-in.

'You're going to be a famous young lad tomorrow.'

My tomorrow was still a long way off. I walked home. I was glad Bob had mentioned my impending loss of anonymity; it made me really appreciate that evening. St James's Park was quiet and full of shadows. I strolled by the lake, watching a painted duck, brown, black and grey. What neat colours for a winter outfit: grey silk shirt, brown waistcoat, black Shetland jacket. The brown was the key, I decided, the clockwork paddler's brown feathers were chocolate, without a taste of red.

I crossed the blushing tarmac in front of the palace and slipped on to the shaded grass carpet. There was a hush beneath the giant planes, but then there always was – Green Park is the contemplative link in the chain of parks that stretches across London. Knightsbridge was still warm and populated; a few girls were even braving the May evening in summer cottons. I floated through the window-shoppers in a world of my own, suspended between reality and illusion. One of them, but at the same time apart, aware of a sense – like the one that stopped me from bumping into anybody – that I was about to join an exclusive club, whose membership I'd hankered after for many years.

I came into the mews via the hole in the wall at Rutland Street. As I turned the corner into our road proper I saw Doug's car parked at the top end. A shower had started and the first raindrops were giving the cobbled street a shine. Then I saw Doug sitting on the doorstep. He jumped up when he saw me and bounded up like a puppy who'd arrived home first.

'Man, you were great.'

'Did I do it?'

He giggled, 'Did you do it? I was proud! Me, was I proud!'

I let us in. Once inside I collapsed on to the sofa, momentarily exhausted. Doug stood by the TV that we'd perched on the cupboard behind the armchair. He pointed at the box.

'On that screen, that screen, you shone out, like...' He paused. 'Like a Mazda bulb.' He stopped, astounded by the fiery tongue that had descended on him.

'Pink, you mean? That's something on a black and white set.'

'That guy who was interviewing you, he was blown away.' He beamed at the memory.

'He dropped his questions,' I said.

'Come on, man, you were great, own up.'

'I did feel pretty good up there, Doug, to tell you the truth.'

'And the press conference, how did that go?'

I realised he was gasping for details, anything that constituted success. I'd have been the same. Our life had been so devoid of it.

'It was a breeze,' I said. 'Where's Caine?'

'He went out, pulled a mystery. Oh, he left a note.' He pattered into the bedroom and came back with two scraps of paper. One in Mike's hand said, 'Couldn't have done better myself. See you later.' And, as an afterthought, 'If you feel flat out, aim my mattress in the living-room.' Whenever one of Mike's dates looked like staying the night the sleeping arrangements were subtly rearranged. Mike had perfected a technique of picking up the top mattress complete with all his bedclothes, running it into the living-room and dropping it neatly so that it fell ready to use behind the sofa. By the expressions on their faces, some girls must have wondered what they had let themselves in for as they witnessed this expertise. The other note, also in Mike's writing, was from my brother Chris, who was working as a prop man on what was to be Gary Cooper's last movie. 'Superb, glad you didn't change your name. The first famous Stamp not on an envelope.'

I put the notes in the left inside pocket of my jacket, and then realised I still had it on. I started to take it off.

Doug said, 'What would you like to do?'

'I dunno.'

'Come on, Smiler, think about it. What would you most like to do?'

'Anything?'

'Anything, your carriage awaits.' He pulled his backless driving gloves from the angled pocket of his fave-rave Jimmy Dean windbreaker. I could see he wanted to drive, wanted it to be like old times for one last evening. Neither of us knew if it would be the same again.

'I'd really like to see Ethel and Tom – Christ! Did you get the message to them?'

'Done!' He spread his hands. 'All done.'

'OK, ace, let's go.'

We skimmed over the cobbled backdoubles heading east, Doug at the wheel. He knew the way from endless trips we'd made to enjoy Mum's Sunday roast, but he let me call the route, conscious I might want to look at special landmarks, as though leaving for good. We left the West End via the Tower of London and drove down the Highway past Meredith and Drew, where Bernie Wilson and I had fried crisps. I wondered if he'd seen me on telly. Past the block where the Cosgrove family lived – long Sunday afternoons spent playing cards with Johnny Bradford and Ken Jude with Brian's mum supplying rounds of tongue sandwiches cut in neat triangles. It was funny the things that came back to me and in the end I asked Doug to turn his radio on: I didn't like the look of the feelings that kept surfacing and thought I'd blot them out. If I'd known myself a bit better I'd have almost wondered if I was having second thoughts about what I was doing.

As we slipped into the Commercial Road, passing Cable Street where it becomes East India Dock Road, it stopped raining. Doug, doing his best to accommodate my fast-changing moods, said, 'Would you like the top down?'

'No, we'll take it off for the run back if it holds up.'

The enclosed space comforted me, offered me protection against the tigers that roamed outside. The lightness I'd felt all day was dimming.

I'd taken off from the East End without giving a thought to what fame would be like, only concerned with achieving it. Well, I'd soon know. Over Silvertown Bridge, right at Beckton Road and into the top end of Chadwin. It didn't smell the same, somehow: it was gearing itself for the move into middle class. Fake leaded windows were erupting and a carriage lamp proudly adorned the house of the local coalman, the handsome Mr Diprose. It didn't seem possible, Plaistow becoming ponsified. My mind went back to the first car we had parked in our street, bought by old Jim Letton. He couldn't drive but it made no difference. He would be in or around it from dawn to dusk, painting, polishing, but mostly sitting grasping the steering wheel, staring out through the wind-screen, motoring to God only knew where.

The light from the sitting-room shone on to the lace curtained front-door windows as Dad answered our knock. We had an overhead light and a shade for the passage, but Dad used electricity sparingly, and the light was never switched on. He was still in his work clothes, so they hadn't been out.

'Hello, son,' he said, 'come on in.'

Mum rose from the armchair by the wireless as we came in, but when she caught sight of me she stopped and stood not quite square on her feet, as though a wasp, which she couldn't see, had entered the room. It was a moment before I took in how alien I must have looked to her, with my bleached curls and elegant outfit. Her eyes kept flicking to the twelve-inch Ferguson on its stand and I realised that, more important than any of this, they had seen me on the magic box. I was no longer their Terry with his tantrums and moods, but a glittering stranger beamed into their home by the cathode tube. I moved across to where she stood and gave her a hug. I heard Doug say, 'What d'you think?'

I turned to face him and Dad, putting my arm around Mum's shoulders. There were two bottles on the table, a quart of light ale and a pint of Cream Label milk stout.

'Did yer see him on the news?' Doug added.

Dad looked at Mum and they nodded at each other.

'Did I do OK?'

They nodded again.

'Didn't let you down, did I?'

They nodded no. This is terrible, I thought. The room appeared dim, small. Doug and I seemed to fill it.

'What about a cuppa?' I said, putting things on familiar ground. I followed Mum into the scullery where she told me about Mrs Straffon showing her the newspaper. Was that only this morning?

In the living-room Dad said to Doug, 'Turn up for the book, eh?'

I could almost hear Doug grinning. 'You can say that again, Mr S.'

I was glad Doug had come. What is it that allows the Jewish race to corner the market on sentiment? How naturally they share emotions. Even a stoic, like my dad, with a shell as thick as a landcrab, presented no problem to old Doug. He went straight in, cutting the iron bun with one swipe.

'Mates at work mop you up, did they? Wait till tomorrow.'

'Tomorrow?'

'Yeah, press launch this afternoon. In all the papers tomorrow.'

'Blimey,' said Dad.

I smiled at Mum, who was warming the pot, and whispered across to her, 'Hope Dad doesn't mind, all the journalists wanted to know about his job on the river.'

Mum turned at the sink. 'He loves it, really,' she said, 'but you know what he's like.'

'How about you, were you pleased?' I asked.

Mum nodded and looked me over.

'Oh Terry, what have they done to your lovely hair?'

'It's your fault,' I said. 'You should never have let me have that Toni. That's what started me off.'

Mum had helped me to perm my hair when I first started at grammar school – I'd been taken in by the 'Which Twin has the Toni?' campaign and pestered her until she'd bought the pack. I'd slept in the curlers and the next morning my hair looked like I'd had a near escape with an electric chair. I couldn't get a comb through it and had been frightened to attend school, but Mum had made me go.

'You made your bed, you lay on it,' she'd said.

I'd gone, but the most unnerving thing was that nobody at school mentioned it, even though I looked like Mr Therm for weeks. We chuckled, re-living it. What a brew of events our scullery could have recalled.

'I might have missed all this, Mum, if I had done what you wanted and never left home.'

'I know.'

'Why? Why didn't you want me to leave?'

She didn't speak for a moment and then said, 'I was frightened you wouldn't eat properly and you'd wear damp underwear.'

As we were leaving, Dad said out of the corner of his mouth, 'Don't let it go to your head, son.'

I awoke the next morning to hear Mike answering our phone.

'It's for you, Tel,' he said, holding out the receiver as I stumbled across the bedroom to take it. He turned over in his bed and tried to go back to sleep. I sat on the floor at the foot of the delicate

Tugboat Terry at the Savoy.

table whose only purpose was to hold the telephone. 'A right nancyboy table,' my dad would have called it. My warm pyjamas made contact with the not so warm carpet. I remembered I was famous. For a split second I thought Brigitte Bardot might be calling me.

'Hello,' I said, trying to sound as butch as possible.

'Hello, love.' It was Mum. 'Have you seen the papers?'

'No, haven't bin out yet.'

'Oooh, it's everywhere, neighbours pushing 'em through the letter box, even the toffee ones, pictures of you everywhere. Oooh, can't believe it.'

'What does Dad say?'

'I dunno. He's on early shift this week. Tugboat Terry, it calls you in the *Mirror*. Oooh, whatever will his mates think?'

B.B. didn't call that morning.

When I finally put down the phone it was past eleven. Mike had bathed and used the hot water so I settled for a wash in cold. Cleaning my teeth it occurred to me how ordinary everything felt, like any other day. It couldn't be true, could it? Fame hadn't appeared to change anything. I put the crushing thought out of my mind and dashed off down to Knightsbridge to buy all the papers.

3

Filming isn't all it's cracked up to be, even under the best circumstances. It's said that shooting on a train presents the most problems, but whoever said it has *never* made a film at sea. The galleon left Alicante at five-thirty every morning and by sun-up we were out of sight of land, ready to make the most of the usable light. That and the roll and pitch of the ship were Robert Krasker's first problems; the struggle with motion sickness and the effects of my first jab for smallpox were mine. There were subtler psychological burdens but these didn't even take shape until later. The first weeks were unnerving: all the cast were a good deal older than me and most liked a drink – if I didn't head straight for the bar after work, nobody sought me out. After the immunisation made me really ill, Suzanne Ustinov insisted I move into the spare room of their apartment, but they were busy and I spent most of my free time alone. I cadged sticky Polaroid prints from the wardrobe department or the continuity girl (the only people allowed to use the expensive instant camera) and posted them to Mum and Dad; writing home was the only thing that eased my feeling of homesickness during the six long weeks of location work. I missed Mum's cooking too; the plump steak and kidney puds and steaming roasts I'd grown up with had in no way prepared me for Spanish coastal cuisine. The answer to some of these difficulties came in the form of an American photographer who'd been assigned to cover the film. No ordinary smudger, no ordinary guy, but Sanford H. Roth from the Magnum Agency – the man who had been with Jimmy Dean when he'd driven the Porsche Spyder to the Salinas races.

'I think I'll just take her out and warm her up a little,' Jimmy had said to Sandy a few minutes before the crash. I didn't know any of this when I first met him but he must have noticed how lonely I looked and how skinny I was becoming as he made it his business to hang out with me when we docked in the evening. Sandy took me on excursions to great local markets, loaded me with fresh fruit and introduced me to paella – it was the first Spanish grub which, to my insular British palate, didn't taste as though it had been cooked in Brylcreem.

Carrying out Ustinov's instructions to shoot 'special material' on me, he dreamed up all kinds of schemes that entailed getting out and about along the coast. At that time, Benidorm was a deserted beach with one modest hotel; I shot there one Sunday with Sandy and a local beauty he'd brought along.

'Don't want the folks in the US to think you're a faggot,' he said.

(Until then I'd thought faggots were something that went into stew when you couldn't afford stewing steak.) He saw everything we did in terms of layout: this for *Life*, that for *Stern* or *Paris Match*. He was determined to give me a spectacular launch and I was a willing accomplice. Sadly, he died before placing any of his material but his pictures are a testament to an extraordinary fella and a document of the beginning of a golden section in my life.

The situation I found myself in during the location shooting of *Billy Budd* was like nothing I had encountered before. In a foreign country for the first time and without old chums to turn to, I had nothing to grab hold of, was even deprived of the everyday comforter, a cup of tea. 'Up shit creek without a paddle,' I'd heard my dad say of similar conditions. I found it difficult to sleep in the heat of the night and hard to wake up in the morning. I kept telling myself: This is a film I'm part of – all my heroes must have gone through this, how else *Captain Blood* or *Against All Flags*? But the movies I'd loved as a boy seemed so different from what I was facing every day on the rolling ship, that all comparisons were pointless. My sense of presence, that dreamlike quality I'd always retained when experiencing a dislocation of environment, was the one constant in the uncontrollable sequence unfolding all around me.

During the first few weeks I clung to this token of stability and, once I'd begun to understand the pace dictated by filming, the

Leaving Chadwin Road for location shooting.

All at sea.

sheer technicality of the work involved, I noticed odd things thrown up by my psyche which complemented the role I was to play. My only experience prior to location work in Alicante was the screen test that landed me the part: I'd been so hyped up I'd hardly noticed the mechanics of filming. On the second day out I'd watched John Neville, the matinée idol of the Old Vic, splendid in blue and white officer's costume, step up to his mark. Somebody hit a switch and the big lights – brutes, the electricians called them – crashed on. Even at midday, their power countered the sunlight on John's classic profile and everyone on the boat became quiet, still.

The first assistant, the Honourable Mike Burkett, whispered, 'Ready, sir.'

Ustinov said, 'Turn over.' The camera started whirring gently as Ustinov nodded to Neville and then said, 'Action.'

The small, illuminated corner of the ship became everyone's point of focus and, under the pressure of such combined energy, the atmosphere in the set-up area seemed to condense, become palpable, almost a mist. John Neville appeared to acknowledge the platform it provided as he went to work. The alchemy of movie acting, the scale and intimacy, became clear to me. It wasn't cold, formidable or threatening, as I'd heard, but the opposite: warm and encompassing. Something to wrap oneself in, to rely on. Be supported by. I couldn't wait my turn, or could I? Mike Caine had said often enough, 'The close-up *is* the movie, son. If you can't cut the mustard in the close-up, forget it.'

It turned out my first scene was with Claggart, Robert Ryan himself. Ryan kept himself aloof from me, I'm sure to make my job a bit easier. In the shot I come upon him unexpectedly, and the surprise causes Billy to stammer, the first evidence of the young sailor's impediment. I had based my stutter on that of Ken Tynan, the critic, who was the only person I'd met who had one. I wanted to portray it as an emotional difficulty and had tried to work out what sort of problem would block speech. When we were all set to go, a wisp of melancholy settled over me which would have been the perfect underlay for the action, but a boat drifted into camera-frame and Robert Krasker called a halt to the shot until it sailed on. As we waited, my mood deepened. Before I knew it, I was in tears and hid myself in a deserted part of the boat. Ustinov soon found me and asked what had happened. I tried to explain but felt overwhelmed by the thought that I wouldn't be able to capture the moment again when the camera was set.

Ustinov appeared to understand. He said, 'Of course you will, and if you're not ready we'll wait until you are.'

Even so, Mike Caine's statement on close-ups had played on my mind during that week's shooting, particularly since Ustinov appeared to be easing me into the work as smoothly as possible. He spent the first few days' filming establishing shots of the ships with me climbing the rigging in the background, but by the time he came in close on me I knew how long it took the film to be processed in Madrid and the precise moment the cans were returned to Alicante for Ustinov to view the rushes. That evening I hung around the restaurant on the ground floor of the apartment where Peter and Suzanne were staying, picking at one of those pale Spanish steaks and watching the door for the Ustinovs' arrival. They finally came in with a whole junket of journalists whom Allied Artists had flown out to cover the start of the film: Peter didn't even see me, let alone tell me if my close-up passed muster.

The following day I wasn't on call so I had a lie-in and listened to Peter's new Aston Martin taking off for the dock. Although most actors complain about the early calls and long hours of film scheduling, I've always found the days not called to location far worse, in spite of the extra sleep.

On my first and, as it turned out, my only day not wanted on location I was moping (sulking might be more apt) in the same restaurant where I had jealously observed the press basking in the Ustinov warmth and gaiety, when Suzanne came in to have lunch. As it was only one-thirty – the locals didn't start lunch till three – we had the place to ourselves. She soon realised I was down and wouldn't let it drop until I told her why. I confessed my worries and Mike's thesis on the movie as close-up.

'Who is this Michael Caine?' she wanted to know.

'He's my mate.'

'Is he an expert, this Michael?'

'Well, it's only his theory, but he's a smart cookie, you know.'

'I don't know, that is why I ask.'

'You don't agree, then?'

'Look, I think it is not as simple as this, but that is not the point here. You are depressed, probably because you are homesick. You 'ave not been invited to rushes. Nobody 'as told you if you are any good. Right?'

'Yeah, I guess . . . '

'Homesickness is one thing you will have to get used to. It is like that if one is an *artiste*. Your home is not a place, it is your head. Excuse me, in your head. Second, Peter thinks, as this is your first film, it is better for you not to see the rushes. It is, how you say, magnified, the image on the screen. He feels it might disturb what you are doing, you might start to change things if you look now, because you will only be watching you, getting everything out of proportion. Always remember, Peter is a genius; if you're not good, he will make you good. So you have nothing to worry about. Just relax, enjoy this film. If he doesn't speak, this is the best, it means he is happy with what you do.'

Gradually my despair focused on a direction in Ustinov's screen-play describing the moment before the innocent Billy is to die. In this key scene the noose is dropped around his neck and the script indicates various shots of the crew's agony, their outrage quelled by Billy's serenity. Ustinov had only directed me obliquely, so it felt indelicate to approach him about it head on, yet I couldn't think of a way to broach the subject. The scene festered in my mind, bothering me whenever I thought of it.

On the Sunday before flying out to Spain to commence work on the film, Lionel Bart had asked me over for a morning cuppa. When I arrived at the mews he took me round to Anthony Newley's house. I'd been impressed by Newley, or Newburg as Lionel called him, ever since we had been shown *Oliver Twist* in the air raid shelter which doubled as a cinema at Plaistow Grammar, and I jumped at the chance to meet him.

The grown-up Artful Dodger opened the door and, before I could be introduced, dashed to an open piano in the living-room and proceeded to play and sing the score of a new show he'd just collaborated on, *Stop the World I Want to Get Off*. Lionel and I stood in the doorway, entranced.

As each song ended Lionel would try to speak but Tony would say, 'Oh, and what about this one?' 'What Kind of Fool Am I', 'Gonna Climb a Mountain' and many more were sung to us hot from the sky, Tony's plaintive voice squeezing the high notes into falsetto.

It was so rich, so unexpected a privilege, that we were left speechless. Lionel finally said, 'Groovy, man, real groovy,' as they started a composer's rap, with me standing there like a lemon.

It was only when Lionel was about to leave he thought to introduce me.

'Oh, Tone, this is Terry Stamp. He's off to Spain tomorrow to start his first film.'

Tony Newley focused on me, empathising, instantly aware of what I was feeling. He smiled but his eyes were rock-steady.

'First film, eh?'

'Yeh.'

Silence. The eyes were still locked on to mine.

What to do? I floated across the tracks of our glance.

A moment, then he said, 'If in doubt, do nothing.' Newburg lowered his eyes and crooned, 'You gotta pick a pocket or two', cockily beaming at the lyric's composer. The *prasad* (nourishment) had been offered from the table of a master.

Whenever I thought about the difficulties of my key scene I remembered Newley's advice but I didn't have the guts to let it go at that and the worry kept returning like a moth to a flame.

Wilfrid Lawson came out to Spain to play the part of the Dansker, Melville's old salt who is aboard the ship on to which Billy has been press-ganged. All the cast were overjoyed at the prospect of such a distinguished player joining the ranks. I remembered how sweet he'd been when as a student I'd met him on the Underground; I sat near him the evening he arrived in the hotel bar, although I didn't know what to say to the great man and spent a long time staring at his highly polished lace-up boots. The silence didn't appear to bother him. He smiled reassuringly at me across a table of empty glasses, then stood up. I thought he was leaving, but he turned round and clasped his hair together at the nape of his neck.

'I thought I might wear it like this,' he giggled, 'tied in a little tail. What d'ya think?'

One of my greatest ambitions – to be in a film with Wilfrid Lawson, to watch him work – was not to be. The doctor hired by the insurance company examined him and judged him unfit for the rigours of the work at sea. He wasn't ill, only fragile. The company insurance wouldn't cover Wilfrid and although Ustinov wanted to play him anyway, Allied Artists put their moneyed foot down. Peter had to send the marvellous actor home. After he'd told Wilfrid he came and told me; we were both close to tears.

I said, 'The irony is when the film is finished and out, Wilfrid will be around and wonderful.'

'I know, I know. That's what drives me mad.' We were right. Long after the movie had been released I went to the Arts Theatre Club to see Wilfrid play in Gorki's *Lower Depths*. He was up there, the greatest British actor not to be offered a knighthood, doing it in the way only he could.

The day dawned when I was to hang.

Over six long weeks I had pondered my past, trying, without success, to recall the most peaceful moment of my life and hoping to dredge up a memory which would power an emotion intense enough to quell my mutinous shipmates. I hadn't succeeded. By the time Ustinov had shot all the set-ups he needed to proceed with the execution, it was four o'clock. The sun was hot but dropping. I pulled on the fur-lined jerkin that Anthony Mendelson had designed for my final scene and put on a pair of shoes: the only time Billy is seen without bare feet. It was Ustinov's idea that the 'good sailor', conscious of the fact that he is appearing in public, as it were, makes an effort to look his best.

I stepped up to my mark. The noose was blowing a little in the wind just over my head. I hadn't come up with anything. I'd have to follow Tony Newley's advice and do nothing. Bob Krasker did his final checks. The sun was beating on my right cheek, balanced by the light from the brutes on the other side.

Ustinov asked if I was ready.

I shrugged. Nothing in my head.

The first assistant nodded to the sound engineer.

'Sound turning,' he replied.

A little gust of wind fanned my face, momentarily cooling the heat of the sun. The opening notes of a tune started to come into my head. Anxious, I tried to push it away. Then I recognised the melody. It was 'Little Dolly Daydreams', the song Granny Kate would sometimes sing to herself as she made my marmalade sandwiches in the kitchen at Barking Road. I could hear the camera rolling and feel its subtle presence, but I went with the song. All sorts of memories came crowding in: long afternoons during my first summer break at Plaistow Grammar spent on the holiday

Captain Ustinov.

assignment, given to me by Miss Fowler, the lovely art teacher. I'd gone to my gran's house every day and worked on the mat in front of her black Zebra'd stove, laboriously re-creating a scene from the Beckton Road Lido with a box of Derwent water pencils. I listened to my Granny Kate, Kate, who I loved most in the world, singing her lullaby. The camera was rolling. I slowly turned my head towards my fellow shipmates. Was this how it would be if I were to die? Would Kate be there waiting for me on the other side, wiping the excess Golden Shred from her knife on to the top of the quartered sandwich? The hangman placed the noose over my head. I felt the rope rough on the skin of my neck. He squeezed my shoulder and stepped back. I breathed out the feelings inside of me towards the sailors in the well of the ship. I looked at Ustinov.

'God bless Captain Vere,' I shouted.

4

I was overjoyed to be back in London. Thin but tanned by the long days at sea, all I wanted was to see my family and friends and to wear my black leather jacket. The Sixties had started without me; I was determined to catch up.

'There's a new dance, Tel,' said Mike Caine. 'It's called the twist. Nobody's cracked it – everybody's in the same boat.'

'Spare me the boat, Mike.'

'You gotta learn it, son. No one can do it, see. I've been practising.'

He grabbed the living-room doorknob, and executed the few passes he'd mastered.

'It's the twist, see,' he said.

'Looks downright pony to me.'

'Exactly. No one can do it, except John Fenton.' He named the scourge of the Café des Artistes who could dance anything.

'And he taught you?' I enquired.

'Well, I've bin clocking him, haven't I? That's how he does it.'

He grabbed the doorknob again and did a re-run.

'There's this new club as well, in Park Lane, called the Saddle Room. Can't get in there. It's a real toffee place, full of high-class crumpet.'

'Why can't ya get in?'

'They have to know you, it's membership, I think.'

'I'll get us in, we'll go tonight.'

At last, I thought, a chance to put my new fame to use. Mike put on a tie. I put on my leather lounge-jacket and we both wore the black elastic-sided boots I'd treated us to.

The film stunt-man done up in a tight uniform on the door said, 'Are you a member, sir?'

'I'm Stamp,' I said, 'and he's with me.'

'Sorry, Terry, didn't recognise you for a minute.'

'You're excused. This is Caine, Michael Caine. Remember the name.'

'I will, I will, mate. Any work going on that picture of yours?'

'I should think so. Give Judith Jouard a buzz at Elstree.'

We were in. It was as simple as that.

The last I saw of Caine that night, he was twisting the night away like a corkscrew, with a blue-blood in black silk stockings and a mouth that would have roasted chestnuts.

The £900 I received for *Billy Budd* soon went. Ustinov was appalled at the exclusive contract I'd signed with ABC. He'd given me the break, gone to bat for me with the Americans but now found himself in the unenviable position of having to pay ABC if he wanted to hire me in the future. He read my contract, then had his US lawyer, Lee Steiner, give it the once-over and together they had it cancelled. (Ustinov had been paying Bob Lennard a salary to cast *Billy Budd* when he'd signed me to Associated British.)

I was free but broke, when a call came from Jimmy Fraser. I went to the Regent Street office to see him.

'I've had Jennia Reissa on the phone, she's the casting director for Romulus and Remus. They'd like you to go along to their offices in Park Lane to meet Peter Glenville, the director, and James Woolf, the producer: the part isn't big but it will be a distinguished film. Laurence Olivier is starring with Simone Signoret and a new girl, Sarah Miles.' He pushed a script across the desk.

As Jimmy was giving me the brief I began to get that chill in my chest, a feeling I had when things weren't right. I played for time.

'James Woolf. Isn't he the fella who masterminded Laurence Harvey's career?'

'Yes, he's a powerful man. Probably the most powerful producer in England.'

I flicked through the script. I could hardly find the part they wanted to see me for. Fraser lit a cigarette rather nervously, I thought. It was out of character for him.

'Blimey, Jim,' I said, 'it's about as big as No Smoking in the auditorium.'

'I know, but it will be distinguished.'

'Yeah, maybe, but I won't. The part is a yobbo schoolboy, strictly one-dimensional stuff.'

'Just go and see them, all right?' he asked.

'You know, man, if I go and they want me, it'll be worse.'

'Meet with them, O K?'

'O K,' I said, 'I don't want to do it, but I'll meet them.' I didn't feel good about it.

Jimmy was already on the blower. 'Can you go this afternoon?' he was asking me, his hand over the receiver. I nodded and Jimmy beamed: he was delighted.

James Woolf was something of a legend. Few actors, the ones I knew at any rate, had ever met him, which only increased the speculation. James and his half-brother, John, had been born into the film game; their father had owned cinemas before selling out to Rank. The brothers were the major shareholders in Anglia TV, which was Remus, run by John, whilst James ran the film division, Romulus. John, the elder, was happily married and said to own one of the world's great collections of jade. James was a bachelor with few possessions. The power he wielded in showbiz was massive. I approached the building on the corner of Brook Street and Park Lane with foreboding. I kept telling myself how silly I was as I made my way to the first-floor office. Three men waited in the spacious room: Peter Glenville, the director, a chum of his, Bill Hardie-Smith, and, sitting behind a desk with his back to the view over Hyde Park, James Woolf. A cigar clamped between his teeth showered flakes of ash on to his waistcoat as he rose to shake hands with me. He didn't brush them off; I don't think he even noticed.

'I wonder if you'd be kind enough to do a little reading for us?' said Mr Glenville. 'If you could manage a bit of a Northern accent . . . ' He smiled a big pantomime smile.

Oh God, I thought, they want me to audition for a walk-on. I'd recently watched Albert Finney do the *Face to Face* interview with John Freeman. Mike and I had mimicked Albert explaining to Freeman 'I can read, but I'm not a avid reader' in a broad Mancunian dialect. As I had no intention of playing this part (Glenville had trouble finding more than a couple of lines of dialogue for me to read), I did my imitation of Finney, really codding it up, clenching my teeth and rolling my eyes like an Albert's brother who was completely off his rocker.

Leslie Caron visits us at Elstree studios.

I thought I'd go over like a cup of cold, but they giggled. Bill Hardie-Smith clapped and James Woolf waggled his knees sideways as if rehearsing a step from a seated charleston.

'We'd like to offer you the part,' Glenville concluded.

'Oh, well, you'd better speak to my agent,' I replied.

I rang the agency from an outside phone but Jennia Reissa had already contacted Jimmy.

'Well, I hope you told her no.'

'She offered £2,000,' he said.

'Jim, I don't care. It's nonsense. Ustinov said we'd done something special on *Billy Budd*. He said to wait for good things.' He'd actually said, 'If you do good things, good things will come to you.'

'It's a lot of money for ten days' work, young man.'

I had this funny feeling Fraser was intimidated by James Woolf, was perhaps nervous of offending him, yet I couldn't believe Woolf would refuse to see other agency clients because Fraser couldn't deliver one actor for a walk-on part.

'Listen, Jim. I'd rather pass on this, if you don't mind. Something better will come up; I can get by without the money.'

When I related the events of the day to Caine, he shook his head, but didn't comment.

A few days went by. Fraser received another call. This time from James Woolf himself. He wanted me to go to Grosvenor House for tea – purely a social visit. He understood my feelings about *Term of Trial* – the name of the new film – but of course there were other things he was doing. Fraser advised me to go. He'd heard talk about another film prepared with Laurence Harvey in mind, but as Harvey was floating around the Med on a yacht as a tax exile he seemed an unlikely contender for the part. The film was *The L-Shaped Room*. It was Fraser's theory that if it had been written for Laurence Harvey it had to be good.

I had no misgivings on my way to the famous Park Lane hotel. I even had ideas about landing the plum role conceived for Mr Harvey, which just goes to show how naïve I was, and how little I knew of the formidable Mr Woolf. The minute I showed a glimmer of interest in his project, or any project, for that matter, it was as if I'd provided him with a large brass ring into which he immediately snapped a grappling hook.

After that tea with caviar in his service flat at Grosvenor House with Glenville and Hardie-Smith and a subsequent one with Jimmy

Term of Trial hooligan.

alone, I left with a guaranteed £4,000 fee for the ten-day job on *Term of Trial* and the promise of a contract to star in *The L-Shaped Room*.

Caine was delighted. You could see he thought I'd come to my senses as last. Neither of us realised how out of my depth I was. For one thing, the ten-day assignment was spread out over twelve weeks which meant being on call in freezing Bray outside Dublin, and even Jimmy Woolf had reckoned without the wily Bryan Forbes, who was set to direct *The L-Shaped Room* and had casting ideas of his own.

I went to Ireland, paid the price of working for the bread and grew up a bit. I spent many hours in Jimmy Woolf's company during the endless days of being on call and I grew fond of him. He became the super-bright adult I'd always wanted in my life but had never had; a night figure, with all the mystery and intrigue such characters possess. Many of my friends saw the negative effect he was having on my career. Some pointed it out or advised me to cut myself loose, but my vanity was flattered by his interest, and I was dazzled by the man's brilliance. Other friendships appeared child-like by comparison. Although I knew he was some-how preventing me from working, I didn't care: I thought I could handle it. Jimmy Woolf must have laughed. He read me like a book. Spun me like a top. Even if I had my life to live over, I don't think I would sacrifice my friendship with him.

While I had been completing location work in Paris on *Term of Trial*, Mike had found and taken an opulently furnished flat for us at 5 Ebury Street, spacious enough for Mike and I to have a bedroom each on different floors. Judy Huxtable, a red-haired deb I'd been out with a few times, helped him make the move.

To celebrate my release from bondage, I bought myself a lovat-green Mercedes 220 S E, convertible with antique red leather seats. I drove about London for days with the hood down, freezing cold, but very pleased with myself.

One evening, finding myself at a loose end with both Doug and Mike otherwise engaged (I still hadn't managed to find myself a steady girl), I accepted a last-minute invitation to some kind of advertising executive's celebration. My interest was part architec-tural as the address I'd been given was the St Ermine Hotel –

somewhere I'd always been curious about but had never managed to visit.

I put on my Cyril Castle suit, one of my made-to-measure sea-island-blue cotton shirts and a wide-knitted silk tie. 'All dressed up and nowhere to go' is how my dad used to describe me. Except now I had destinations, lots of them. I placed some evil Boyards in my gun-metal cigarette case, an affectation borrowed from Ian Fleming's literature, and set off. The interior of my new acquisition smelled exactly how a car should smell, although the hotel was so close that I hardly had time to enjoy it. In no time at all I sauntered into the large ballroom on the ground floor. It was filled mainly with suited ad-men, some dancing unusual variations to Chubby Checker, others swilling short drinks. Then I spotted a blonde being danced around the floor in tango-time. She was cool: I felt myself losing mine. I heard somebody speak nearby.

'Something, isn't she?' a lyric baritone commented.

The question didn't seem to warrant an answer. I turned and looked at my unintroduced accomplice; he had the shoulders of a Robert Mitchum devotee.

'I'm Wayne,' he said, offering me his hand.

'Terence,' I said, shaking it.

'What are you doing here, slumming?'

'No. I'm looking for her.'

He smiled. 'Yeah.'

'Do you know her?'

'Not really, but I know she's taken.'

'Aren't they all?'

I offered him a maize-paper special. He took one. A man of discernment, I thought. I finger-snapped my Zippo and we lit up.

'Who's the taker, then?'

Wayne looked around. 'That stout fella over there.'

I followed his glance. By the makeshift bar was an overweight dude with a ruddy, drinker's complexion.

'Looks like he's with,' I said.

'That's his wife.'

'I see, so that's his girlfriend and that's his wife. Do they know about each other?'

Wayne seemed to feel no pain from the effects of the French tobacco. He smiled through the smoke.

'She knows about the wife, but the wife doesn't know about her.'

'So, actually, he's at a disadvantage tonight. Wasn't expecting both to show.'

'Probably, he's a top account man. Has to be a control freak. You know, organised. Wife in the country. Pad in town. Has a lot of fantasies about modules.' He pronounced the word as though he meant a component of a space rocket. 'Those guys wield a lot of power at casting sessions.'

'Which is how he came on this one. What's her name, by the way?' I said.

'You don't know? I thought you came to find her. I'm surprised, she's the stuff of legends in the schmutter trade.'

'I haven't cracked that yet; strictly actor's equity fare for me.'

'They call her Sexy Betsy. Her actual name is Elizabeth.'

'Sexy Betsy. You're pulling my leg?'

'No, it's true, too. Supposed to be sensual beyond restraint.'

'Sounds too good to be true.'

'I heard a story about her,' he began. His voice descended to the one-to-one, boy-to-boy level. 'She was modelling in New York and needed a lift to catch a plane she was late for. The camera man's assistant said he'd drive her but he wanted a favour in return.'

'So when they arrived at Idylwild . . . ' I chimed in.

'Exactly,' confirmed Wayne.

'I think I'm gonna ask her to dance.'

'Nothing ventured,' said Wayne.

'You're a philosopher as well as well dressed,' I said. 'Who's your tailor?'

'Potter and Mendoza, Romford Road.'

'No kidding? I haven't seen those two for yonks.'

'I'll go and chat the big fella, while you steam in,' said Wayne.

'Thanks.'

He cruised over towards the bar. I moved towards where Betsy was being incorrectly danced. The truth was Betsy (sensual beyond restraint) bore a noticeable resemblance to my tutor and initiator, Nurse Grace, although the ages didn't tally. Grace had been in her mid-twenties when she'd seduced me at the convalescent home. It had speeded my recovery no end and the light of my young life had been an object of affection ever since. I'd often followed women who simply reminded me of her, but I'd never come across her again. As I focused Sexy Betsy in close-up, the similarities became striking. I could see she was taller, with long lanky legs and an altogether different body, but her face and hair colouring were uncannily like Grace's. The music changed to Ray Charles's 'I Can't Stop Loving You'.

'My name's Bond, James Bond,' I said in my best Edinburgh accent. 'Would you like to dance?'

I stubbed out my cigarette and fastened my three-button roll-to-two jacket, while Betsy looked me over.

'I don't mind if I do,' she said with a slight Lancashire accent.

It was a thrill just to look at her. I knew it wasn't Grace, of course, but I had the feeling I'd manifested someone, pulled them to me by the strength of my wish.

'I'm Elizabeth,' she told me as we drifted on to the floor. I steered her to the middle so we could get lost in the crowd.

'And you're James,' she said.

'No,' I replied. 'I'm Terence.'

'I thought you said . . . '

'I did, but it was a joke; sorry.'

'Oh, a joke.'

I was never a great exponent of ballroom dancing, but I loved the way it enabled me to hold a complete stranger intimately within seconds of saying hello. Elizabeth and I were soon feeling hot under the collar.

'Why don't we take a drive?' I suggested, reverting to my double-zero grading.

'Ooh, have you a car then? I love cars.'

'I have. It's a Merc. 220.'

'I love cars, will you let me drive it?'

'Well, I haven't comprehensive insurance.' The third party had cost me a small fortune. 'But I'll risk it, if you'll pay a forfeit.'

The Sexy Betsy part of her gave me a long look.

'OK,' she said. 'Oh, I have to tell someone I'm leaving; d'you mind?'

'Nope, I'll wait by the cloakroom.'

I didn't. I nipped up the circular stairs and stood by the balcony rail overlooking the dance floor. In time to watch her walk over to the fella with the porky pink chops. Wayne was still chatting him up. He backed off a few paces when she arrived. The guilty face

looked round anxiously, no doubt checking his wife was safely out
of earshot. The conversation became animated. Wayne saw me
and motioned me down.

'Well done, sir,' he said, 'the gov'nor's not too pleased, I can
tell you. He knows who you are. When I left he was mentioning
that he'd heard you'd contracted an incurable syphilis.'

'Well, he's an ideas man, after all, isn't he?'

'She's mad about cars. Drives a jeep. Passed her Advanced
Driver's Test.'

'I'm in good hands, then.'

Wayne grinned. 'Did you promise her a ride?'

'I did,' I said, 'I did.'

'See you at the tailor, then,' said Wayne. 'He's got my number.
I live out Chingford way.'

'All the best people do.'

Betsy came gliding towards me. I watched the long thighs moving
like an athlete's, beneath the silver belt she wore slung low,
medieval style. I unlocked the car and gave Betsy the keys.

'You're on. It's a steering column shift,' I told her. 'I had a bit
of trouble with it at first.'

'I'm familiar.'

'You are.'

She shifted smoothly into first, clicking the indicator on the
steering wheel as we eased out into traffic.

'Do you wanna stop for a cuppa?' I asked as we passed the stall
opposite Westminster Abbey.

'Perhaps later. I'm enjoying the drive now.'

So am I, I thought, watching the knees pump the foot pedals
and Betsy's model hand with Chinese Red nails manoeuvre the
gear stick. We took a long circuitous route, along the dark oily
Thames reflecting the lights of Battersea Fun Fair and two laps of
Hyde Park before heading north up the Edgware Road to Maida
Vale. Betsy knew routes I didn't know myself. I wondered how
somebody from out of town could have learnt the city so well.

'Did you do the Knowledge?' I asked.

'Almost. When I arrived in London and bought my first motor,
I followed cabs whenever I had free time – I picked up all their
short cuts in no time. Sometimes when I take a cab and tell the
driver the route I prefer, he's blown away.'

'I bet.'

She pulled the car to a halt, backing with ease into a space I'd have passed on.

'You drive well,' I complimented.

'I do.' She looked at her make-up in the driving mirror. 'This is a nice motor,' she said, patting the walnut facia as though congratulating it. 'The clutch's tasty, though. I'd say your left foot is a trifle heavy. You should get it adjusted.'

'Thanks.'

'Do you want to come in?' she asked.

'No.'

She looked taken aback.

'You've had a drive, and we haven't even discussed the forfeit.' She smiled. 'No, we haven't.'

'We haven't.'

'Wot's your game, then?'

'What's yours?'

'It's all the same to me,' she replied, drawing herself away across the seat and swivelling sideways, her back against the driver's door.

'You gotta girlfriend?' she asked.

'Not tonight.'

'Oh.'

'You have a chap though, I believe?'

'Sort of.'

'He was a bit upset about you leaving. Probably told you nasty pork pies about me.'

'How do you know?'

'Little bird told me.'

'Did he tell what I like?'

'No.'

There was a pause. I reached for my fags.

'Has he a member problem, your guy?'

'A member problem?'

'Yeah, isn't he very well endowed?'

'I think that's classified.'

'Let me put it this way. Is it noticeably smaller than mine?'

'I dunno. I haven't seen . . . '

'Well, that was part of the forfeit I was coming round to, and as we both enjoy being in cars . . . '

Later that night I asked Betsy how she wound up being a mannequin. She told me that when she left school she'd wanted to be a nurse but she was fired from her first post at an exclusive boy's boarding school when it was discovered that more than a few pupils had been molested in the first-aid room. It made me smile and bore out my theory that look-alikes often have more than their looks in common.

5

Much to my disappointment, the opening of *Billy Budd* was delayed. ABC, who'd agreed to release the film in Britain, went cold on their promise and Ustinov had to conduct delicate negotiations with the other distribution giant, J. Arthur Rank. Rank were hoping to show the film on their Odeon circuit but had a batch of movies already stacked up for release. Ustinov's film had to wait; *Term of Trial* would open first. It turned out for the best. The newspaper critics reviewed Jimmy Woolf's production and the next week were shown *Billy Budd*. Although my performance passed unnoticed in *Term of Trial*, many of the critics picked up on my change of pace when *Billy Budd* was screened. My personal notices were nothing short of wondrous. I was in the happy situation of attending the première knowing I'd had a personal triumph in a film that most critics agreed was Ustinov's masterwork.

As the first night was a dress affair, Jimmy Woolf introduced me to his tailor in Sackville Street, Maxwell Vine. The man, who in his youth had cut for Cary Grant, created a dish of a dinner suit, a single-breasted, lightweight barathea with a rolled collar and watered silk lapels. At fifty guineas, one of my better investments.

In fact, my only problem was a partner for the evening. I had asked Betsy, who'd gracefully declined: I think the idea of becoming an item in the newspapers might have cramped her style. As luck would have it, Samantha Eggar, my old drama school chum from Webber Douglas, rang me the day before the opening in tears, woefully explaining that her latest beau, one Albert Finney, hadn't called. Why didn't she let me take her to the opening? Nothing like a little rivalry to add spice to life, but she would have to follow my instructions precisely. An eyecatching gown was required, in green, perhaps, or turquoise. A dress with a good line (as there would be lots of photographers), and fast. It would be aired the following evening. She was game.

My family were going, too, although on the night it was touch and go for a while. My dad was a man of great moods. As I grew older I saw there was a part of him that was a natural loner, a side that loved the life at sea with its long solitary hours on watch. Quite young in life he'd fallen head-over-heels in love with my mother and settled for a cramped family existence with little privacy and little or no time to himself. The man who worked boilers and steam engines and knew everything there was to know about pressure took a drink instead of blowing a gasket. Although the core of his personality was as solid as cast iron, the outer man was modest and, for such a handsome fella, curiously lacking in confidence. The smallest thing could make him withdraw into himself like a tortoise, leaving others only a shell to deal with. I'm sure this enforced isolation was even more uncomfortable for him than it was for us, as some of the qualities he loved in my mum were the antithesis of his moodiness. Mum was so gregarious and outwardly sure of herself, she would ignore the fact that he had retreated into himself and behave as though he was co-operating in full. Often, at the very last minute, he would be compelled to go along with her wishes – which is probably what he wanted to do anyway, but somehow couldn't manage unless pressured.

The *Billy Budd* première was one such occasion. The Leicester Square theatre had been booked for the opening night: the film would remain there for a month before going on general release. On the afternoon of the big day, Dad announced to Mum he wasn't going. Mum acted as though he was and went about the business. As the hour of departure became imminent Dad became so comatose that even my mother's fiery resolve faltered. She went next door and rang her sister Julie from the neighbour's telephone. Julie, although her junior, shared Mum's natural ebullience.

'Go on your own, Et. Come with us.' Julie was going with her husband George and Maude, my youngest aunt. 'Better still, I'll order a car, one of those lovely Humbers, from Joe Magnus at the Boleyn.' Julie knew the dark-haired owner of the fleet of luxury limos from the numerous weddings and funerals he'd supplied transport for and wasn't above flirting with the swarthy car man to get a good rate. 'I'll put my coat on and go over there now. It's better than asking him on the phone. The film starts at eight o'clock. You should arrive by seven-thirty. I'll ask how long the driver will need, and have him pick you up at 124, so's not to rush. We'll see you in the foyer.'

'I can't believe Tom's not going to go,' Mum said.

'Don't worry about it, sis. Them Stamps are all a moody bunch.'

Julie was as good as her word. It was only when the spick and span Humber Pullman was sitting outside the house that Dad was galvanised into action, putting on a clean shirt, suit and tie in a few minutes. These dramatics were unknown to me as I struggled nervously with my bow tie. While the chauffeur-driven black Rolls purred outside, Doug and Mike, like seconds at a duel, checked and double-checked my wardrobe. Mike was holding it in, Doug unashamedly excited.

'Should we invite that fella in for a cuppa?' He was identifying heavily with the driver. 'It's nippy out there.'

Mike said, 'Doug, he's a chauffeur. He's used to it. Got the motor running, heater on. It's a Roller, not a bloody Sprite with a hood like an elephant that's got the wind behind it.'

'I'm sure he's cool, Doug,' I said, not wanting to dampen his spirits. 'He's bin hired by the studio, bound to be a pro.'

''Course he's a pro, he's got a hat, hasn't he?'

Doug and I looked at each other. We were accustomed to Mike's non sequiturs.

'You haven't got a big head, son. Nip out and get us a few pounds of spuds in yer cap.' Mike laughed at the old joke. It was his way of easing the tension. A première – we were in unknown territory here.

'Why don't you put your record on, Doug?' I said.

Doug grimaced. He'd recently covered an American hit, 'Runaround Sue', but the original by Dion had hit the charts. Caine put the disc on our record player and gave the introduction a few twists. With bow and hair fixed, there was nothing left to delay my exit.

'Well, chaps, I'd better be off to pick up the lovely Sam.'

'You got readies?' asked Mike. 'You might need a few quid extra to bung the driver. You know, if you keep him later.'

'Right.' I checked my notes. 'I think I've got it covered.'

'Right, take it easy, then,' said Mike.

'Yeah . . . ' Doug was lost for words. 'Let's see him off.'

'Don't be wet,' Mike said. 'We don't want to look like the three

Dad, me, Mum and Sam.

bloody stooges. Go on, son, off you go. It's your night tonight.'

Samantha looked wonderful. Her dressmaker, Daetwyler, had knocked up the dress in record time. The fact that her single piece of jewellery, a brooch, had a dodgy catch and kept coming undone, only added to the incident-filled evening.

Mum and Dad were already there in the crowded foyer to meet me. We posed self-consciously amidst the crowds for the press photographers.

I don't remember much about the actual screening but I think I had the only dry eyes in the house at the end. The cinema emptied slowly. We were the last to leave, and when we reached the top of the stairs to descend into the foyer I realised the place was jam-packed, with people standing shoulder to shoulder. I could see Ustinov and his wife amongst them. As our little group started down the carpeted stairs, the onlookers lifted their arms above their heads and clapped. I managed a glance at Mum and Dad on either side of me – they looked so vulnerable, so overwhelmed, that it was my turn to have a lump in my throat.

Outside, the applauding crowd spilled on to the pavement. Bob Webb was there to push us into the Roller.

'The chauffeur knows where to take you,' he said with intentional calm as I had a last look around before climbing into the jump seat.

We were driven to the White Elephant in Curzon Street, where the Ustinovs had reserved the best table in the back room. Suzanne Ustinov placed Tom and Ethel with their backs to the mirrored wall facing the room. Peter and Suzanne sat opposite them, Samantha and I at either end. Peter and Suzanne were brilliant, treating Mum and Dad as though they were their own kin. When I recall all the wonderful times the Ustinovs brought to my life, I think the charm and understanding at that dinner were their finest gift to me. We didn't roll out of the restaurant till three a.m. Coffee and cognacs had flowed for hours. Samantha and I drove with my folks back to Chadwin Road: it was nearly four o'clock when we waved them goodbye.

Twenty years later my mother told me that after they'd watched the Rolls disappear and let themselves into 124, she'd asked my dad what he wanted to do.

'It's too late to go to bed,' he'd replied, 'let's have a cup of tea. I have to leave for work in an hour. Then you can have a kip.'

Robert Lockwood, now a leading supplier of artists' materials, with premises near where I live, was my dad's apprentice on the river at the time. He told me my dad turned up for work as usual, did a full day's work on the tug and none of his workmates had a clue of his escapades the night before until they docked and read the evening papers. And Samantha's Mancunian hero was on the blower, as promised, the next day, wasn't he?

'You're not keeping your end up, Tel,' Mike said. I'd been moaning about the lack of women in my life. 'It's no good us being known as the hammers of Ebury Street if you're not up to it.'

'I wonder you've still got an end to keep up, the rate you're going at it,' I retorted. 'I've got my work cut out. I feel like I'm running around holding a glass slipper.'

He took a drag on his Disque Bleu. 'You don't know how to look, mate, that's your trouble. I'll find you a princess.'

After a significant pause during which he looked at the exhaled smoke as if expecting a visitation, he said, 'Well, what do you say?'

'What?'

'I offered to find you a royal of a goil.'

'You're a poet and don't know it, mate.' I counted the words of the unintentional rhyme on my fingers: A B C D E F G H I J. 'J. Who do we know with a name that begins with J?'

A week later I went over to Paris for the French opening of *Billy Budd*, staying at the Hotel Lancaster with the Ustinovs. The day after the première François Truffaut sent me flowers. What a compliment: he had directed one of my favourite films, *Jules et Jim*. Suzanne bought me a glowing silk paisley dressing-gown from Christian Dior. Outsize. 'Comfortable is chic,' she said.

On my return, Mike greeted me as I came up the stairs to the first floor. We were living above a ladies' hairdresser's, with accompanying peroxide fumes.

'I've seen one for you,' he announced.

'At a bus stop?'

'No, on the box.'

I dropped my overnight bag, walked back down half a flight to the galley-like kitchen, and refilled the new electric kettle that Mrs Michael Wilding had provided for us. The ex-Mrs Wilding was our new landlady. Mike followed me in.

'On the box, eh? Stay in, did ya?'

'I met a fella who needed a background to do some photos with a model. Ron, he's called. I let him use the bedroom.'

'My bedroom?'

'Actually, I offered him the choice. He thought yours was more in keeping.'

'I bet.' The big advantage of our new quarters was that both double bedrooms had bathrooms *en suite*, but Susan Wilding's taste in décor was sumptuous, to say the most, and lady visitors did wonder about the pink-silk-tent dining area and green cabbage crockery that went with it.

'Stayed over, did she? After the session finished, or should I say started?'

'I offered her a drink. Ron, the photographer, had to leave.'

'Actress or model, was she?'

'Model.'

'What for, broken biscuits?'

'Fruit, actually. She was very fruity.'

'And you watched TV?'

'We did. Which turned out fortunate for you, because I saw a girl that in my considered opinion is right up your alley.'

We returned to the dining-room. I lay on the black sofa and looked up into the semi-circular bits of mirror that formed part of the moulding around the ceiling. I waited for Mike to divulge more details of his discovery.

'You don't seem too interested,' he said.

'Well, if she's anything like the last one you unearthed, what aimed ashtrays all over the place . . . '

'If you ain't . . . '

'Tell me, I'm interested. I'm all ears.'

'We caught the last episode of a science fiction serial, *A For Andromeda*. The girl played a computer, beamed in from space and assembled on Earth.'

'A computer, Mike?'

'Yeah, some sort of machine, but wait, don't fly off the handle. She was absobloodylutely gorgeous. I even wrote down her name 'ere.' He gave me a scrap of newsprint from his robe pocket. 'Flossy thought she was gorgeous, too!'

'Flossy?'

'The module.'

I looked at the hastily pencilled name on the paper.

'She's a blonde,' said Mike, with a triumphant smile.

A week later, the new magazine, *Town*, featured a startling cover and I saw what Mike had meant. The colour photograph, credited to Terence Donovan, portrayed Julie Christie, wearing an open blue denim shirt and holding a Sten gun. Readers wrote into *Town* complaining that the pose was indecorous: it takes all sorts, I guess.

I drew a blank when I tried phoning *Town* for Miss Christie's whereabouts. I didn't know this Donovan or anyone who knew him and for a few weeks it looked as though Caine's inspired thinking would die the death.

The Discothèque had opened in Wardour Street and Caine, Doug and I, now passably proficient at the twist, often went there. It was a sparse, dark place approached by an equally dark, dingy staircase. Inside, the tiny dance area was flanked by old brass bedsteads with bare mattresses. Good-looking girls danced there: one who moved like a leopard on slim, graceful legs caught my eye particularly. I heard she was called Christine Keeler but I was advised to stay clear of her as she and her best friend, Mandy Rice-Davies, were thick with Rachman, a wealthy property dealer whose Lebanese minders kept an eye on them when he wasn't around.

I thought the place might be a hangout for a modern-looking girl like Miss Christie but, although it was rumoured she'd been seen there dancing, I didn't catch sight of her. When I'd almost given up on the project, Mike asked a writer named Derek Marlow round for a drink. He acted a bit too and I remembered seeing him in a production of Alun Owen's play *Progress to the Park* at the Theatre Royal, Stratford East. During the drink and subsequent chat, Derek referred to a Julie. It took me a while to latch on but, with Caine gesticulating behind Derek's back whenever the name was mentioned, the penny finally dropped. Derek agreed to introduce her to me and, after some frustrating postponements, a date was fixed for dinner at the Seven Stars restaurant in the Coventry Street Corner House.

I was hours getting dressed, finally slipping on the gold Rolex that Jimmy Woolf had passed on to me when Larry Harvey presented him with an identical new one. I felt sure Miss Christie would find my gold bracelet watch, worn loose, extremely impressive, which only goes to show how wrong preconceived ideas can be. At that time I knew she'd studied for three years at the Central School of Speech and Drama, done the television series and worked as casual labour at the Post Office, but nothing else.

I arrived at the Seven Stars early. Moray Watson had introduced me to the place while I was still at drama school and, as I'd eaten there whenever I could afford it, I felt on home turf. Selecting a cosy horseshoe banquette with a good view of the room, I waited. Derek arrived with Julie who looked fierce. She wasn't dressed to kill, either, and I realised immediately that I'd overdressed. She sat down in the booth without speaking. For a few moments I went through that change as notions made way for reality. The eyes were brilliant, almost turquoise and, although she glanced down at the tablecloth a lot of the time, whenever I caught her eyes on me they were defiant and glittered like a dragon's. When she finally spoke her voice was low and husky. It wasn't the easiest blind date I'd had. It didn't occur to me that perhaps she was as unnerved as I was, so while I put on a brave, talkative front, Julie ate her meal and didn't say much. I thought I'd blown it. We walked through the crowded street towards Piccadilly Circus where Julie and Derek intended to catch the tube. I plucked up the courage to ask for her telephone number.

'Have you a pencil?' she growled.

'No, haven't.'

'You won't remember it.'

'Try me.' I did. I also remembered something else. During supper we had discussed the things we most coveted, objects we would acquire first when our ships came in. Julie had always wanted a rocking chair. I left it a few days and rang her number to invite her to lunch. To my surprise, she accepted, and we fixed on the Casserole, a funky eating place that had opened recently in the King's Road. The following day I went to Harrods and chose a wooden rocking chair, making it clear to the salesman that the sale hinged on delivery to the Casserole restaurant between one and two-thirty the next day. He assured me it would be there.

'Wrapped or unwrapped, sir?'

'Wrapped, but nothing fancy.'

Purely functional. It needed to be in travelling order for the onward taxi ride. I left her name with the Chelsea address.

Harrods were as good as their word: Julie and I had started coffee when a green-coated man, looking for a Miss Christie, entered the café. Julie felt certain there had been a mistake; I had to encourage her to go outside and look.

'I'll come with you,' I offered.

In the doorway stood the object, wrapped up as if for autumn.

'But what is it?' queried Julie, standing with her toes dug in like Eeyore, biting the side of her lower lip and frowning deliciously. She looked at me for back-up.

'I can't imagine,' I replied, sidling up to it and tilting it like a see-saw, 'but it sort of rocks.'

The mouth that was to launch a thousand ships split into a grin.

'Ooooh, you,' she said.

It was the first Christie smile I'd seen. It was worth the wait.

Our romance blossomed. After Julie received her big break she was taken up by the media as the girl who epitomised the Sixties, but to me she will always be a bohemian from the Fifties. She had little or no regard for the trappings and finery I sought to bolster up my success, and when I first saw where she lived I was taken aback by the proportions of her little room, with its broken window through which stray cats crawled. I had shared flats all my student days, still did, but Julie's lifestyle was a forerunner of the hippy communes: in that sense and in many others, she far outstripped the traditional lifestyle I was seeking. She felt as out of place staying with Mike and me as I would have been mucking in with her chums; yet she was a delight to be with and, as I began to get to know her, I became aware of the clash of backgrounds our friendship threw up: she the daughter of an Assam tea planter, nursed by an *ayah* in the last days of the Raj, and I the eldest son of two warring cockney clans. Julie was the only professional artist I'd met who found public appearances more harrowing than I did. When I mentioned that I'd been invited to attend a première followed by supper at the Savoy, Julie blanched.

After a moment she said, 'I've nothing to wear.'

'We can buy you a frock,' I said. 'That's easy.'

'It's a coat,' she admitted finally. 'I haven't a suitable coat.'

'OK, let's buy you a coat. What about a fur coat? It's winter, you'd look wonderful in fur.' I visualised her in a Persian lamb, styled for the Twenties.

'But . . .'

Julie.

Escorting Sarah Miles in Venice.

'The do is Saturday. You have all week to find a coat you like. When you see something, tell me and I'll buy it for you.'

She didn't look convinced and as the days passed I heard nothing more. On the Friday I said, 'Listen, Miss Crystal. You have today and tomorrow to locate a winter outfit. I don't care if it's not a fur coat. As I'm running about tomorrow I'm giving you a signed cheque. When you find the coat, fill it in and buy it. OK? Don't turn up tomorrow without one,' I chided her.

She nodded, sticking out her jaw and delectable lower lip.

On Saturday evening I had just scrambled into my dinner jacket when Julie arrived wearing a fur coat. It was unusual, but nice, somewhere between an astrakhan and a beaver lamb.

'You look beautiful. It suits you,' I told her. She looked as cuddly as a teddy in Hamley's window.

'Where did you find it?'

'In Portobello,' she said. 'I gave them the cheque. It was a fiver, was that all right?'

At the reception she nearly passed out with nerves. Sarah Miles saw it coming and helped her into the powder room. While Julie was recovering Sarah came out and chastised me.

'She's a good one, Terence, and you're not looking after her. You'll be sorry. She's rare. Now pull yourself together.'

I guess I didn't. When Julie was unexpectedly asked to take over the role in *Billy Liar*, the movie that proved to be her launch pad, it was all a bit hurry up. I went to King's Cross Station to watch her night shooting. She looked so cold and forlorn that I wrapped her in my sheepskin and told her to take it up north on location.

While she was away she wrote me a letter. It wasn't exactly a Dear John, but enough of one to hurt my pride. We didn't see much of each other after that, which proved to be a big loss for me because Ruby Crystal, as I called her, was one of the most lovable creatures I ever met. She would have made a steadfast friend, rare – as naughty Sarah so clearly saw.

6

Most men have a dream girl – an ideal they push before them like a ball, always out of reach. As the years pass, this phantom either fades in the face of reality or becomes refined in the imagination, accommodating attributes, known or wished. By the time I reached twenty-five, the woman of my dreams had become so exquisite I'd acknowledged that, bar making a pact with Beelzebub himself, she wasn't about to enter my life. Then she did, albeit through the media. I wasn't a paying customer of *Harpers* or *Vogue*, but whenever I came upon a copy on a coffee table or in a waiting room, I ogled the mannequins. I had no interest in the couture. In the Fifties the models were anonymous, lissom clothes horses. My interest was academic, part of my search for Cinderella with perfect legs. When I saw her, I didn't know who she was although the face rapidly infiltrated the fashion pages. Titillation until the Sixties had been limited to specific magazines. Among the popular press the *Daily Mirror*'s Jane was the most blatant. Yet here was *Vogue*, the bluebloods' favourite monthly, regularly featuring a creature who made the other fashion plates look just that. Her cover shots were pinned to the underside of prefects' desks and bedsit walls across the country. None of us knew her by name: for months she was 'that girl with the big eyes and the legs'. Of course, it didn't take Condé Nast too long to cotton on to the fact that they had given birth to a substantial commercial entity. They broke a cardinal rule and personalised the first of their models: Jean Shrimpton, alias the Shrimp. (My previous daydreams had centred on Marilyn and B.B. archetypes.)

This girl looked as though a fairy godmother on tour had sneaked into an Oxford Street store and blown life into a window dresser's fantasy. Initially my interest was purely aesthetic, although that changed abruptly one afternoon as I strolled through the

The Shrimp.

rush-hour traffic. Mike and I were still living at 5 Ebury Street. I had walked alongside the high brick wall of Buckingham Palace Gardens and down Grosvenor Place, overtaking the bumper-to-bumper Friday commuters. I enjoyed the fact that I lived in the West End and could walk home.

The little stretch of Lower Grosvenor Place, before the Ebury Street corner, housed a row of puzzling shops. At least, they looked like shops but they were never open for trade, and the items exhibited in their windows were often dusty and yellowing from neglect. As I reached them something in the centre window caught my eye – a newspaper folded and laid as if to lure the attention of a casual passer-by. The tabloid carried a full-length picture of the Shrimp wearing a leotard and holding hands with a small child by her side. I caught my breath and felt my throat becoming dry. It wasn't an indecorous pose but it hit me where it hurt.

Mike was engrossed in a novel entitled *V* as I staggered into the pink-ceilinged sitting-room. I related my chance encounter and its effect on me.

'I think I've got it bad, Mike.'

'You and a million others, mush.' He leaned forward and tapped an open magazine in front of me. It contained a full colour picture of the same girl, her mouth holding a shrimp, her eyes looking up at me beguilingly. The photographer's credit said David Bailey. Soon after that, Bailey and Shrimpton became items in the media. Apparently, he had discovered her after she'd completed a modelling course. He then masterminded her launch in *Vogue*, leaving his wife to set up a new home in Primrose Hill. She worked exclusively with him.

Mike Caine, who could be relied on to give impartial objective views on almost anything, said, 'I should forget about her, mate. Sounds like they're almost cut and carried. Besides, I hear he hails from down your manor. Probably a nice bloke.'

It was funny how blasé all the great pullers I knew were about women. I tried to be most of the time but, now and then, one who plugged straight into my obsessions would come along. In this instance I could actually see how bizarre it was, particularly since I hadn't even met the girl. I did as Mike advised and got on with my life.

*

There was plenty to distract me from the fact I hadn't worked since *Term of Trial*.

Mike was seeing a scrumptious girl called Edina Ronay regularly and, when her friend Caterine Milinair returned to London after a spell in France, Edina introduced her to me. Caterine was the eldest daughter of Nicole Milinair who had married the Duke of Bedford. Caterine Milinair had a great smile. She had a great mouth, too, but not all wide mouths smiled like hers. Caterine's sweetness surfaced in her smile. She brought a sparkle to my life and taught me to jump to her version of 'La Bamba' at the Saddle Room, breaking for ever the bands that encompassed my chest whenever I was dragged on to the dance floor. She lived in Chesham Close in a pied à terre as feminine as she was – it became a haven for me in those sometimes fearful early days of fame and fortune, and I was never to forget the joyful grin that lasered support across a crowded room and put me at my ease.

Caterine was also the first of surprisingly few women to draw me a bath, blending a mixture of pine essence and Badedas that always gathered the strands of my blackest moods and changed them to aromatic pleasure. Although she'd lived in England for some time and spoke the language perfectly, it would have been like trying to take the sweet out of sugar to separate her Frenchness from her. Rising early, we would step out to the new Kenya coffee bar in Knightsbridge, which in those days sold '*bons croissants*' and '*pas mal café*', and take breakfast '*à la française*'. At the time Caterine and I met, the Duke – Ian or Yan as Caterine called him – and Duchess were on an extended world tour showing the 'Treasures of Woburn' in Australia. Their stately home, Woburn Abbey (Ian Bedford was one of the aristos who'd originated the ingenious scheme of opening his pile up to the public), was the playground of the combined Bedford and Milinair kids, and what a playground.

As a small boy, I'd been obsessed with having a title, even fashioning an enigmatic calling card based on Leslie Charteris's hero, the Saint. I called my stick figure the Duke, and I must confess I often felt like a duke when Caterine brought weekends at Woburn into my life: flashing up the newly opened M1 in Caterine's car on Friday evenings or seated alongside the lordling Rudolph Russell in his Mini Cooper S if Caterine was busy in

London at _Queen_ magazine. The Duke's eldest, son and heir Robin, was attending a university in America, no doubt chosen by his dad to equip him for the rigours of running the huge estate that he would inevitably inherit. Word among the children was that Robin didn't relish this post, didn't feel too cosy in the Abbey and was going along with his father's ideas in a manner befitting a first-born but with little enthusiasm. The Lord Russell, the second son, loved the place to distraction, however. It was probably this passion, fuelled by the knowledge that everything would fall to his older sib, that made Russell so cranky. I was warned of this whilst being filled in on the other guests that first weekend.

He and I hit it off straight away. His pale complexion and carroty mop of hair would have been more at home in _Just William_ than Debrett. When we met he could only have been seventeen or eighteen, with an extremely pronounced stutter which I found endearing.

The first time we spoke I said, 'Blimey, I wish I'd come across you months ago. I could have used that in the film.'

He giggled and we were friends. I hadn't been away for a country weekend before and it was certainly a memorable introduction.

When we arrived it was already dark and all the sightseers had gone. The car crunched over the gravelled approach to the front of the building and a liveried man bearing bee motifs on his gold buttons let us in. The Abbey, a successful business operation, was always fully staffed. Caterine's whippet, Melkior, bounded up to meet her. Mike and I were relieved of our bags.

The footman said, 'I'll put the luggage in your rooms, gentlemen.'

He was obviously a past-master of tact. Our combined possessions would have hardly warranted a delivery by Melkior, let alone a burly manservant. I watched him disappearing down a hall thick with gilded side-tables, my holdall, a remnant of my table-tennis days, in one hand and Mike's carrier bag from British Home Stores in the other. Mike and I grinned at each other: wolves in new sheepskins.

It got better. After our pre-dinner drinks – I'd nonchalantly doused a generous snifter of Napoleon brandy with a bottle of Coke, the 'in' drink of the time – I went up to look at my quarters, only to find my toothbrush already contemplating the marble bathroom and my pyjamas, which would have also fitted Caterine's

Evening with Caterine.

whippet, laid out on the bed. Further investigation revealed a bedside bottle of Malvern water, a bar of French Fern soap and a large bottle of bath essence. This elegant scene was completed by the discovery of a dashing black silk robe with white polka dots hanging behind the padded suede door.

As the kitchen staff had no idea of our arrival times, a cold buffet had been arranged on trays in the small dining-room at the southern end of the lounge on the first floor. Before we went to bed our wake-up times were left in the ante-room to the main kitchen.

Creeping back to my room in my borrowed dressing-gown the next morning, I found a breakfast tray complete with newspapers already placed on my undisturbed bed.

Mornings in the great house appeared to be leisurely. Caterine, with her fashion world employment and twenty-hour day, slept late. I had breakfasted, bathed and shaved in the sumptuous bathroom by nine o'clock and was combing the corridors and public rooms of the Abbey, scrutinising the furniture and paintings in close-up before the punters arrived. I was half under a particularly striking but simple Georgian table when I realised I wasn't alone. A pair of cowboy boots and tapered blue jeans were waiting for me to re-emerge. It was the young Lord Russell.

'Hhhhello,' he said finally.

'Hi,' I replied from the floor, 'lot of good gear you've got here, built to last.' Rudolph lowered himself into a Louis-Quinze chair opposite me.

'Gggood gear.' The statement rebounded like an echo, as the young beanpole mentally converted it into standard English.

'Yes, my dad put it all into shape when he inherited the tttitle; there there were only two rooms open. A bedroom and a ddining-room. Most of this stuff was in the cccellars, accumulating cob-webs.'

'I'm glad he did, it's wonderful.'

'The Ddduchess, Nicole, mmy stepmother, wants to have all the furniture re-gilded,' he said rather disapprovingly. 'I ththink it's beautiful as it is, bbut nobody cares much what I think.'

I had no idea what new gold leaf would look like so I didn't comment. He took my silence as tacit agreement.

'Come,' he said, 'I'll show you round.'

It was nice seeing the great house through Rudolph's eyes. It

James Woolf.

wasn't a national monument to him, just the home he'd grown up in, the priceless portraits that covered the walls of the stairwell, his ancestors'. He identified them in much the way I pointed out my relatives in our photo album to Sunday lunch guests at Chadwin Road. After he'd shown me his room on the top floor where the studded doors were covered in brown baize and bore the children's names in copper-plate behind polished brass frames, we set off for a tour of the park in his Mini. Paying visitors were already arriving, but Rudolph knew corners others didn't, along tracks prohibited to the public.

'You must come in the spring when they're in flower,' he chirped proudly as we power-slid through the forest of rhododendrons. 'My great-grandfather brought them back from China.'

Back at the Abbey the staff were busy. The crisp aroma of burning fruit-wood greeted us from the log fire in the main hall, but this was ignored by Rudolph, still intent on showing me the things and people he loved. I was introduced to Mrs Cook, or Cookey, who, needless to say, was the cook. No ordinary one, as we discovered later in the Canaletto dining-room, and no ordinary woman, either. Everything about Cookey was big, most of all her affection and understanding for the motherless young Lord. She didn't stay at the Abbey, preferring to be an independent native of Woburn village, where she lived with her husband and kids in a compact two-up two-down, and where Rudolph spent almost as much time as he did in the ancestral seat. I suppose it was because I obviously liked Rudolph that Mrs Cook approved of me. Certainly, I was the only guest who was made welcome in her fiefdom, the biggest kitchen in the world, over which she reigned with a considerable iron hand. Later, even Rudolph was impressed when Cookey offered me the recipe for the yard of apple strudel we had demolished at lunch.

Rudolph Russell and I made an odd couple; but I always had the feeling he would have gladly exchanged his privileged boyhood for the warmth and companionship of my early family life.

That first wintry afternoon, the whole gang, Edina, Caterine, Mike, Rudolph and I, rode all the rides at the permanent little fair-ground protected by the Abbey walls. Of course, as the guests of His Lordship, we weren't asked to pay – another of my childhood fantasies come to pass.

7

'Why don't you come out to Hollywood with me?' Jimmy Woolf suggested in early 1963. 'We can stay at the Beverly Hills Hotel. There'll be lots for you to do when I'm busy. Lots of pretty girls in California. You'll have a wow of a time. Besides, be a good move to let the studio heads see you in the flesh. I don't see Jimmy Fraser getting lots of offers for you from America.'

'It's a great idea, Jim, but I'm not exactly flush at present.'

'Oh don't be silly, Terence. I'll pick up the tab. Think of it as an advance. When you finally decide to let me manage your career we can settle up. Now get off round to the American Embassy and pick up a visa. We'll take that new non-stop polar flight. It's direct, painless.'

That's what we did. Jimmy was as good as his word. The hotel wasn't as I'd imagined it, but he was treated like visiting royalty and the same service was extended to me. Years before, Wolf Mankowitz had told me a story about Jimmy Woolf and his adoration of Larry Harvey; the key to the relationship was in a book that Jimmy had written when he was young. He'd been invited to Hollywood by someone who had promised to take care of him and pick up the bills for the trip. Jimmy had sailed to New York and taken the train across America, but when he arrived in Los Angeles his chum was not to be found. Jimmy was stranded. He'd set off without informing his family and didn't want to cable them for money. He checked into a suite at the famous hotel in Beverly Hills, sat down and started writing a book, living on room service, charging everything he needed to the hotel until he had it finished and had done the deal, whereupon he settled his bills and purchased a ticket home from the advance. On publication, the book received so many threats of libel from characters recognisable in the text that the publishers were forced to withdraw it. Wolf

Mankowitz had read it and he told me that the hero, who Jimmy obviously saw as himself, was the spitting image of Laurence Harvey: tall, dark, handsome and debonair. Harvey (who'd started life as a poor Lithuanian, Lauruska Mischa Skikne) was as ruthless with himself as he was about his career. It was said that early in his career he had had his back teeth removed to give more emphasis to his cheekbones. In Wolf's opinion, Jimmy considered Larry his idealised alter-ego, loved him as one would love oneself.

I often tried to draw Jimmy out on the subject of the book but it was heavy going as he didn't much like speaking about himself. However, he did admit to being 'given the bum's rush' on his first visit to Hollywood and having to 'roust about a bit' to get out of trouble.

I went to bed early the first evening. Early, that is, by California time. 'The coast' was eight hours earlier than England. Of course, I awoke at some ridiculous hour and couldn't get back to sleep. I rang down and asked if Mr Woolf was taking calls. Apparently, he'd already ordered coffee so I dressed and nipped along to his room. He was sitting up in bed in one of his sleeping coats made by Dale Cavanagh and was delighted to have company.

'What do you want to do today?'

'I haven't the faintest, Jim. It's all a bit unreal to me.'

'This is Hollywood, you can do whatever you like. Let me introduce you around. I know all the beauties: Rhonda Fleming, Gypsy Rose Lee or Natalie, cor!' He did what he thought was a cockney accent. 'Now, Natalie, you'd like her.'

'I'm sure I would.' Natalie Wood: Jimmy Dean's co-star and friend. She'd have some stories to tell.

'We'll ring Natalie, soon as it's polite,' Jimmy said. 'Cor!'

What we didn't know was that Natalie was being escorted by a young millionaire businessman, although I did get to meet her at Minna Wallis's house on Foothill Drive.

As things turned out, my first night on the town brought me in sight of one of the most splendid creatures I had ever seen. To be fair to Jimmy, he didn't tell me that she was my blind date for the evening.

He'd said, 'I've arranged for you to meet some young people. One girl who's going to be there is Edgar Bergen's daughter. I hear she's a cracker.'

He was right. I reported to Ray Milland's house at seven sharp.

Of course, as soon as I laid eyes on the lovely Candice I couldn't focus on anybody else. She was with one of those confident young property tyros who didn't even acknowledge me as a possible contender. All I can recall of the evening is the looks of the seventeen-year-old Candy, and an Alsatian dog that could switch the telly on and off by running past in his metal collar. I didn't get a look-in and my first US trip was soon a memory.

I'd been in the limelight since *Billy Budd* and had worked with a number of photographers, among them Antony Norris who, whilst not as famous as Bailey and Donovan, took terrific snaps and made me laugh. Although enjoying this deluge of publicity, I'd been turning down subsequent job offers, worrying instead about Doug and Mike. Doug was still covering American hits and I'd often noted song titles that I thought might suit him. None of us realised that the tune I'd jotted down a few months before going to the States heralded a revolution in the British music scene. I'd watched a TV programme *Take Five*, which dropped into a five minute slot before the six o'clock news, showing an enchanting clip of a baby primate with its mum, accompanied by an irresistible song that suited the black and white images perfectly. It was 'Love Me Do' by the Beatles.

Mike, for his part, had always advocated patience whilst waiting for that elusive break, but he also had a saying, repeated at regular intervals, that anyone who hadn't made it by the time they were thirty wasn't going to. When I realised his own thirtieth anniversary was near I tried again to give his career a push, repeatedly taking it up with Jimmy Woolf until Jimmy said finally, 'Look, Terence. I think your friend is extremely nice and probably a very capable actor, but he hasn't got what it takes, believe me. Now let him sort his career out himself and you get on with yours.'

13 March 1963 was a Wednesday. It sticks in my mind because on the Tuesday Mike Caine had done a screen test for Cy Enfield who was about to start work on a film produced by Stanley Baker called *Zulu*. Mike's new agent, Dennis Salinger, had squeezed Mike in to see the director on the understanding that Mike would read for the part of Private Hook, a corblimey cockney and one of the soldiers decorated at the Battle of Rorke's Drift. It turned out that when Cy Enfield saw Caine he recalled Mike's opening speech

in the play *Next Time I'll Sing to You* at the Criterion Theatre. Michael had delivered the lines in a rather cod upper-class accent. Enfield, an American by birth, had been impressed, and read Mike for the part of Lt. Bromhead, which was actually a starring role along with Stanley Baker. Mike had read well and won himself a screen test. There had been great excitement back at Ebury Street but, by the Wednesday evening when Mike's agent hadn't called, we were all a bit downcast.

Someone rang and invited us to a party. The address was a stone's throw from Park Lane, the host a Mr De Havilland. Mike, Edina, and I togged up and set off. Although the partygoers had the run of the large apartment everybody was congregated in one crowded room. I grabbed us some drinks from the bar and returned to find Mike looking paler than usual.

'What is it, Mike?'

'He's here.'

'Who?'

'Cy. Cy Enfield.'

'So what?'

'Well, he, he's bound to think . . . '

'Oh, yeah, he's bound to think you're hounding him, right? To convince him you can play the part. Fast! Point him out to me.'

He did. A rotund man with alert eyes, blinking through owlish specs.

'Looks a nice guy. Go and say hello. You've got nothing to lose. Want me to come?'

'No,' Mike declined. 'No. I'll er, perhaps you're right. I'll go and say hello.'

He walked, a bit dazed, in the direction of the director. The gramophone played the Stan Getz version of 'Desafinado' as Edina looked at me, very much a nineteen year old. I pushed her off after Mike. I saw a girl I'd met once or twice called Martine Beswick and we talked about great drummers. In between the chat I looked across at Mike. He and Cy appeared to be hitting it off. Both were laughing. Someone asked Martine to dance; I glanced again in Mike's direction. He came towards me through the crowd, towering above them like a schooner under sail. Tears were streaming down his face – I didn't move. His lips curled back: he was speaking but I could hardly hear the words, only a tense, high-pitched whisper. He came closer.

'I've got the part. He liked my test. I've got the part. I'm going to play Bromhead!' His face was wet. I hadn't a handkerchief and he wasn't aware he was crying, anyway. I looked at my Rolex: eleven-thirty. Mike is thirty tomorrow. He's made it, with half an hour to spare.

8

I was becoming more dependent on Jimmy Woolf's friendship. Long days out of work were spent in lazy convoluted discussion in his offices or over expansive lunches. Hardly a day passed when we didn't touch base. One evening we were talking in the sitting-room of his apartment in the Grosvenor House, a rare event, as whenever he returned home he liked to get into a sleeping coat and lounge in his bedroom. However, Dr Buki, who regularly dropped by for a drink and to give James an injection, wasn't expected: Jimmy had an evening rendezvous. The ash from the burning Romeo and Juliet fell on to his suit, as usual. He took no notice.

'You're becoming such a slob,' I said. 'You've got to stop swallowing those Tuinols, they're doing your brain in.'

Jimmy ate the highly coloured pills kept in a big jar in his bathroom cabinet like sweets. He flicked the ash off his chest disdainfully.

'Oh, be quiet, Terence. You don't know what you're talking about.'

'I know barbiturates leave a residue in the body that gets compounded. You're not aware of it until too late.'

I'd seen this in *Time* and *Newsweek*, which Jimmy encouraged me to read. He'd said the US editions were the only way of finding out what was actually going on in Britain.

'Sshhh,' Jimmy hissed as the waiter arrived with our high tea: china pots and Grosvenor House crockery laid on a silver hotel salver. Jimmy and I called him Dizzy because Jimmy said he'd worked on the railways for twenty years and still bumped into passage walls as if compensating for the trains' motion.

'Will that be all, Mr Woolf?' Dizzy asked.

Jimmy slipped him a pound.

'Thank you, Donald, that's all for this evening.'

We waited until he closed the front door behind him, and then we nipped over to it smartly. As we peeped out Donald was bumping his way back along the corridor.

I'd heard Jimmy Woolf had played bridge for England when he was eighteen. He wouldn't deny or confirm the honour, but playing cards was still a passion; he would have been considered a world-class card man, if such a category had existed. As it was, he played in showbiz circles only, using his ability as a medium for gathering information and spreading his considerable charm to the right effect. Right, in Jimmy's case, meaning doing what amused him most, making films, films he fancied, and having a say in everybody else's.

One of Jimmy's card-playing circle that evening was Binnie Barnes, whose husband, Mike Frankovitch, had just been appointed world-wide head of Columbia Pictures. She would thus be a useful ally as well as a formidable gin rummy opponent. During the years I was Jimmy Woolf's mate there wasn't a film produced in England without his know-how being used. Whoever wanted to make a film sooner or later wound up on the phone to Jimmy, usually sooner, as the crucial ingredient needed was always money. Jimmy knew more about finance than making a straight flush – I don't know how he coped with the multiplicity of deals and the intrigue they involved, considering the quantity of pills he swallowed at night. His brain obviously moved at a speed that was impossible to slow down.

'My problem,' he once told me, 'is that I can't sleep. If I didn't have an injection now and then I would stay awake for ever! You can't imagine what it's like to take a few pills (Seconals and Tuinols) at eleven o'clock and wake up realising you've only been to sleep for a couple of hours. It's so dark.'

This was the moment that the people who loved him feared the most because it was in this depleted, semi-conscious condition that Jimmy would stagger into his bathroom and gulp down a handful of five-grain barbs. I had often wondered how he had managed to acquire such a big stash of these lethal downers.

One afternoon, after we'd had our ritual Tuesday lunch at Les Ambassadeurs, I found out. Jimmy made a point of taking me there regularly on a Tuesday when the chic restaurant boasted a selection of large doughnuts from Grodzinski's, served from a dessert trolley.

Mike Caine and Edina Ronay twisting the night away.

Jimmy loved to shock the staff and fellow diners by ordering only these jam-filled bumper editions for lunch. He would egg me on to ask for seconds and sometimes we managed half a dozen between us. Our schoolboy antics had been eclipsed this particular lunch-time as the garden at Les A. had been booked for the launch party of a new film based upon Rider Haggard's *She*. A hush fell over the place, and even I squirted jam on myself when the two stars, Ursula Andress and John Richardson, glided through the room. It was hard to say who was the more eye-catching. Ireland, Jimmy's chauffeur, had been waiting for us in the Jaguar – Jimmy bought a new one every year – in Old Park Lane. Jimmy climbed in the back and I slipped in front next to Ireland.

'Put your hat on, Ireland,' said Jimmy, knowing that Ireland hated wearing the chauffeur's cap. Without it, in the bespoke suit Jimmy had bought him, he could easily have passed for a successful male model, or a writer of bestselling thrillers, which Ireland would have probably preferred. He was working on a book, scribbling down pencilled notes during the hours when he wasn't required.

'Yes, Mr Jimmy,' replied the driver with a feigned grimace of long suffering: all Jimmy's close associates indulged him in his penchant for living theatre.

'He knows he looks fetching in his cap,' said Jimmy to me as though Ireland wasn't there, at the same time firing up one of the Cuban torpedos he'd acquired from the wine waiter on our way out.

Ireland, who was only a few years older than me, smiled at me in the mirror. He and I were quite matey when Jimmy wasn't present and I'm sure Ireland and Jimmy weren't so formal when I wasn't in the car, judging by the stories Jimmy concocted about his driver.

'Cor, that Ireland really fancies Haya Harareet,' or, 'You should have seen the meal he made of helping Anne Bancroft out of the car.'

When Ireland dropped us at Grosvenor House, Jimmy handed him an envelope. I heard him mutter something about a package from the hotel chemist. Jimmy headed directly for the lift and we shot up to his flat on the second floor. He appeared excited, shuffling off to his bedroom and returning minutes later in a pale blue sleeping coat, made by 'the boys' in Kinnerton Street who also ran up his exotic velour dressing-gowns with wide astrakhan lapels, which he rarely wore. He sat in an armchair, flapping his knees. Now I knew something was going down. Knee flapping was his body language indicative of high excitement. Ireland returned holding a paper bag which Jimmy snatched, scurrying into the other room. Ireland grinned at me and left – he wasn't wearing his cap.

Jimmy came back into the living-room still clutching the brown bag.

'OK,' I said, 'what's up?'

'Oh, it ain't nothing,' he replied in the quaint East End accent he used when he wanted to tell me something, but needed persuading.

'My mum says if it ain't nothing, it must be something.'

Jimmy's smile just widened. He hadn't managed too well with his razor in the morning and tufts of hair bristled on his chin.

'Well, if you're not going to tell me what you're clutching in your hot little mits, I guess I'm going to have to find out, mate.'

I advanced towards the sofa threateningly. He put the bag behind him on the sofa.

'Mandies,' he said.

'What?'

'Quaaludes. It's a new one. Marilyn gave me one in Hollywood. She said it was the best, didn't have many.'

'Marilyn?'

'Monroe. They've only just come on the market here.'

I was lost for words for a minute. Marilyn, my teenage dream of carnal ecstasy, a downers freak?

Jimmy continued, 'Buki wouldn't give me any. Said the withdrawals were horrific.'

'But you're not contemplating withdrawing, are you, Jim?'

Jimmy kept grinning and drew the jar out of the paper wrapper like a conjuror working a rabbit from a hat. The neat little time-bombs shone cosily in their gelatine husks.

'Marilyn told me when she first saw one she just couldn't resist, it looked so pretty.'

'How d'you meet Marilyn?' I asked with mixed emotions.

'Simone introduced us when Yves was doing *Let's Make Love*. She thought we'd get on.'

'And you did, eh?'

'Oh yeah, oh yeah.' He did another cockney diphthong. 'She loves swapping new barbies.'

Like finds like, I thought. Astute of Signoret to see that, although I doubt that she did either of them any favours. Jimmy had mentioned that Marilyn and Yves Montand were getting along too well and Madame Montand, Simone, had thought it wise to turn up during the shoot. Jimmy was still grinning. He hadn't reached for a cigar which usually meant he still had something to reveal, and wasn't bored.

'That all?'

'You're a smart cockney boy, ain't ya?'

'It's no secret.' I slumped into the armchair opposite him.

'I bet you can't guess.'

'What?'

'How I acquired them.'

'What?'

'Oh, Terence.' He feigned impatience.

'How did you get Buki to come across?'

He beamed, placed the jar – it was about the same size as the one my mum used to pickle onions – and the bag separately on the glass-topped table in front of him, and smoothed the bag flat.

'If you guess right I'll get you a date with Kim Novak.'

'I've had a date with Kim Novak.'

'You can drive the new Jaguar on Ireland's day off.'

I shrugged, unimpressed. We often played these charades. It amused him to try and press my buttons.

'There's this new tailor Bryan Forbes told me about. He comes to your house . . . '

'I can only wear one suit at a time, Jim.'

'I'll talk to Harry about you playing James Bond. Sean's bound to only want to do a couple.'

'I know – you told Buki you couldn't sleep.'

Jimmy snorted, and started searching his pockets for the gold cigar trimmer.

'You told him your aunt in Marble Arch, who fries the fish for you, has trouble nodding off.'

'She should be so lucky.'

'I give up.'

'You don't want the part?'

'I used to want the part. It's too late now, he's done it. I can't think how you did it, that's all. I give up. You win.'

He slowly slid his hand on to the paper bag and whisked it away,

94

stuffing it into the little pocket of his gown. He grinned, immensely pleased with himself.

'You didn't?'

He chortled, like a schoolboy.

'You didn't, Jim, you didn't?'

He nodded his head, a grinning mandarin.

'You didn't nick a prescription from Buki?'

'Better.'

'What?'

'Whole pad, took it while he was washing his hands.'

'He'll notice.'

Jimmy shrugged his shoulders. 'He's got plenty.'

'Who wrote it?'

He lifted a cigar from the Dunhill humidor and pointed it at himself.

'Bloody hell! And you sent Ireland in with it?'

He was shaking with pride and laughter.

'He could have been caught.'

'Noooo. I took the first one in myself.'

'But this is the big score,' I said, picking up the packed jar of red devils, 'a big score.'

'Lovely, aren't they?'

I grimaced.

'Straight flush in diamonds, eh, Jim?'

'Better,' he said. 'Have you got lots to do?' he added timidly.

'Why do you ask?'

'If you're not too busy, I thought perhaps you could watch *Coronation Street* with me. Ena's on tonight.'

Jimmy was fascinated by Ena Sharples, the old dragon played by Violet Carson. He knew I couldn't understand what he saw in it, nevertheless, the evenings the show was on were the highlights of his week. This man who'd produced *Room At The Top*, master-minded *African Queen* when Sam Spiegel was blacklisted and worked out of London as S. P. Eagle, whose prowess at cards was probably second only to Richard Conte on the hot Californian circuit, loved nothing more than to lie tucked up in his king-sized bed and giggle at the antics of a pot-boiler which bubbled endlessly from Granada TV.

'You can have Ireland drive you, when I drop off.' It was almost a plea.

I sat in the mock Louis-Quatorze chair next to his bed as Ena bullied and barked at her neighbours on the street, too naïve to understand the behaviour of the sad genius, the nerves of fire that inflamed his system, and his need for that last little window of awareness, unaffected by the sleeping draught, to be soothed. I sat with him as he slipped into a desperate oblivion, lulled by the flickering black and white images on the screen in much the same way as a bedtime story calms an anxious child.

I knew the showbiz community regarded Jimmy and me as a bizarre combo. It didn't bother me at all: the few people who knew Jimmy well thought the world of him. We were bound together by our concern over his health but it was a problem without answers. Bill Hardie-Smith had often spoken with me about Jimmy's intake although when I suggested hospitalisation Bill said, 'It wouldn't do any good. He'd have Minna Wallis under the bed shoving a hypodermic up through the mattress.'

The indomitable matron was the sister of producer Hal and a long-time card-playing friend of Jimmy. She thought she could boss Jimmy around but she always wound up doing what he wanted. Shortly after my conversation with Bill, Jimmy checked himself into the London Clinic in Harley Street. It wasn't for a rest, it was for surgery. Jimmy wouldn't discuss his condition, neither would Buki, his doctor. Ireland finally told me that the problem was haemorrhoids, not serious but fearfully painful, often resulting in the patient breaking his own stitches. The day after the operation, a weak-voiced Jimmy rang me and asked if I'd like to visit him.

He was grey with pain when I arrived and he seemed so frail that I spent the hour trying to cheer him up. Jimmy told me that I should make myself scarce when his surgeon turned up. In fact the surgeon recognised me, saying, as he strode across the room, 'Of course I know Mr Stamp, he's exactly the person they would choose to portray someone like me in a film. He probably has the kind of long artistic hands that film directors imagine surgeons have, but as you see . . . '

He stopped speaking as his hand clasped mine and he glanced down at them – a matching pair.

'My God!' he said. 'You've missed your calling.'

*

Julie Christie by Terence Donovan, 1962.

I think Jimmy Fraser, my agent, felt much the same. The continual stream of offers I had turned down worried him, although guilt probably played a part too. He'd, after all, insisted that I meet Jimmy Woolf, who had promptly taken over my career and seemed bent on masterminding me out of the business. Fraser compensated by taking me to lunch regularly, trying to interest me in new projects, knowing full well he had to find a subject which would intrigue not only me but get Jimmy Woolf's approval as well. He had received a call from an outfit entitled Blazer Films who wanted to see me. Of course, I was happy to see anyone. There was a level on which I needed to work very much. It was only when I was with Jimmy Woolf that his negative logic blanked out my intuition.

Blazer Films had a small suite of offices at 13 Wigmore Street. In those days would-be producers cultivated publishing houses in the hope of getting tipped off about any new books that were potential movie material before they became popular and therefore expensive. Tom Maschler, the whizz-kid at Jonathan Cape, had sent John Kohn and Jud Kinberg at Blazer the proofs of a first novel by an unknown writer, *The Collector*, by John Fowles.

Nobody knew that Maschler had instigated the million-to-one chance that every film producer dreams of – a novel purchased for spit which becomes a world-wide number one bestseller. I started to read the proofs on my way home and from the first sentence was hooked. It wasn't until the 73 bus reached Knightsbridge that I glanced up from the closely printed text and realised I had missed my stop. But the further I read the more miserable I became. I was convinced that the wonderful part in this riveting tale was not for me: it seemed physically impossible to fold myself into the part of the collector.

The story turned on the fact that the boy was small, grey and nondescript, symbolic of the anonymous mass who lived their lives unnoticed by others. He was spotty, his nose ran. He lived with his aunt, worked at the local bank, collected butterflies and had fantasies (which was all I could identify with). There were really only two parts: the clerk and a local beauty on to whom he transferred his butterfly fixation. Feeling sick, I rang Jimmy Fraser and told him no. He was sick too, and he hadn't read the manuscript.

9

In January 1964 Antony Norris married a statuesque redhead called Paulene Stone at the church along from Hatchards in Piccadilly. I was invited but went alone as Caterine had a date with George Hamilton that Saturday. Weddings always made me cringe: even when I'd sung in the St Cedd's choir at sixpence a go I'd been suspicious of the glow that emanated from couples as they promised to do things for ever and ever. Things I knew I would be unable to give my word on for five minutes, let alone 'as long as ye both shall live'. I put on a suit and went, however. Bob Dylan once told me, 'I don't feel good if I don't work, Terence,' and to be honest, although I wouldn't have admitted it at the time, it had been fourteen months since I'd worked and the round of publicity and cocktail parties was starting to feel like a drip-dry shirt. I thought that the wedding and the instant grat of being recognised might be welcome distractions, might stop me considering that this choosy resting actor was getting perhaps a touch gun-shy.

The church was high, the occasion reverent and the pews were filled with Tony's friends. I saw Terence Donovan and David Bailey; Bailey was accompanied by my dream girl. I scrutinised the hobbady from East Ham – an irreverent black polo sweater, tight jeans and dusty, high cuban-heeled boots, which, like my dad's trilby, made him appear taller than he was. My first impression was of the young Citizen Kane. He was good, though. Even from a distance I could see what people saw in him, especially a rose from the counties, more accustomed to local horse trials than the cut and thrust of the Ilford Palais. He'd been lucky to cross her path, all the same. He leaned forward. I caught a glimpse of her as the sunlight, broken up by the coloured glass in the chancel windows, fell upon her face, still angel-innocent.

The traffic noise outside was suddenly a long way away. My

heart seemed to shrink as though protecting itself from the new sensation vibrating through it. My head was hot and I was certain my ears were red, but I couldn't move. The least distraction might have dashed the feeling which was distilling my blood. The church organ played us out. By the time I reached the courtyard a group had formed. Messrs Donovan and Bailey were snapping away with modest cameras, for all the world like wedding smudgers. The only evidence of the blissful turmoil I'd undergone was a dampness on the front of my voile shirt.

I walked to the reception at Quo Vadis on Dean Street, taking my time. I tried to calm myself, attempted to reconcile excitement with reticence whilst prolonging anticipation. When I arrived the bash had started. I congratulated Tony, kissed the bride, accepted a flute of champagne, sniffed at my carnation and found a spot against the wall where I could observe the action.

Over the years I had become quite accomplished at closing myself down: it was a practice I'd worked at to cope with being uncomfortable at parties. I had the idea from watching a cat in our yard at Chadwin Road. It sat so still; after a while it seemed the birds no longer saw it. I developed it a bit, switching my brain off and keeping the energy low so it didn't reach out and stimulate interest. I moved my head slowly from time to time so I wouldn't draw attention to myself by being too still, but I hadn't allowed for the camera. Bailey, focusing on a couple to the left, saw me through the viewfinder. He clicked the shutter and came over, grinning as though he'd known me all his life.

'You must be the Orson Welles of Soho,' I quipped.

''Orse and cart, you mean,' he quipped back without a beat, his grin getting wider.

He knew he didn't know me. I knew I'd never met him, but we fell easily into the new convention of assuming a familiarity with fellow mediarites. I remarked on the humble size of his camera.

'Inconspicuous, ain't it? Don't wanna make everyone self-conscious, do I?' He angled his lens at a girl falling out of her frock in an effort to load pasta on to her plate.

'Good exposure?' I asked.

'It's only album stuff. Norris couldn't afford my Hasselblad.'

He chortled to himself, a high-pitched 'he he he'. It was a comical sound, infectious.

'You're laid back,' he continued, 'not what I expected.'

'What d'ya expect, Dave, the black raper?'

He laughed again. 'Sort of.'

I looked around the room. Tony and Paulene were preparing to leave.

David said, 'I'd like to take some snaps of you . . . '

I didn't answer. Tony was smiling at me across the room, his eyes contorted like upside down crescent moons.

' . . . for *Vogue*,' David continued. 'You game?'

She was coming through the other guests.

'For anything,' I said.

'Bailey,' she said, 'Paulene and Tony are leaving. We should go and wish them . . . '

'Jean,' said Bailey, 'this is Terry Stamp. He's game for anything.'

I looked at her quickly, half hoping to catch the black of expanding pupils. Just the opposite, the famous eyes were almost completely blue.

'Hello,' she said and looked down, as though I was somehow intruding.

'Shall we go and see them off, then?' she said, reaching for Bailey's free hand.

The voice was high, like a schoolgirl's. It wasn't thin, only pitched incorrectly. Nothing a few sessions with my old voice coach, Kate Fleming, couldn't fix, I thought, wanting her to be perfect. I realised immediately the crassness of my intention. She had slid alongside Bailey. Unless I moved I couldn't see her, only her slender fingers clutching at his arm.

'I'm going to get another swig,' I said. 'Can I get anybody a glass?'

'No, we're pure. Thanks, anyway.'

I grimaced.

'I was a vegetarian till I met her. She started me eating chicken. Didn't you, Jean?' I bet she did, I thought, making my way to the bar. I couldn't resist a backward glance at the exquisite ankles. I bet she did.

After my second glass of Moët ordinaire I was feeling light-headed and quite philosophical, considering. I wished old Mike Caine had been with me – I could have used a bit of back-up. I joined the crowd on the kerb waving off the newly-weds. Donovan was getting his bulk behind a few snaps. He smiled at me when he saw I was watching him.

'Another good man gone,' he said. 'You'll be the only single geezer in town, at this rate.'

'It's a good life, if you don't weaken, Terence,' I retorted.

'Tell me about it. I wish I'd stayed single. I didn't know all this was gonna happen, did I?' He opened a surprisingly delicate hand, acknowledging the feminine beauty around him, amazed at his own position in the midst of it all.

'Didn't know I was gonna be a top man, did I? Jetting all over the place, smudging delectable crumpet every day. Earning a wedge, to boot.'

I remembered how Lee, my old mate from Plaistow, and I always went to his home late on Monday nights to see the Bob Cummings TV show, the sit-com about an American fashion photographer we'd both wanted to emulate. I wondered if T. Donovan had had the same fantasy. It had come to pass for him all right.

'So you want to be single now, do you?' I asked.

Passers-by were gathering across the road, looking at the goings on. Some started to recognise me and I began to feel uncomfortable.

'I wouldn't mind,' said Donovan.

'You're not the type, I've heard about you. You've gotta have balls to be a moving target.'

'You're a bit steely, ain't you, for such a skinny geezer?'

It was odd how cockney boys used mild insults to show they approved of one another. Donovan's prowess with the ladies was known even before he left Stepney. He pointed back into the restaurant.

'I'm grabbing some more bevvy while it's going, you coming?'

'No, I've had my limit.'

'Cheap date, eh?'

'Yeh, depletes my sperm count.'

'Funny, does the opposite to me.'

Donovan's alcohol intake was also legendary. I'd heard that he'd held a New York model out of a twenty-storey window at arm's length to 'cool her off'.

Bailey cruised over.

'Got it covered then, Donovan?' he said.

Donovan slipped his little camera into his charcoal suit pocket and patted it. He moved off. A volcano of a man, I thought.

'What are you up to, then?' Bailey said to me.

'Me? Not much.'

'We're going to pick up my Morgan and drive down to Jean's folks in Bucks. Wanna come?'

'Sure.'

So we picked up his natty racing green sports car from a mechanic in a mews off Wigmore Street and motored to Rose Hill Farm. Bailey drove and I sat in the only passenger seat with Jean on my lap.

That was how it started. I had the impression of being dragged feet first into their circle and truth was, I felt uncomfortable in Jean's presence. She was indifferent to me. It was a re-run of the one-sided romance with Ethel Proud, my grammar school heart-throb, except that now I was the flavour of the month and expected everything to be different. Also, the model image in the media needed some adjusting. Jean was serene, and certainly didn't chatter, hardly spoke. She carried wool and knitting needles with her and when Bailey and his friends were gassing away, out came her pastime. It was the last thing I expected from the fast-rising sex symbol. Jean had eyes only for Bailey, or so it seemed, and it didn't take long to figure why. He was one of those rare archetypes, rare in my experience, anyway, who chose to be with their women twenty-four hours a day. As he was blessed with a wickedly comical sense of humour, making frequent references to his National Service nickname, King Cory, I had little reason to believe Jean would ever look seriously in my direction. I was increasingly taken by his charm, and the friendship that blossomed was between Bailey and me. Jean made a beautiful, albeit passive, adornment. I rarely saw Bailey alone. Even when he first photographed me for *Vogue* Jean soon joined us and that became the trend. I don't think he was wary of the company of men and on those rare occasions when Jean was working for someone else, he and I had some hilarious times, but on the whole he gravitated naturally to women.

Jean struck me as a country girl giving town life a whirl. She had a Yorkshire terrier that usually stayed with her mum on the farm and the times I accompanied them to the country were the occasions I witnessed Jean at her most animated, amongst the horses and prize Welsh white porkies of her changeable and explosive dad, Ted Shrimpton. I became very fond of Mrs

The Shrimptons and Bert.

Shrimpton, and studying her gave me lots of insight into her eldest daughter.

As my friendship with Bailey developed it was easier to sublimate my feelings for his girlfriend. Where I grew up there had always been a code about messing with mates' wives or lovers. When I started travelling, foreign acquaintances often referred to the English penchant for affairs between friends. I was aware of the erotica these clashes promised, but I'd always exercised restraint. My growing comradeship with Bailey dissolved the passion I felt for Jean, replacing my obsession with a less explosive affection. I could gaze at the polished limbs without getting into a frenzy of desire, and be objectively in awe of her beauty as though coming upon a rare orchid. When she began showing me her facial imitations of other models she'd worked with, I felt I'd somehow earned her trust.

THE GREAT MIDDLE

10

In May 1964 I went to Hollywood to start *The Collector*. Bailey had offered to drive me to Heathrow in his new E-Type Jaguar, and *en route* he told me Jean and he would soon be in New York shooting for American *Vogue*. We should try to link up. I thought it doubtful I would have any time for jaunts to the East Coast. He suggested they might visit me.

During the flight I had thirteen hours to ponder the events that had led to this project. Jimmy Woolf, who always encouraged me to turn work down, had agreed I shouldn't attempt to play the seedy bank clerk. Jimmy Fraser hadn't been so sure. Time was passing and, although I was still blazing a media trail, my agent knew that every day without work made it harder for him to get me any. I was also short of funds. This was making me increasingly susceptible to Jimmy Woolf's constant offer of an exclusive contract. At the moment I felt most desperate to work, John Kohn called. William Wyler had agreed to direct *The Collector*.

'Are you going to say no to Wyler?' he asked.

As Wyler was one of the all-time great film directors – *The Best Years of Our Lives*, *Wuthering Heights*, *Roman Holiday* – my certainty faltered.

'Does he want me, though?'

'That's the point,' rasped Kohn. 'He does.'

'Who is set to play Miranda?'

'We are doing some tests.'

'Let me sleep on it. John, I'll call you tomorrow.'

Even Jimmy Woolf was taken aback when I told him.

'Wyler,' he exclaimed. 'Why would Wyler want to do it? I thought he was set for *The Sound of Music*.'

'Well, the book's number one in the *Time* bestseller list. It's not exactly uncommercial.'

Jimmy agreed. 'Why don't you offer to test with the actresses? That way, you'll see how you go, and it will give Wyler an opportunity to see you in the role.'

'Yeah, that's a thought.'

'In the mean time, I'll talk to that Jimmy Fraser of yours and see what sort of money is involved.'

At last he's thinking positively, I thought to myself, but I said, 'Mike Caine thinks I should do it.'

'Terence, Michael Caine is not you. Michael Caine would do anything. Stars are choosy, they only come out at night. There are lots of fine British actors, but not so many stars. Don't be in such a rush.'

I'd heard it all before, but I couldn't pass up a chance to work with Wyler. I called John Kohn. Jud Kinberg, his co-producer, answered. I told him I'd like to test with the girls. He was delighted.

So I tested with Samantha Eggar and Sarah Miles. I believe Julie Christie was also approached. A director named Bob Parrish shot the footage. I took it seriously, went to Morris Angel the costumier in Leicester Square and found a tight, blue pin-stripe suit with one or two moth holes. It was perfect for an underpaid, underachieving bank clerk. A pair of heavy, highly polished Oxford shoes gave me the right footing.

The test – a complete scene shot in the collector's cellar – went well. The girls featured but there was enough of me to give Wyler a good idea of the line I intended to take.

The great director arrived in London a few days later to view the footage Robert Parrish had shot. He invited me to the Columbia building in Wardour Street to meet him. I was in a corridor on the first floor when Wyler heard I'd arrived. He came out of an office to greet me – smaller than I'd expected, tender eyes in a grizzled face. We stood looking at each other in the passage. John Kohn and Jud Kinberg started to come out of the office, but hesitated and stopped in the doorway. My first impulse was to get hold of him. He wasn't at all like I'd heard. Every actor I'd met related gruesome tales from artists who'd worked for him. He looked like a big pussy cat to me. It was rumoured he was hard of hearing, but the eyes sure twinkled a million times a second. Was this the guy who'd given Montgomery Clift his film break, the director who'd taught Laurence Olivier how to act on film?

'I've seen the tests,' he said simply, his voice husky, accent American, but intonation something else.

'Which girl did you like?'

He drew closer. 'I haven't looked yet. I've only been able to look at you.' He smiled. It was more than warm.

'Do you . . . do you really want me for this part?' I stammered.

'No one else.'

'But the, in the book . . . '

He cut me short, putting most of his fingers over his mouth. It was a gesture I would get to know well. Then he placed his arm around my shoulders, his mouth close to my ear. He smelled spicy – leather and French tobacco.

'I'm not making the book,' he whispered. He paused, his arm still enclosing my shoulder. 'I'm going to make a love story. A modern love story.' He turned my face to his and looked me directly in the eye. 'And you're going to be . . . just purrfect.'

I'd only known him a moment but I was a conspirator already. I drew back warily. In a grave tone I said, 'I've heard about you, though. They call you the velvet glove with the stainless steel fist. I've heard you strangle actors. Make them do fifty takes, without telling them why.'

He just smiled the big monkey smile. I went on.

'I have to warn you. I only like to do one or two takes.'

Without a beat he said, 'You give me what I want in one take and we'll get along just fine.'

The two Jimmys did the deal, including a point and a half of the net profit and $1,000 a week expenses. Even Caine was impressed.

Once in Hollywood, I stayed in the Beverly Hills Hotel for a few days, then found myself a flat in a compact apartment building south of Sunset. Sunset Boulevard, surely the street with the most romantic name in the world. My address was 1006 Doheny Drive. I hired a Studebaker Lark from Milt Friedman, took my driving test, which lasted about twenty seconds, and called the only person I knew in town, Harry Cohn, son of the late mogul, Harry Cohn, who'd started Columbia Pictures. Harry, jun., had little interest in movies himself, other than watching them, but he took me to a Malibu Point beach house that belonged to Tuesday Weld. It was

Samantha with William Wyler, Hampstead.

being thrown open to celebrate her homecoming from a forces tour of the Far East with Bob Hope. The high-rafted studio was one enormous room whose décor looked as though it had been conceived around a large leopardskin-covered bed. Now I know I'm in Hollywood, I thought. I was standing looking at this monster, when an impossibly cute blonde approached me.

'Hello,' she said, offering a silky tanned hand. 'I hear you're the new stud in town. I'm Tuesday.' She was all of seventeen. In the background, Harry was killing himself at my loss of words.

We were to rehearse the picture in the Columbia studios on Sunset and Gower. Sets of the interiors were already under construction on the sound stages. I had always visualised the movie as small, a black and white subject shot on location in an English cellar. I hadn't allowed for Mike Frankovitch who had recently become head of Columbia Pictures world-wide. He wanted to be known as the strongman who had ended European-based productions – many film-makers had crossed the Atlantic to avoid escalating labour costs in Hollywood. *The Collector*'s budget was $2,000,000. As a conciliatory gesture, Frankovitch had agreed to allow Wyler to shoot the exteriors in the English countryside after the studio work was completed. It was a risky way of doing it, as if the weather in England was bad we would be without weather cover (movie terminology for scenes that can be shot inside if the elements don't match the shooting schedule).

The first week of rehearsal went well. I was introduced to the art of Bud Westmore, who designed my make-up. I particularly liked Friday when I reported to the little hatch, not unlike a ticket kiosk in a railway station, and was handed a thousand dollars that I had to get by on for seven whole days. Wyler rang me on Saturday morning.

'You were at acting school with Sam?' he asked.

'Yeah, I had a crush on her, as it happens.'

'Don't get too friendly, now.'

'Why?'

'I want a real tension on film. OK?' he said tersely.

'OK, if you say so.'

Half-way through the second week, Willie hit a hitch. He took me aside.

'I want to stop work for a little while. Don't look worried, you're doing fine. It's something I need to work out. You take off

Rehearsal without rain – *The Collector*, 1964.

somewhere, relax, you'll be on expenses. Have a holiday. Let me know where you are and I'll call you when I want you back.'

I'd met a girl in Hollywood at a Sunday brunch who could have been the model for a Christmas tree fairy. Everybody called her Angel. She'd starred in a TV series playing a French maid of that name. Her real name was Annie – a Parisian, with an accent to prove it. Annie turned out to be an Aries, and was as petite as my grandmother, Kate, had been.

At the time of the picture's postponement, Annie was in New York. She rang me frequently, sounding full of beans, languishing in a friend's spacious apartment which was empty, save for her five-foot-two frame. I thought I'd go east and keep her company. She hadn't told me she was dating French director, François Truffaut, who was also in New York.

However, I didn't suspect anything when she told me sweetly, 'Eet is not proper for you to stay in friend's apartment lended specifically to 'er.'

I checked into my old stomping ground, the Drake Hotel, where I had stayed for the US première of *Billy Budd*. Finding Annie had more business to attend to than me, I rang Condé Nast on the off-chance that my mate Bailey had hit town. That evening I located him at the Concord Hotel.

As Jean was in demand in New York and working for photographers other than Bailey, he and I often hung out together. The three of us went to parties and I was introduced to the fashion world of New York, including some well-scrubbed young models from *Glamor* magazine. I was quite sorry when, after ten days, Wyler recalled me to the coast. The limousine sent by Columbia to take me to Idylwild arrived early and, as I had plenty of time and only hand-luggage, I asked the driver to stop by the Concord to say cheerio to my chums. Bailey was up but Jean was still in bed reading the Sunday papers. I had never seen her completely without make-up: she looked younger than ever, but appeared uncomfortable. I felt that I was intruding so, after giving them my telephone number and offering to put them up if they felt like a vacation, I left.

The picture started smoothly. I had based my character on the lonely tailor's apprentice I'd met years before when on tour with *The Long and the Short and the Tall*. Wyler seemed pleased with me and I with him, but my evenings were lonely. Although not short of company, there was that something inside me that never seemed to be nourished. I was more aware of it away from home. I would look at couples linking hands and strolling along the Strip and wonder if they were in love, wonder if they felt like me or if there was something special inside that lit their faces on their languid twilight walks. Driving home from the studio after work one evening, with a radio rock station playing full blast and both windows open, enjoying the early evening breeze, I caught sight of Vita Health Foods, near the corner of Fairfax. I'd seen the shop before: a small building shaped like a toy fort, divided into two premises with a sign on the roof proclaiming Natural Vitamins and Minerals. Cosmetics. Herbs. Organic Produce. It looked interesting yet out of place on Sunset Boulevard, and I'd been planning to give it the once-over.

That night I had nowhere to go, no engagement to keep. The store was still open. I parked the car and went in. There was something out of step here, or perhaps it was because I'd never been in a real health shop before. It was the only one I'd seen other than the tiny premises in Barking Road across from the florist's at the Abbey Arms, and I hadn't set foot inside that one, although as a boy I must have spent hours looking at the windows arranged with small dishes containing unnamed dried seeds and fruits. The interior of Vita Health gave me the same feeling I'd had gazing into the shop in Plaistow. I cruised the stacked aisles, wondering at the eclectic collection of food and pills that made you healthy. It was all interesting but I couldn't overcome the vague sadness I kept feeling. I always suffered away from home. It was like the moods I'd had as a boy, which I imagined would evaporate when I grew up and met a girl: a Grace my own age or a Toni who loved me – not someone else. Yet here I was, twenty-five years old, making my first Hollywood film, fulfilling most of the fantasies I'd dreamt would make me content, and that same feeling, that same unfulfilled space was still there. Worse. I purchased a basket of minute tomatoes, my favourite size, from a lady who told me she was Betty Von Breck and had run the store for ten years, and left. During the remaining mile or so to Doheny Drive I asked myself about this feeling. I switched off the dashboard radio and spoke direct to the part of me that felt tender, talked to it as though it was a small child. No answer.

That evening I was trying to fathom my multi-channelled television set when the telephone rang. It was Bailey. He sounded upset – Jean had left him. I was amazed. It had seemed an ideal partnership. He was shattered, lost, with no idea of what to do.

'Well, what did she say?'

'She wants to spend some time apart. I don't know how, where to go. I should go back to London but I'm not sure. She's spending a few days away. I'm . . . what d'you think?'

I didn't know what to say, either.

'D'you think I should go back home, Tel?'

'Dave, I never think it's good for a woman to see a bloke when he's down. I think you should take yourself off. Don't hang up behind the door. You're a top man. If she's found someone else it'll be humiliating for you to be hanging around getting kicked, and maybe if you're not there, chances are she'll see what she's missed and come to you. I think you should split. Come out here if you like, or go back to London if you feel better on home ground. You know, you've mates there.'

I'm not certain he was listening. He must have been inconsolable. I promised I'd ring him the next day to see what he'd decided. I didn't. We worked late and when I arrived home I felt, with the time difference, I might wake him.

I rang the next day as soon as I'd finished work. I was put through to their room. There was a click and a female voice answered. I was taken aback. It was Jean.

'Er, hello, it's Terence. I, er, is David there?'

I expected her to put on a cheery Bailey and discover everything patched up.

'No,' she said. 'He's gone back to London.'

There was a long pause.

'Stamp,' she said, 'are you still there?'

'Yes, I'm here.'

'Are you busy? Have you got a moment?'

'No. Yeah, I'm fine.'

She began to speak to me easily, like a friend. Although I'd spent time with them both, I felt uncomfortable, as if I was betraying Bailey. I had to keep bringing my attention back to her voice. The least I could do was to give my ear a hundred per cent. I tried to picture her in the untidy hotel room. I couldn't. She kept asking me if I was listening. I suggested perhaps it was a mistake for her to stay in New York, that it might be a good idea for her to go back to London, too.

'Listen, Stamp. I know you're fond of Bail, but it isn't how you imagine. I don't want you to feel bad, me talking like this . . . I know he's your friend, but I'm a person, too, you know.'

It occurred to me we hadn't really spoken, only hellos and cheerios. She'd laughed if I'd said anything funny; she'd listened while Bailey and I solved the world. I had no idea of what went on under that fringe yet now she was revealing a little of herself, a different Jean.

I heard someone knock on her door. She excused herself and I hung on. I heard her answer she would be right down. I wondered where she was going.

'Stamp?'

'Yeah.'

'I've got to go out now. You know you said we could come and stay with you in Hollywood. Did you mean me, as well? I'd like to, if it's no trouble. I need to get away for a bit. Word is out Bailey's gone back. I'm a bit of a moving target. You know what photographers are like.'

'Sure, that'd be fine.'

'Can I ring you towards the weekend, to let you know?'

'Yeah.'

'Can you give me your number, then?'

I gave it to her, and hung up in shock. Trying not to think about it, feeling bewildered, excited but guilty. On Wednesday night the phone rang.

She said, 'What's brown, weighs a ton and lights forest fires?'

'Don't know.'

'Smokey, the firebug,' she chuckled, pleased with herself. 'Is it still OK? I've booked a plane that gets to LA at six-thirty.'

'That's fine. Give me the flight number.'

I scribbled it down.

'Listen, Jean. I generally finish work at six. With a bit of luck I should be able to meet the flight. Now, if for any reason I'm not there, take a cab and go to 1006 Doheny Drive. It's just below Sunset Boulevard.'

'I'm looking forward to getting away,' she said.

'I'll try to be at the airport, OK?'

'Are you all right? No second thoughts?'

'No, no. I'll see you tomorrow. 1006 Doheny Drive.'

'Yes.'

We hung up and I glanced around me. My quarters looked decidedly small. There was only one bed, large, but one. Perhaps I could sleep on the sofa in the living-room? It was big enough but, as I walked around the apartment visualising it housing two strangers, I knew it wasn't on. Jean was probably hurting so I should give her space, make her feel comfortable. I had two days to find a house.

The next morning I rang Jimmy Woolf in London. I was vetted by the Grosvenor House switchboard, announced and then put through. I explained my problem to Jimmy.

He said, 'Call my actor friend, Lee Paterson. No – I'll call him and call you back.'

'Jimmy, I have to go to work.'

'What's got into you? It will only take a few minutes.' The line went dead.

He was right, I was nervous. There was no real reason. I could always book her into the Beverly Hills Hotel. I had to be careful, though. In Hollywood, hotel clerks and waiters in restaurants actually phoned in bits of gossip to the papers for money. It wasn't like England. The telephone rang.

Jimmy said, 'Lee's house is free. It's beautiful, on Doheny but high in the hills. It has a pool and wonderful views.'

'Two bedrooms?'

'Two bedrooms, with bath *en suite* and separate guest quarters upstairs. Who are you trying to get away from?'

'As long as there's plenty of room.'

'There is. Now, I have given Lee your address and telephone number but, if you don't hear anything to the contrary, be at the house at seven o'clock this evening. An agent will show you the place and give you the keys. You can move in straight away. It's not expensive. Lee has made you a special price. Any questions?'

'No.'

'Don't you want the address?'

'Oh yeah, yeah. Sorry.'

'My God! 1706 Doheny Drive. Got that?'

'Yeah, Jim. Thanks, mate.'

'Any time.'

I saw the place, as arranged. It was splendid but the three-car garage at the top of the steep drive reminded me that Jean would need transport. It was almost illegal to walk in Beverly Hills.

I packed my things, intending to move my stuff into 1706 before I went to work, but I didn't have time. I left my suitcase in the hall.

I had a very sympathetic dresser on the picture, named Jack. He and the make-up man had taken care of me since day one. When I told Jack that I had a friend coming to stay who would need a car, he said he could arrange for one to be delivered to my apartment that evening. If I wasn't there the keys would be left on the sun visor. I could sign the papers later.

'What time is she arriving?' Jack asked.

'Six-thirty from New York.'

'Why don't I have a word with the first assistant, see if he can get you sprung a little early?'

'If you can.'

'No problem.'

It seemed nothing was a problem in Hollywood. Jack spoke to the first. The first spoke to the cameraman, the great Bob Surtees, and he said he'd set it up so I wasn't in the last shot. I could lose my make-up and be off just before six. It should only take me thirty to forty minutes to drive to the airport.

That's how it worked. The make-up man rubbed a dash of Sea Breeze aftershave on my face and I left. 'Freshen you up,' he said. On my way to the car I noticed the ground was wet. The car park attendant on the lot said there had been a sun shower, rare for the time of year. He wiped my windscreen and I was off. Pulling out on to Sunset I saw the giant arc of a rainbow, one foot planted into the eastern end of the famous boulevard. Driving west I could see the colours in my mirror. I hoped it wasn't a bad omen to be driving away from it.

I hadn't worn aftershave for years. My face smelled overpowering. Would she approve? I arrived at the airport with ten minutes to spare and messed about with the radio trying to find a station with mellow music, in case conversation proved difficult. Then I climbed out of the car and walked a witch's circle around it to stop anyone giving me a ticket. The afternoon flight from New York was on time.

'Should be de-planing any minute, sir,' affirmed a Lana Turner look-alike from the airways. I was feeling all right, but as soon as I caught sight of her tall body stepping out ahead of the other passengers, her head held high, the eyes and lips filled with light, my heart hit the roof of my mouth. She saw me. Her blink rate went up, she was nervous, too. A couple of truants meeting up in the park. Well, I thought, I'm the man, it's up to me to make her feel at ease.

I said, 'What's orange, pointed and travels at a hundred and twenty miles per hour?'

'An XK1 carrot,' she replied.

'Gosh, you're so smart.'

She flushed and I didn't know where to put myself.

'My luggage is all in here,' she said, pointing to a tobacco suede weekend bag.

'You mean, we can split?'

'Yes.'

'How wonderful. A woman after my own heart.'

We climbed into my lucky Studebaker Lark and took off. By the time we'd left the San Diego freeway and headed east, the rainbow had moved. She was in my car. The sun set during the drive to the apartment. By the time we arrived it was almost dark. The man with the car was waiting. I signed and received the keys.

'It's for you,' I said.

'Oh,' she replied.

'You can't get anywhere on foot here. It's too spread out.'

'I'm . . . '

'What is it?'

' . . . not sure I can drive it.'

''Course you can. You love to drive.'

'But it's left-hand drive and so big,' she said, looking doubtfully at the finned Belvedere.

'It will take you two minutes, believe me. I, er, asked for a real American car, because I thought you'd like . . . '

'OK,' she said. 'I'll manage.'

We went upstairs to the apartment. She saw the suitcase in the hall.

'Let's go.'

She looked bewildered, but followed.

'Now you drive your car and follow me. We'll take it slowly. It's only up the hill.'

She twitched her lips like a mouse.

'It's nothing. Come on.'

I'd no sooner climbed into the car and started backing out, when I saw Warren Beatty arriving at the front door. I don't know if he recognised Jean: I realised I was a bit paranoid about keeping her visit a secret.

The nervy caravan edged up the twisting road of Doheny. We both made it up the steep drive of 1706. I unlocked the front door, left the suitcase by the stairs, and proudly showed her the house. The view was wonderful, an illuminated map of L A. I turned the pool lights on and off, pointed up to where I would be sleeping and took her bag into the master bedroom, laying it on the queen-size bed. I opened the drapes to reveal the pool and another fanfare landscape.

'These are your quarters,' I said with a flourish. 'Your bath and shower-room, here.'

She looked around, overwhelmed, I thought.

'I haven't had a chance to buy any provisions yet. I thought we could do that together, tomorrow.'

She hadn't moved. I rambled on.

'We can go out if you're not too tired or we can have tea here. I have some packed in my case. No milk, though, but it's good tea.'

No answer.

'What do you think, hmm?'

She walked back through the passage and looked up the stairs.

'You can stay up there if you like; it's nice, a bit smaller but . . . '

She gave me a blank look and walked back into the gigantic living-room across the white wall-to-wall, thick as a West Highland terrier's fur. She switched on the lamp at the end of the massive sofa. The static electricity in her fingers made her flinch.

'I should have warned you about that,' I said.

She sat herself into the far corner of the sofa, slipped off her shoes and folded her blue-jeaned legs under her. She looked small.

'Stamp,' she said, 'there is something I want to tell you.'

I couldn't think of anything I'd done to give offence.

'Do I need to sit down?' I joked, trying to lighten the atmosphere which was curling the hair on my neck.

Jean at the dolls' hospital.

'You may, if you please,' she said, like a teacher of English grammar.

I hunched into the matching armchair by the big fireplace. Everything else in the room was white. I messed with the chain curtain which hung in front of the grate. It was loaded with logs atop a fixed gas bar, a key set into the floor to turn it on. Silence. I realised she was waiting for my attention.

'I know you're bad with girls. Into one night stands and that. I just want you to know, I don't care.' She looked down. 'I like you, that's all.'

She stood up. I felt weak as I stepped across the room to her. She took a pace and stopped. Her bare feet sank into the pile up to her Levi bottoms. She was wearing her favourite heather sweater from Liberty's, the knit so thin in places that the pale blue of her shirt showed through. When I was only a foot or so from her, she lifted her deep lids and I saw a light, a thin line of fire come from her left eye. I felt my hands grip her arms but I couldn't move my eyes from hers. The expanded pupils covered almost the whole iris, leaving only a rim of blue. I had no will left of my own. I kissed her. It could have been my first kiss. I felt as though I'd reached home. Guilt set in immediately. My friend's girl. She felt it and drew away.

'What?'

'Jean, I . . . ' My voice sounded dry. Distant. My knees couldn't support me. I slid down to the carpet. She held on to my right hand and lowered herself to sit in front of me. Again, the hot line of vapour from the expanded cat's eyes.

'Oh, Jean,' feelings bombarded me. 'I've waited for . . . but Bailey, what's he going to say? I know how he feels.'

'Of course,' the long fingers stroked my hair, my shorn *Collector*-style hair.

'It's short,' I said self-consciously.

'It'll grow.'

'Yes.'

'What would you like to do, then?' she asked.

'I could make some tea.'

'I don't mean that.'

'I know, but . . . ' I was lost for words again, looking at the face before me.

'We'll make some tea,' she said, suddenly practical.

'We might get ginger twins,' I said automatically.

'I beg your pardon?'

'Oh, nothing, a superstition, something my mum used to say, if more than one person made the tea.'

We brewed a pot of Earl Grey and sat formally across from one another in the stark dining-room, never used, off from the kitchen.

'What would you like to do, then?' she repeated. I breathed in the steam of the scented fumes rising from the cup in front of me. It smelled unusually strong.

'How long can you stay?' I asked finally.

'I'm booked to work in New York on Wednesday. I could cancel. It's only advertising.'

'Good photographer?'

'Very. Bert Stern.'

I poured some tea into my saucer, blew on it and drank down a draft.

'How much work d'you have?'

'It's my New York season. I can't make any money in London. I only work for *Vogue*, they pay practically nothing. Eileen Ford, my US agent, knows that, so she gets me in July and usually books me solid – I make enough to keep me for a year. I shifted a few bookings to come this weekend. Bill Hellberg, he's a chum. He didn't mind.' She looked at me. 'It's not really important. It's only what I do. I like to be independent.'

'So you have two weeks' work from Wednesday?'

She nodded. I heard myself saying, 'Let's not make this heavy. If it's important, let's be sure – get started on the right foot. We'll have these few days like mates. We'll do something, go somewhere funny. You go back to work. If we both feel the same, I'll send you a ticket, you come and stay here for the rest of the shooting. How's that sound?'

'You're a funny boy,' she said.

'That's well known.'

'I heard.'

'It's the least we can do. If it wasn't for David, we wouldn't be here.'

'I know.'

'Do you?'

'I know now.'

'OK, settled.'

In her only evening gown.

'Stamp, there *is* something.'

'Anything.'

'Don't commit yourself.'

'Almost anything.' I poured another cup. It was looking strong.

'You make a serious cup of tea, my friend. My new friend.'

'I'm a serious girl. Stamp?'

'You're so wonderful to look at.'

'It's only make-up, my face is too square. Wait till you really see me . . . '

'I have.'

'Stamp. Don't sleep upstairs. Don't make me sleep on my own. We needn't do anything. Only, let's be close.'

We were. After the first moments it wasn't difficult. She wore a nightdress, me pyjamas. It was wonderful, actually. A current seemed to flow between us. A circuit connected.

We went to Las Vegas. It was my choice, not the right one, but we had fun. Saw a show designed by my chum, Sean Kenny. Jean had never been to a dinner-show before. I kept finding myself gazing at her.

'What?' she would ask quizzically.

I couldn't answer; how to explain my empty-headed wonderment? She would grin and look away, blushing, mystified. I had a terrific urge to dance with her. We found a hotel with a bar and minute dance floor. I no sooner had her in my arms when the hotel detective accused her of being under age and wanted an ID. We didn't know what it meant, let alone have one. The days flew by. It was time for goodbye. I awoke before sun-up, watched her sleeping, then climbed out of bed carefully and made us a farewell cuppa. I brought the specially designed tray for bed back to the bedroom, woke her, and we watched the sun rise, lighting the mist, filling the room with that clean smell. As I left I could see her by the little jade tree, its leaves polished by the rays of the early sun. It liked being close to her, too.

I arrived at the studio late by ten minutes and Wyler was waiting. He looked at me without speaking. I apologised and patted my chest.

'It won't happen again, sir. I'm sorry.'

'That's all right, then.'

We went straight into a long scene. It was ten o'clock by the time I could get to a telephone. I was fretting to hear her voice. There was no answer. She had already left.

Jean Shrimpton by David Bailey, 1963.

My favourite photo of Jean.

11

The day passed incredibly slowly as though compensating for the previous four that had sped by. It was six-fifteen by the time I pulled into the steep drive of 1706. Everything was clean, everything put away, save two cups and saucers on the table in the position where we'd sipped our tea the first night. I made a pot and poured both cups. The telephone rang. It was the AD confirming my call for the following day. I drank my cup, then sat in her seat and tried to look across at myself.

Stamp. She had only ever called me that. I did like the way she said it. It sounded special, like Cadogan or Jaipur. Perhaps I'd made a terrible mistake sending her away. The more I thought about what I'd done the more insane it seemed. I had not only let her go, I'd sent her away, practically forced her back to New York.

'You know what photographers are like. I'm a bit of a moving target,' she'd said.

Oh God! I thought, please, please let it be OK. It had all felt so right at the time. Don't let her meet anybody else, I said to myself. The telephone rang.

'What is yellow . . . '

'Oh, Jean, you called.' That lump swelled in my throat.

'Stamp,' her voice sounded shocked, 'is everything all right?'

'Yes, yes, it's OK now – it's been a long day.'

'It has. Stamp, how do you feel?'

'OK.'

'Stamp, tell me how you feel.'

I couldn't speak. Chain mail enclosed my chest.

'Are you there?' the small voice from faraway New York, like paper being crinkled.

'Yes, I'm here.'

'Stamp, do you miss me?'

'Yes.'

'Tell me, Stamp, let me hear you say it.'

'I miss you. Jean . . . '

'Yes.'

'I . . . feel, you know . . . '

'I don't, tell me.'

'Jean, I – I think I'm . . . '

'Tell me.'

' . . . very much in love with you.'

The pounding in my head rushed away and a breeze drifted in, cool, touching the place that lamented, that had lain fallow, dormant, thirsty, all through my boyhood. A tremor – the unseen announcing itself.

'Are you there? Stamp, you there?'

'Yes.'

'Darling, it's the same for me, you know that, don't you?'

'I . . . '

'Don't speak now . . . '

'No.'

'Let's talk tomorrow, you ring me, this time.'

'You staying home?'

'I'm staying home.' She hung up.

Darling, had she called me darling? No one had ever called me that.

So it continued. My work during the day became light, effortless. I was happy. Wyler was pleased. One-takes abounded. Everything was different, changed. This was IT, the thing that transformed people, made them glow. I'd seen it on their faces and now it had happened to me.

We spoke nightly, but by the end of the first week I couldn't stand it, it was too frustrating. Unable to see her or hold her, I felt drained by hearing her voice and I asked her not to ring.

'Jean, just tell me when you're coming, let's not speak any more. Just arrive.'

There was a long silence.

'You are such a funny boy,' she said.

'Funny peculiar or funny ha ha?'

'Both. I'm coming on that same flight, Friday.'

'Yes.'

'Stamp, don't hire me a car.'

'OK.'
'Good night, then. See you Friday.'

There is a tree that does well in California's desert air. It bears
soft mauvy-pink blossoms that soon fall. Sometimes these fragile
bells float down without impact, and it's possible to smell a delicate
perfume, barely discernible and only for a moment. The damaged
ones have no fragrance. You can wait a long time for one to fall.

When I was little it was rumoured that if you caught a falling
leaf in your left hand and made a wish, the wish would come true.
I was born a lefty, in a world that was geared to right-handed
tin-openers and scissors, but my cack-handedness came into its
own during autumn in the Beckton Road Park where seven winds
blew. In autumn, the ground rose, enriched with the shades of its
temporary carpet. But even in November with the excitement of
Guy-Fawkes (in those days, a treat in its own right, as no one dared
to promote Christmas until well after the last sparks of bonfires
and fireworks) whilst kids of all ages stuffed the tough leaves into
discarded sacks, old trousers and sweaters producing eye-catching
effigies for threepenny joeys or even silver tanners, I was always
less industriously occupied. Or so everyone thought. I was, in fact,
exercising my one big advantage in a right-handed world, but then
I had such a lot of wishes to be granted. When others' rockets,
catherine wheels or giant roman candles had long gone the way
of all pyrotechnics, my boyhood requests were slowly being
answered.

This particular Beverly Hills tree, which I came to think of as
my wishing tree, used to stand in a garden which formed a triangle
at the junction of Swallow and Doheny. I'd discovered it the night
after Jean left Los Angeles that first time, bathed in the light which
fills the air as the sun sinks and tends to make everything look like
ice-cream. I'd climbed out of the car and smelled one or two of
the fallen blossoms before driving on. You have to be careful when
you stand still in Beverly Hills – you can often experience something
called armed response if you loiter anywhere too long.

The night before Jean's proposed return, I drove up to Swallow
for some left-handed expertise. Throwing caution to the rarefied
breeze, which is all that is allowed to blow there, I kept my eye on
a pale blossom as it drifted down from a high branch right into my

palm. It fell like a sigh. I inhaled at the moment it released its delicate scent and made my perfumed wish.

On Friday I returned to Los Angeles airport, to find the same spot vacant by the kerb. This time I noticed it was painted red. I made my circle and then, realising Miss S. would probably have a suitcase, I walked round the motor a second time. I stood by it until I saw her. She had a frock on and the curve of her calves was intensified by the small heels of her navy blue shoes. I kissed her. We set off. Radio? No. She rested her left hand lightly on my right thigh. We turned off the freeway before Sunset.

'Where are we going?'

I glanced across at her. She looked fragile that evening, even though she wore lipstick.

'Surprise,' I said. 'Dinner.'

'Oh.' She didn't sound too keen to be surprised.

At Trader Vic's we were shown to an intimate corner table on the ground floor of the Polynesian room. I ordered her a Banana Cow, a funny non-alcoholic drink. In the half-light she looked uneasy.

'Are you OK?'

She nodded, jaw fixed. I associated the expression with first days of rehearsal when I've studied the lines but I'm not sure of their delivery. The drinks arrived.

'We'll order in a moment, thank you.'

'It's over, isn't it?'

'What?'

'You've changed your mind, haven't you?'

It took me a moment to fathom what she was saying. I placed my hand over hers on the table.

'Stop. Stop right there. This is the most wonderful night of my life. I haven't breathed properly all day. I'm nervous. You're nervous. I only wanted to take you out to supper. I thought you would like that. Kinda romantic. If you don't, we'll leave. We can do whatever you want. I'm sorry if you misunderstood. I'm a clodhopping scrubber from the East End. Whatever happens, you've given me feelings I haven't had before, wonderful feelings. Did you hear me? Would you repeat it for me, please?'

I produced a small gold cross and chain. I'd had the modern design made for her. I pushed it across in its little box. She smiled, and the warmth returned to her face.

'I'm sorry, Stamp, it's me. I'm being silly. I am silly.'

She was the sixth-former again. She knew. She had my number. Maybe she didn't know. Maybe that's what devastated me. The Scorpio eye approved my token gift. She put it on.

'Don't order much for me,' she said. 'I can't eat much when I'm . . . like this.'

I drove home through the Toytown centre of Beverly Hills.

'No car for you, this time, right?'

'Right. I don't mind staying in. I can amuse myself.'

'You drive me to the studio in the morning, you come and pick me up at night. I teach you the route. Right?'

'Yes, I'd like that.'

As we arrived I scraped the back of the car, tilting up the steep drive too quickly.

'Tea?'

'No.' Her lower lip quivered but she turned it into a grin.

'OK, your choice tonight.'

'Ours?' she says.

I kiss her. I've wanted to so badly.

'Straight to bed, then?'

'Yes.'

She went into the bathroom. I lay on her side of the bed to take off the chill, and heard her switch off the bathroom light although I couldn't quite believe it was happening. In a waking dream I tried to keep my breath even as I trembled. I watched her slip off her robe.

Early in the morning I woke up to find myself alone. Then I saw her in the garden wearing only her nightgown, pink in the early light. She had her arms around herself, but she didn't look cold.

'Love, are you all right?'

She looked at me. I felt clumsy, naked beside her.

'I'm more than all right. I'm so all right I don't know what to do with myself.' She hugged herself tighter.

Later that morning, I discovered her writing a letter. 'It's to my mum,' she said. She read it to me. It was touching, a letter from a woman to her mother. I felt doors opened for both of us that night. Through mutual attraction and delight she touched an emotional chord embedded deep within my psyche. I know of nothing with which to compare it, only that she came into my life and allowed me to fulfil myself through her. I needed no explanation and sought none. My hand didn't need foreknowledge of a flame: it is hot, that is all. Hard to put into words, even today.

Outwardly, we behaved the same as we had done before we met. We didn't do anything unusual, but the ordinary was charged with a new feeling that flowed between us. She would arrive for breakfast with a thick belt of cloth tied tightly around her damp fringe (to prevent it curling) – her squaw look. We'd avoid each other's eyes, but one of us always gave in and we'd collapse in unstoppable giggles.

Investigating the Californian supermarkets became a magical shared experience. We would loon about in one of the massive constructions with hypnotic rows of food rising high above our heads. On Saturday morning we were in the giant market on the outskirts of Toytown. I was fascinated by a glossy black china jar of oven-baked beans. I couldn't believe this high-class ceramic went into the oven and was used only once. Engrossed in the detailed instructions on the label I failed to respond instantly to Shrimpton's yelps from further down the aisle. By the time I looked up she was running backwards and forwards, towards me a little way, stamping her feet to get my attention and then back again. 'Look, look!' In her floppy hat teamed with baggy Desert Rat shorts she looked so irresistibly girl hockey captain that I began to laugh and couldn't stop. I never knew whether she had actually played the game.

'Don't laugh,' she said, 'come and look, Staaamp!'

She dropped the end of my name, so I knew she was serious. She had found a whole range of dressings for salad, something that didn't exist in England. When we rattled our bottle-filled trolley to the check-out, the cashier looked at us as if we were dolally. We knew we were. Didn't give a hoot. We ate nothing for days without a huge accompanying salad, both chopping and chomping away in an effort to try all the varieties before it was time to leave. Mornings, I would drive us down Fountain to Gower, kiss goodbye and wait for her long-fingered wave as she cornered on to Sunset. After work I could hardly wait to get out of costume and run across the street to the little parking lot where she would be waiting in the car, head lowered over a magazine, her hair tumbling about her face. As I neared she would look up, and every day I gasped at the perfection of her.

I noticed she didn't go out without making-up. I asked her about
it.

'I don't like to.'

'Why not?'

'Just don't.'

'But, why?'

The large eyes clouded, looked down.

'I'm not much without it,' she murmured.

'Not true.'

''Tis. It's OK for you. You're a natural.'

'Actually, you are most beautiful without make-up.'

She stared at me, unconvinced.

'Jean, why would I lie to you? I prefer you without. I understand,
when you work, but you're here with me. Nobody knows you're
here, except me. You're my secret. I've ensnared you like Miranda.'

'I'm too nervous to go out without it. It's a habit.'

'Well, that's easy, we won't go out until you can.'

She lasted a whole day. Sunday morning we went to Scandia
for a long, slow brunch. She shone. I felt proud of her, proud to
be with her. Happy that she had eyes for me. Heads turned as she
walked in.

'They're not looking at me, love,' I said.

It was a triumph. We celebrated with a swim and cuddle in our
heated pool. Like real Californians.

Somebody leaked the news to the papers. I heard later that Annie,
my angel from Paris, had told Bailey herself. Studio shooting
finished, we took off for Nassau, without so much as a look back
at the house where it had all happened. We rented a straw-roofed
hut on the beach. She'd found a bikini, a gasp of white with pale
blue check that exaggerated the forward lean of her pelvis. I became
fascinated by the high-stepping way she moved, like a pacing foal.
She noticed me watching from the shadow of our hut.

'What you looking at?' she asked, wet with salt water.

'What year were you born, Jean?'

'Forty-two, why?'

'Year of the Horse,' I said to myself. 'An elegant water horse in
the water.'

'Horses?' she asked, obviously not quite hearing. 'I didn't know

you liked horses,' she said, putting her scuba mask over her eyes.
'I can't wait to show you our horses at the farm. Come on, lazy
bones.' She beckoned me to join her. I went to fetch my mask,
thinking about my teenage idol from my Boys' Club days, Roy
Studd. I'd love to take Jean home for Sunday lunch, drop in and
show her off to Roy *en route.*

Why was I dragging my feet about returning to London with the
goddess? I suppose I'd had a feeling. It wasn't only confronting
Bailey, his friends, the heat. Deeper, I felt that Jean would drift
from me, catch too many eyes. Or was I afraid of the happiness,
frightened, perhaps, to measure this new intoxicating emotion
against familiar surroundings? I watched the slow movements of
her brown body in the clear, turquoise water. When I wasn't with
her, I longed for her, yet near her I worried about absences to
come. I didn't realise the implications of what I'd started doing to
myself. We put off leaving our haven until the last minute, dashing
to the shanty airport in a hired topless Triumph to catch the
afternoon flight to London.

Mike Caine had written to me: 'Don't worry, Tel, it's my turn
to find a pad. I've scored a corker. 28 Albion Close, W2.' He had
been moving in whilst my life had changed.

Mike's life had changed too and the place reflected it. He had
secured the corner mews unfurnished, and had done it up himself,
plush, modern. If I'd had eyes for anything but Jean I would have
seen the set-up straight away – his house with a guest quarter, a
box-room for Jean and me. I didn't pay too much notice. The bed
in our room was a pine single, squeezed in with a hastily purchased
cupboard and chest of drawers. Jean, only two inches shorter than
me in bare feet, found it 'cosy'. I grinned and bore it. Edina spent
a lot of time there and she and Jean seemed to get along well, but
the little mews house was crowded.

One of the things I'd always associated with luxury, a throwback
to my days as a delivery boy, was to have the morning papers
pushed through my letter box and to scan them in bed with a cup
of tea. As soon as Jean and I took up residence in Albion Close I
trotted round to the local newspaper shop and placed an order for
a daily selection. Something for Jean, something for me. We had
lots of morning giggles reading tit-bits aloud to one another,
squashed in our military bed. One morning, the papers didn't
arrive. I went to the shop in Connaught Street, notified the lad

there and picked up a few. They arrived on time the next morning but, the day after, no papers again. I left Jean sleeping in bed and nipped round a second time. I'll fix this once and for all, I figured, and spoke to the gov'nor.

'I'd really prefer to live without this constitutional every morning, John,' I said. 'The geezer who covers Number 28 is a-kip on the job.'

'Number 28, sir?'

'Yeah, Albion Close, round the corner.'

He consulted his ledger.

'Cancelled.'

'Don't be soft, I came in day before yesterday, specifically told the boy what I wanted.'

'Yeah, but your china came in again yesterday and told me to cancel them.'

'My mate? You sure?'

'Yes. Big blond geezer. The one with the bins.'

The penny finally dropped. I went back to Jean, who was sitting up in bed.

'You working today, love?'

'Not till this afternoon.'

'OK,' I said. 'Get packed, we're out of here.'

I made my last call from Mike's, to Jimmy Woolf.

'Your guest-flat vacant, Jim?'

'Yes, any problem?'

'Am I all right there with my girl for a week or two?'

'My pleasure,' said Jimmy. 'Stay as long as you like.'

'We'll be over in half an hour.'

That was how the famous Caine–Stamp team ended. Mike was still in bed. I left him a note, explaining we'd moved to Grosvenor House as he didn't appear to hear us packing. He never mentioned it and nor did I, but then we saw surprisingly little of each other after he'd cancelled my order. I stopped reading the papers in bed. It didn't seem so luxurious any more and, besides, I had better things to do with my mornings.

12

Jean and I moved into Jimmy's spare room at Grosvenor House. Although he referred to the space as his guest-apartment, it boasted only a bedroom and a bathroom. He was kind enough to invite us to share the sitting-room. The flat could be entered from this room but we did have our own front door, 36A. We also had a splendid double bed and a sizeable TV. That first morning we loaded my belongings and the contents of Jean's suitcase into the back of her mini-traveller and we were in. We spent the morning exploring the hotel, our new home. I knew most of the staff from my daily visits to Jimmy; they waited on us hand and foot. Jean couldn't believe everything was being done for her. She'd never had 'help' before.

'It's like living in a hotel,' she whispered. I grinned.

'It is, love, that's where Jimmy Woolf is so shrewd. It's the ultimate luxury. An apartment in a hotel. No problem with temperamental cooks or chars, here.'

'He doesn't mind us, me, being here?'

'No, no, he'll love you and you'll love him, he's an original. We'll have tea together when he comes home from the office.' Which is precisely what happened.

Jean and I went to the movies that evening, returning late. The room wasn't cold, but it had an unoccupied feel to it. The maid had hung up our things and turned the bed down. I pointed to the bathroom.

'Why don't you investigate?' She went and cleaned her teeth. Then it was my turn. When I came back, Jean was sitting up in bed sinking amongst the many outsize pillows. She was wearing a T-shirt type of vest with the faintest traces of what looked like a strawberry design. It was obviously an old favourite, worn paper-thin. She looked so breathtaking against the raw apricot silk of the bedhead, lit only by parchment light spilling from the lamp on the side-table, that I was stilled.

'You don't mind if I wear this, Stamp?' she asked, her little-girl voice unsure. 'My shoulders feel cold tonight.'

'No,' I replied, drawing the heavy curtains and stumbling to my side of the bed, finding it hard to contain my urge to hold her. 'I'll give you a cuddle, and when you're warm you can slip it off.'

She would sleep in my arms like a creature from an ancient forest. Turning in the night I would stir, her perfume reaching into my subconscious, and I'd become aware of our breath in unison. If I traced the outline of her delicate shoulder with the inside of my wrist I didn't know where her skin ended and mine began; often, in that dark closeness the layer of separation between us would dissolve and I would be her.

It was a pity my mind wasn't steady more often. What a life we could have had, if only I'd learned my lesson sooner. I was so intent on dragging the concepts I'd formed in childhood to fruition in manhood I hardly realised the life I was living now was Nirvana. I'd discovered peace, safety and fulfilment for the person I was, but I remained distracted, preoccupied with the image of what I thought I should be. Convinced by respected elders that I was 'different', I'd grown up believing I was smart, that I could handle it all – wealth, success, public acknowledgement and, my most cherished wish, the perfect partner. Heady stuff, considering it practically all came at once. It was as though the Granter of Wishes had discovered my cache in his bottomless well and decided to get me off his back: 'Let's fit up this greedy bastard, right now. Lay it on him, today, all of it.' But, as I said, I was smart, Jack the lad. I was seasoned by a rough neighbourhood and tempered by years of deprived conditions. I would show them.

But, who?

Often, in my early years, I'd witnessed the stress that lack of privacy or mystery could engender in adults, so it followed that part of my treasured philosophy for keeping interpersonal relationships long and spicy was space. Physical space and space through separation. My dream house was to be compartmentalised. Whilst communal areas were to remain – kitchen, sitting-rooms, studio, gardens, even, at some point, stables – the bedrooms and bathrooms were to be suited to one particular occupant. The female areas, perfumed, soft, lacy. The male areas, austere, manly. These locations were to be visited frequently, but visited. Subtle invitations were to be extended, invasions spontaneous. It was Errol Flynn, Katharine Hepburn stuff. 'The best laid plans fall awry,' as the Bard wrote.

Jimmy Woolf couldn't put us up indefinitely, not that we wanted to stay on a permanent basis. I moved into Vidal Sassoon's extremely bijou penthouse in Curzon Street while he was in America, and Jean acquired a room in a property in Chelsea owned by the McEwens, a family of Border aristocrats she knew. We'd meet at Vidal's place after work. I'd found an unfurnished place in Mount Street that needed doing up and Jimmy Woolf masterminded this from his tower in Grosvenor House. I was completing *The Collector* locations in London and Kent. Jean would pick me up in her car after work in Hampstead or journey down to Edenbridge or Westerham in the limo the studio provided. We'd ride back to London at night in luxury. Even these unforced separations increased my need of her. I felt it was mutual, although I never gave Jean a key to my place nor asked her for one. Later, it became apparent she was slighted by this behaviour, imagining I was using my new flat for clandestine meetings. This wasn't the case. I blazoned through our first year together with energy that surprised me. Later, when I fell by the wayside, my desire for Jean continued – if anything, it increased.

I explained to Jean that I didn't actually have any set opinion about the kind of décor I wanted for Mount Street. It was essential, however, that the furnishings be harmonious, as my moods, although I found it hard to put into words, were affected by my surroundings. I always knew instinctively the right feel when looking at properties but, faced with the prospect of making a place for myself and being responsible for those initial choices, I was at a loss. I knew Jean to possess a good eye for line and colour. Of all the women I've known, Jean had the least interest in clothes and adornment in general, although, if the occasion demanded, she would put together an ensemble without a moment's notice that would leave others splashing in the shallows. Even today, I smile when I remember the Melbourne Cup in 1966 when Jean featured in the first sighting of the mini-skirt. Outraged Melbourne matrons protested about her indecorous outfit (lack of hat and gloves). If they could have seen themselves . . . Jean's knowledge of interior design was limited but she was game to learn and so was I. We approached Jimmy Woolf.

'I don't know, Terence. What do you like?'

'Dunno.'

'Jean?'

'Ditto.'

'What don't you like?'

'Jim, I didn't feel right in Albion Close, even before I tumbled we weren't welcome. The furniture, carpets – I mean, it was expensive gear, but Mike only has a lease. He'll have to give that stuff away when he moves on. I do feel easy with old gear, antiques. I knew a family who lived off the King's Road and I always loved it at Woburn.'

Jimmy scoffed, 'My dear boy . . . or should I say, Your Grace?'

'I know. I know I can't afford that sort of clobber, but that's what I like. You asked. I told you.'

'Geoffrey,' he said, 'he's the man for you. Well, almost.' Jimmy smiled enigmatically. 'I'll call him, ask him to help out. He has a wonderful eye. You can't do better. You'll both learn from him.'

That was how the great Geoffrey Bennison, Big Carol, or even Carol Channing's mother, in some circles, came into and enriched our lives – more than even he, with all his feminine intuition, could have guessed. Geoffrey was one of those guys who lead two lives, both larger than life, donning ladies' apparel and 'trolling' at night, dealing in antiques to the gentry by day. The one effect common to this dual existence was a dark brown rug that tilted over his forehead and gave him the appearance of an ageing mop-head, so obviously an Irish that no one had the heart even to refer to it, least of all his hand-maidens, Babs, Agnes and Carlotta (George, Kenny and Christopher).

He operated from modest premises perched on a corner of Pimlico Road, alongside a larger store that sold modern produce from Spain. No one in London, however, had more original stock than Geoffrey. His items were unearthed whilst scouring Britain in a Rover and his beady eye missed nothing, although he couldn't always afford what he spotted. Mayfair dealers cruised his shop in well-heeled droves, yet Geoffrey didn't, like those 'cod polones' or 'grand Bond Street queens', have 'lots of handbag'. He operated, more or less, on a shoestring. It didn't affect his eye, though. It sharpened it, if anything, making him search harder for objects that others with greater funding missed. I suppose if he had a forte, it was art. He more than once asked Jean and I to back a project. Geoffrey always knew when a painting wasn't what it was thought to be and his intuition never let us down.

'A good little earner, dear, some extra handbag for you,' he'd say, dolling out the notes like a provincial madam. Jean and I spent hours separately and together sitting on wonky chairs in the tiny back-room office of his shop, sipping thick tea from thick mugs, spellbound by his connoisseur knowledge and gossip of gay romance. Tales of men the world assumed macho – politicians, gangsters, police, married labourers – all having a night out, all taken by the black fishnets and the water-filled balloons that filled the brassière he donned after dark.

I thought the world of Geoffrey but it was Shrimpton he most impressed. Geoffrey came as a shock to her. She had never come across the likes of him before and had no frame of reference to prepare her. We learned, too. When Geoffrey realised that we both possessed an eye, albeit embryonic, he educated us like the maestro he was; he had the ability to raise the aesthetic awareness of anyone who came within range of his charm and expertise. Being so honest about himself, he must have compelled lots of others to look twice at themselves.

When we entered his orbit he was at a low, living in a basement of an Earl's Court hotel, the Rushmore, which he owned. The hired rooms were clean and cheap but his own quarters were high Bennison, furnished and decorated by himself with Greek and Roman busts set into the walls of his minute garden. Apparently, he'd had a solid career in interior design in the Fifties, but an unhappy love affair with a young man named Blood – 'He was so glamorous, dear, looked like James Dean, you know, moody' – had been so traumatic that he had let himself go when it ended. When a chum finally discovered him (he was, I believe, a lifelong asthmatic) he was dying. The friend flew him to Switzerland and paid for his treatment – a stay of three years. Geoffrey lost a lung in the process but lived to tell the tale. He made it back to the Pimlico Road to find and sell antiques and, of course, his first love, paintings. He hadn't accepted a decorating assignment for years, but agreed to do up my flat in Mount Street.

'I'll show you a few pieces, don't take anything you don't like.

We'll do it together. Don't worry, dear, I won't make it camp. I know how butch you East End polones think you are.'

He was as good as his word. 119A was fixed up in no time. Kitchen modernised, bedroom glamorised, bathroom functionalised and the drawing-room made as slick as fresh paint. Neither Geoff nor I liked mirrors much, but the main room was narrow so he opened it out by hanging a large 'aged' mirror on the wall facing the bookshelves that ran the twenty-foot length of the room. They were painted white and backed by red felt. 'What you see when you come in. Make it feel cheerie, dear.' A few good Georgian pieces, two Mies van der Rohe leather chairs and an Acorn wood-burning stove to warm us and to look at on chill afternoons. It wasn't simple, but made to look so by Geoffrey's wonderful 'throw', as they say in the trade. I loved it. Jean appreciated the craft, but it was my pad. She moved into a flat in Camden Town with a girlfriend.

While Mount Street was being done up, Geoffrey asked me where I would really like to live.

'This is nice, and it's fine for now, but have you ever had a dream place? Somewhere you've seen, never thought you could afford? Money is going to come rolling in for you, dear. You're good, but you're glamorous as well, and that's commercial.'

'What's glamour, Geoff? Real glamour?'

'Can't be explained, love, but whatever it is, you two've got it, that's what makes you such an item. You should see how people look at you. Couples will be trying to emulate you for years. You see if they don't.' He put his hand on his hip, his showgirl posture.

'You're so camp, sometimes.'

'I know, dear, but this old bitch knows what she's talking about; you think about a nice property while you're young, don't let the handbag slip through your fingers. We never know how things will turn out. You don't want to be slaving away all your life, like your mother.'

'My mum doesn't slave away.'

'I meant me, dear,' Geoffrey said with an exaggerated grimace, dragging down the corner of his mouth like a pantomime dame.

'When I was a boy, I had a thing about Curzon Street. You know. I read all the *Four Just Men* books by Edgar Wallace and they lived in a house there, but then I saw this place when I was a messenger boy working in Cheapside. Had a funny feeling about it. I went back there when I was at drama school, don't actually know what it is, often comes to mind though. It's called the Albany.'

'I know it, dear, a bona place to stay.'

'I've never thought about staying there. Love to get a glimpse inside, though. I'm really curious about what it's like.'

'I'll take you there for tea, lovey, I have a great chum who lives on the rope-walk, he'd like to meet you. And remember, you butch thing, enjoy your looks now and make sure she enjoys hers. She's a lovely girl, look after her.'

I've always paid attention to whether or not people keep their word. I've found it to be a sound way of sorting the grown-ups from the not so grown up. Geoffrey kept his, he had offered to have me a sofa made.

'It's a lot of work, but I won't charge you through the nose. I know what's needed,' he'd said.

The day I moved in, Geoffrey came over to 'touch things up'. He'd designed the by now famous sofa himself, to be in perfect proportion to the room – the main item around which everything else would 'fall into place'. He came in the van with the burly upholsterers from Hampstead, where the settee had been covered in skins of untreated hide, so as to remain soft. It was, too, like evening gloves. I've always regarded that sofa as a masterpiece. It was perfect. Geoffrey was actually purring when the tattooed delivery men set it down on its castors. He flirted and cajoled them into staying until he was absolutely satisfied with its position in the room, settled across from the black Barcelona chairs, placed side by side, parallel like a shadow.

'Repetition with variation, dear, always good to remember.'

He shooed the men out with a quid apiece saying, 'Here's a drink, you virile lot.'

'Cor, thanks, mate, you're a prince.'

'Princess, dear, please, I'm a working girl, drop by my shop in Pimlico, any time.'

He threw himself full-length on the settee. The down cushions squished as air was squeezed through the small circular brass ventilators. His lightweight crimson polo-neck contrasted perfectly with the warm Bath Oliver shade of the hides. He rolled his head on the sausage cushion trying to make his feet reach its twin at the other end. He wasn't long enough.

'Come on, dear, it's tailored for you. So you can have a little zzz in the afternoon, without getting too serious.'

He reached over to the French leather-topped desk in the bay window and twisted the telephone on to the floor beside him, bringing it within easy reach.

'That's what an old boot like me thinks is luxury, dear, a comfy sofa by the fire and not having to get up to reach the phone.'

He lifted himself on to his elbow, his tight black trousers protesting.

'Must go on a diet, getting so fat; come on, let me see you aboard,' he said, vacating his masterwork.

I lay down and stretched out on the glove leather. The end bolsters melted under my head and toes. Was this *it*? I felt it was. After long hours of daydreaming on the manky home-made mat in front of the fire in Chadwin Road during puberty, the horizontal champ, as my dad had called me, had made it. I heard Jean bounding up the stairs. She came in the open door wearing her working make-up, her lids heavy with the lashes she stuck on one at a time in her car going to work. She was excited, out of breath, her face flushed.

'Welcome,' I said, 'as always.'

She turned a full circle, taking it in. Sharing the pleasure, hoping for me to be happy.

Geoffrey, never slow on the uptake said, 'I think I'll have a troll around Berkeley Square and Bond Street. Varda what those Mayfair gels are charging for the bits I've flogged them,' and fixing Jean with a dark brown beady, 'just in case you want to try the sofa for cuddle size.' She blushed.

'Oh, Geoff, you say such things.'

'I do such things too, dear. Now don't be a silly girl, take it while you can get it, that's my motto. Oooh, I need a holiday in Morocco. Those blue men . . . ' Geoffrey spun out, pleased with himself.

Jean stood in the centre of the room. She was wearing a pair of beige Chanel shoes with contrasting black toe-caps. The delicate back strap nestled across the hollow above her heel. Her stockings were a touch paler than the strap. I could see her sunburned legs through the sheer silk.

'You know what happens to me when you wear gear like that, gel?' I said.

First night curtain of *Alfie* – Morosco Theatre, 45th St, West of Broadway.

'No,' she said, slipping out of one shoe and gliding a stockinged toe across the new zebraskin at home on the floor.

'You read me like a book, don't you, Stamp?'

'Not always,' I said, raising myself up to look at her properly, 'only when you want me to.'

'That's how it should be, isn't it?' she said, glancing down at the striped skin, momentarily hiding her eyes.

'I don't know. Is it?'

'What do you think? You're mature, experienced.'

'I think you like to be able to catch my attention, when you choose to.'

Jean raised her face to me. Under the mascaraed lids the eyes were becoming drowning blue.

'That's what makes you smart. You know things that matter.'

'Like what?'

'How to turn a clever girl's head.'

'Are you clever, then?'

'I passed eight GCEs. I haven't been tested lately.'

'Move all that smartness over here. You can try for my personal honours. Double first.'

'Only double?'

'You're a hard woman, Shrimpton.'

I stayed prone on the sofa, trying to stop my head spinning. She slipped off her other shoe.

'Get me together, Stamp.'

13

I had booked a table at Wheeler's in Old Compton Street for supper that evening. It was the original eating house of the chain and the table on the first floor beside the open fire was my favourite corner. Jean ordered a Sole Véronique, I, a Colbert. We shared a beetroot and watercress salad. Next to us was a middle-aged American couple, their voices marking them as tourists.

The man said rather loudly, 'We haven't seen any of them beautiful people we read about in *Time* magazine, Shirley.'

Shirley dutifully nodded assent. I glanced up at Jean. She continued eating, but then Jean was endowed with a quality I'd lost somewhere: modesty.

Saturdays were reserved for joyriding in the car up the newly opened M4 to the Shrimptons' farm in Buckinghamshire. Jean's folks, Peg, Ted and little brother Daniel, also had a weekend retreat on the coast and we often canoodled at Rose Hill in their absence, like country folk. We also walked the orchards, gathered cobnuts and rode horses through long grass followed by Jean's scruffball Yorkie, Bert, who had to throw himself up into the air at regular intervals to see which direction we were taking. In Jean's room at the farm, the one she'd slept in as a child, was one of her old dolls. The little terrier had such a passion for this remnant that it had to be kept hidden from him. If he caught sight of the doll he grabbed hold of it and held on with such ferocity you could actually lift him and the toy high in the air, where he would growl helplessly, unable to secure his prize, unable to let go for fear of not retrieving it. I felt like that myself, watching her in her element gathering eggs for lunch, showing me her world. I listened to tales of Tiggy Pig and other childhood pets while we groomed the horses after my riding lesson. Horses had been her first love, the distraction for English roses who hit puberty early. Jean had withstood the rush until she was eighteen, then she'd seduced a local youth her own age.

'He was a dope,' she said, having been left wondering what all the fuss was about.

Sundays, I showed her the world I'd grown up in. I never asked what Jean thought of the memorials from my boyhood – the festering slag heaps, abandoned park playgrounds – locations which held such emotional content for me, and the hero who'd shaped my life, living in his parents' upstairs rooms with his wife and the greyhound he dreamed would sprint them to wealth and escape. Jean liked my mother instantly and my mother liked her. The two women I loved most in the world teamed up. Jean became the grown-up daughter Ethel had longed for and Jean plugged into the dynamo that Ethel was. Jean organised shopping trips to C & A at Marble Arch, deftly choosing items for Ethel's wardrobe. They'd turn up together at Mount Street, late and out of breath, sisters on the razzle. That Christmas she gave Ethel her famous Mongolian lamb coat, and Mum waited for us to announce the day. My mum met Peg Shrimpton, a coming together masterminded by Jean. Apparently, the two mothers 'got on like a house on fire'. Years later, Ethel told me she and Mrs Shrimpton commiserated over modern standards, the free-loving so prevalent in the Sixties.

Peg had said to my mum, 'Well, Mrs Stamp, at least they found each other.'

Mum confided to me that she wouldn't have half minded being young herself, then.

Jean went off to Paris to shoot the collection for American *Harpers Bazaar*, working for the first time with photographer Richard Avedon. Jean had ambivalent views of the world of fashion, but Avedon she admired. His invitation was a hallmark in her career.

'He's asked me to grow my eyebrows and curl my hair,' she said.

'Do anything he tells you, love. It's not an accident his fashion pics are the best black and white in the business.'

When Jean returned in triumph clutching a couple of black and white throwaways she'd picked up from the studio floor and slipped into her basket, I saw why she'd flipped.

*

I was offered Bill Naughton's play *Alfie* on Broadway. There was to be a short tour, New Haven and Washington, then directly to New York. The opening night might well coincide with the première of *The Collector*. I took the chance. Jean had some lucrative advertising bookings in New York where I would have to rehearse, so we planned to meet there. It was 1966, the Beatles had made a movie and they and Jean were centre-stage world media: the start of the English bandwagon. My Broadway debut appeared to be placing me in the right place at the right time.

Alfie is a great part, but a monster to learn. Like Hamlet but with more laughs, the leading character carries the play. Never off stage, he's either getting his leg over, wise-cracking about how he's going to, or philosophising while he's putting his strides back on. There were a couple of bare-chest scenes included in the action. The lines I dealt with using my old Webber D Drama School technique. Five pages a day, come rain or shine, marking the daily consumption in the script and carrying it with me constantly; taking long walks, memorising as I stepped out.

The stripping off presented a different problem. Since my romance with Jean, working out had become a thing of the past. There was nothing for it but to get back into harness. I enquired around and discovered that the latest fitness craze was a system entitled, rather dauntingly, Royal Canadian Air Force Exercises, a daily work-out to be completed in fifteen minutes. It sounded right up my street. I invested 7/6d. In the ensuing weeks, when Jean left the apartment each morning to go to work, I went to work also, cutting through the discipline fairly well. On Saturday morning I waited until Shrimpton was safely in the bath before starting my stuff. Jean, hearing the grunts from the jack-jumps, emerged wet from the bathroom, Navaho maiden headband tied about her forehead.

'What'y'doing?' she enquired, like Peanuts, slumping against the door frame and unintentionally revealing a flawless leg from the towel draped around her body. As I landed, caught red-handed, sweating and flushed, she smiled sweetly.

'You haven't answered my question.'

'I'm . . . doing . . . these . . . Canadian exercises to get . . .'

She stooped and picked up the book open on the floor (placed so I could read the number of the repetitions required without losing momentum), gathering my watch and keeping the place at the same time. She held both objects at eye level and looked from one to the other.

'Timing ourselves, are we?'

'Yeh, it's . . . a system, it improves the . . . breath . . . as well . . . '

'I can hear that,' she said. 'Jack-jumps, I see. You didn't ask me, did you?' she went on.

'Well, they're not for girls, it's for pilots and . . . '

'You didn't ask me if it was all right, did you, Stamp?'

'You can't hurt yourself . . . It's not dangerous . . . '

'It will be, if you don't do what I say.'

'Why? My heart beat is getting stronger . . . '

'It will be dangerous if you upset me. And you will upset me if you continue to do these . . . jerks. I thought your body was changing. I thought you were up to something. Sneaking off out of bed like a naughty child. Well, I don't like it. I like your body as it is. As it is! Understand, Stamp? I don't want you becoming,' she glanced at the page, ' "a super athlete". I like you as you are. There is something about your shape. About your shoulders. They're a little boy's. I don't want you to change anything. Understand?'

She went back into the bathroom. That, as you can imagine, put the kibosh on that, jack-jumps and all.

I took Jean to the airport in her new Mini Cooper. We'd had it re-sprayed, navy blue. She looked nifty driving it, clutching the small wooden steering wheel and throwing it around corners like Jim Clark, whom she'd met and who had obviously passed on some tips. I drove the brainchild of Alec Issigonis back to Mount Street, rummaging amongst the discarded wrappings of sherbet dabs and Mars bars in the glove compartment, investigating the spoor she'd left in the car. I felt her absence already.

I spent the week marching-out the big square of Mayfair. After I'd purchased some sticks of liquorice in the International Stores from the assistant I liked with the memorable name of Alf Flower, I'd open my script at the page I'd mastered the day before and start. North to Oxford Street, west to Marble Arch, down Park Lane, along Piccadilly, up Regent Street and home. Five pages committed to memory. I varied my route by walking clockwise one day, anti-clockwise the next.

When I arrived in New York, I knew the text backwards. Jean

was staying in the Fifties but she had found a furnished pad at the Brevoordt, downtown on Fifth Avenue. We were to move in the next day. I arrived in the afternoon but when I reached the flat it was almost midnight, London time. I had missed her. I didn't realise how much until I held her – my skin tingled as though coming to life after being submerged in Arctic water. It felt like the very blood wanted to get as close as possible to her. I remember almost nothing save the alarm radio of the next-door neighbour sounding through the thin wall the following morning. I awoke, as if from death, to the strains of Herman and the Hermits: 'I'm into something good', encircled safely by her slim arms. I rose up reborn, a phoenix, to make us tea.

Alfie opened and closed in five minutes, or so it seemed. After a splendid tour with packed, laughing houses, we hit a stolid first-night house at the Morosco Theatre. A devout Catholic critic who was reputedly offended by the abortion scene, but too smart to mention the fact, found other ways of making the play seem unwatchable. We closed in a month. It was a remarkable experience for me, nonetheless, to star on Broadway in my twenties, and my only regret was not inviting Jean to see the final performance in Washington. I felt it would be more exciting for her to see the piece for the first time on the opening night in the Big Apple. Mistake.

We attended the gala party held at Lüchow's and bought the next day's newspapers in Times Square on the way home.

'Let's not read them till the morning,' I remember saying in cavalier fashion. 'We'll go straight to bed.'

In Washington I had been stricken with a venereal complaint diagnosed as non-specific urethritis.

'Listen,' I told the specialists, 'I'm clean. I can't have caught anything. I've been abstaining. On the road for nearly a fortnight.'

'It's not like that, old chap, you haven't caught it,' he said. 'It's non-specific. It's the body's warning system. You've been overdoing it. You're weakened. In your condition, you could trigger it by eating asparagus.'

'You're pulling my leg. I don't feel weak, on the contrary, as it happens.'

'Mr Stamp, take my word, rest up, swallow one of these anti-biotics every six hours. No liquor or intercourse until you've finished this course of penicillin. The important thing is the rest. OK? I'll give you the name of a colleague in New York.'

I'd been given a clean bill of health the afternoon before *Alfie* opened. I woke up the next morning to find Jean sitting up in bed surrounded by the reviews and crying softly to herself.

'What is it, love?' I asked.

'Oh, Stamp, they're not good.'

'Let's have a look.'

Actually, they weren't that bad, but the flavour of the era, Walter Kerr, had inserted his stiletto expertly into the play. He wasn't unkind to me personally, but it was obvious that Bill Naughton's text had pushed a psychological button or two. He appeared determined to stop the piece and he greatly influenced theatregoers, who apparently hung on his every word and were bussed into Broadway shows at a flick of his first-night biro. Full houses in London had been cracking up at the piece for over a year.

'Heh,' I said, cuddling her to me. 'It's OK. Look, it's not going to run, but we've had a good time. I've starred on Broadway. Not every lad born within the sound of Bow Bells can say that. Let's get dressed and have waffles for breakfast.'

'Pancakes.'

'As I said, pancakes.'

'With real maple syrup?'

'With syrup and blueberries.'

I made light of it. She'd cried for me. Perhaps she alone knew the effort I'd put into the role. I had misjudged the depth of her support, the identification with her man. She was my invulnerable Aphrodite but that morning I became aware of another aspect of her, the protective, the wife, the Hera.

We ran a month to the day. Lewis Gilbert, who was to direct the movie, came to see the show – he loved it and offered me the film repeatedly. I passed. I'd done it. Instead, I accepted *Modesty Blaise*, a film produced by Joseph Janni, with Joe Losey set to direct. Monica Vitti was to play the strip cartoon title role, I her devoted side-kick, the deadly Willie Garvin, from whose torso weapons hung like leaves. Joe Janni was a native Italian who loved the English and resided in London. He was a creative producer, a rare breed. All the same, when he signed Monica he overlooked two things.

Vitti was the friend of Michelangelo Antonioni, a gaunt Milanese who'd starred her in two of his movies, directing her like Mesmer and carving her performance like his namesake, with whom he reputedly felt a close kinship. Vitti had been haunting, in keeping with Antonioni's iconoclastic black and white visions, but no one had seen her do comedy and no one had tested her reflexes. Janni's other lack of foresight, in his haste to sign the blonde actress, who did, it must be admitted, closely resemble the *Evening Standard* cartoon, was to grant her director approval. It was tantamount to inviting her mentor to pick a director. The first suggestions were politely turned down. I could imagine the austere Antonioni looking down his noble nose and advising Vitti no. In a panic to appease both Twentieth Century Fox with a bankable package and a fussy star in Rome, Joseph Losey appeared as a gift to Janni. His pedigree was elegant and he was approved of by both factions. The fact that he'd never directed comedy was overlooked in the rush to parcel it all together.

Dirk Bogarde, whom Losey had directed with such success in *The Servant*, was cast as Gabriel, the waspy villain. The picture would shoot on locations in Amsterdam, Sicily and Naples, in that order. I would start my shooting, always a dodgy moment for me, alone in Holland. If everything went smoothly, Shrimpton would join me in Sicily.

14

Shortly after the deal for *Modesty Blaise* was concluded, Geoffrey
Bennison invited Jean and me to have tea with him at Albany, in
his friend's chambers on the rope-walk, I1. All the sets, as they
are known to residents, are distinguished by an initial and a
number. Sixty-nine in all. Jean and I met Geoffrey at Mount Street
and drove over with him. We parked the car in the forecourt. It
was Thursday afternoon and there were plenty of vacant spaces,
as most residents left for the weekend at lunch-time. A silver-haired
porter informed us, 'You'll be all right there, sir.'

I had actual butterflies in my gut, as bad as a first night. Up the
front steps, through the first door into the shadows of a high
vestibule with a few shafts of sunlight making it down to the inlaid
stone floor from the skylights above. Geoffrey pushed on ahead
holding the second glossy, dark door open for Jean to pass. I hung
back, pretending to look at the portraits on the wall, admiring a
bust of the poet Byron who had lived here briefly in days long past.
I wasn't really nervous, but needed to approach in my own time. I
didn't know why. For some reason I felt much the same as the
evening I'd been pushed through the glass doors of Fairbairn
House Boys' Club by my mother, fifteen years before. I finally ran
out of logical reasons to linger. Jean and Geoffrey were chatting,
waiting for me on the rope-walk. I stepped mindfully through the
doors towards them. No bells pealed. No banners unfurled as I
set foot into my Shangri-La.

The rhododendrons were without blooms: instead, juicy-ended
strands of Virginia creeper cascaded from second-floor verandahs.
All the ground-floor apartments boasted manicured window boxes
on wide Georgian sills. Tulips leaned out rakishly to take in the
reflected sunlight that bounced from the enclosing white walls.
Under the covered rope-walk the planked arch of the ceiling

held us in shade, protecting strollers from the elements but not excluding them. It also muffled sound – a hush pervaded the colonnade that made me step warily lest I disturb the ghosts that slumbered there. Jean walked ahead, her arm linked with Geoffrey's. Both were appreciative but giggly, like children doing something they shouldn't. He was in his musty polo-neck, she had put on a grey skirt which hung in pleats from mid-hip like a drill skirt. I could see the back of her knees as she walked and the weight of the material swung from side to side. Stockingless, the backs of her legs were lighter. She was always too restless to lie in the sun on her tummy.

For years I'd fantasised about entering this place. Never once had it crossed my mind that the company would be so splendid. John Richardson, our host, was an art critic. I believe Geoffrey and he had met at the Slade. They went back a long way. The Richardson set was on the ground floor where the sun shone directly through the windows for an hour only after midday, on its way over the Royal Academy to Knightsbridge. The chambers were inviting and cool in contrast to the bright scene outside. In the brief moments between conversation, birds flitting carefree amongst the military-trimmed privet hedges a foot or so in front of the glass panes drew attention to the quality of stillness.

I was entranced. Sitting contentedly in a leather-padded cam-paign chair, I took in the high ceilings, the walls festooned with paintings and prints, all surfaces scattered with *objets d'art*. From where I sat I could move my head to the left and look out through the white lace curtaining, see the squared columns of the rope-walk and the tiled roof of the arcade we'd strolled under. If I moved to the right, I faced the door through which we'd entered this main living-room – above its frame John had hung the bleached shell of a giant turtle or tortoise. An open fireplace waited behind my shoulder, and ahead of me the twelve-foot-high wall was broken by a pair of Georgian adjoining doors that made the pair in Granny Kate's front room at 603 Barking Road look stunted. They were ajar, and through them I could see another room identically pro-portioned: mirror image, even to the second fireplace with white marble surround.

'Who would like to cut the cake?' said our host. He was dressed formally with a tight-fitting double-breasted suit, a snappy chalk striped number with six buttons, two for show. He looked rather a card, nonetheless, old John, an in-shape forty year old, I figured.

'Let Stamp do it,' piped up Jean, not at all overawed by the surroundings. 'He's a dab hand with a knife.'

'Dab hand?' commented Geoffrey. 'You're starting to talk like him.'

Jean smiled at me. In our secret language it meant she took it as a compliment. She was always supportive of me in public. I didn't realise what a luxury this was. I stretched forward, slipped on to the floor beside the low table and picked up a sensible knife with a yellowed bone hand. I cut into the rich fruit cake retaining most of the roasted almond halves lined up along the top. It dropped into slices, revealing smatterings of red glacé cherries inside.

'It's a good cake,' I commented, sniffing the just-as-it-should-be Dundee aroma.

'Thank you,' said Richardson, 'deft knifework. Comes from Fortnum's, my tuck shop.'

'He was going to be a surgeon, weren't you, Stamp?' said Jean, letting them know my expertise hadn't been learned in a grocer's. (My initial publicity had so heavily accented the working-class origin, people meeting me for the first time expected some sort of iron fighter poured into a flash suit.) I suppose Jean had had much the same experience with Bailey, as she was quick off the mark in situations like this, anticipating any preconceptions and countering them in advance.

I winked at her. It meant I'm OK. I'm only being quiet while I get my bearings.

'Lady,' I said, offering her the slice I'd shuffled on to a paper-thin bone china plate. I looked into her eyes. Unmade-up, how I preferred her. The delicate skin under her eyes, my bags, she called them (they weren't and I loved them), were a barometer by which I could tell her state of health, mood, energy. Today, they were tinged blue. She needed an early night. I'd promised her we'd go out to dinner, perhaps not tonight. Saturday. John Richardson was telling Jean how he'd become a resident at Albany. It was a revelation to me.

Up until the moment John started to elaborate his introduction to the place (he'd answered a one-line ad in *The Times* offering a bachelor apartment in Piccadilly) I was under a spell. Everything had been moving in slow motion, the people in the room almost transparent, hardly more substantial than their voices, presences that flitted in and out of my consciousness. I let myself drift, rousing myself only once or twice to smile at Jean, to cut more of the cake.

'So I rang the number and trotted along, wasn't expensive. Had to squeeze by a crusty ex-Army type, Captain Adams. References, all that bumf. As luck would have it, I recalled some old scout master he knew, it oiled the way. Another cup of tea?'

He was looking at me, proffering a refill of smoky Darjeeling.

'Thank you.' My voice sounded unfamiliar to me as I poured for Jean and myself, putting her milk in first. She couldn't drink tea like iron filings, the way I did. The jolt of the caffeine grounded me a bit.

'You mean you produced a few references, that's all?' A voice screamed within my head. I drank another draught of the hill station potion and thought carefully about my next remark. I tried to smile self-deprecatingly, but it felt like one of Elvis's top-lip snarls.

I said in a cockney accent, as heavy as I could without making Jean laugh, 'I thought it was just for earls and marquises an' that.'

Jean didn't speak. Her eyes rounded like willow pattern saucers. Richardson sat down on the sofa next to Jean. He didn't undo his jacket but leaned forward in the attitude of an expert whose subject has been broached.

'That's right, my dear Terence. Originally, when Holland developed the mansion – that main house you came through – by constructing the rope-walk sets, he flogged them to his aristocratic chums in the Shires with sons who wanted to come to London to get laid. That's why they're all freehold, you see.'

'You own this?'

'No, no, old fruit, on a lease. Mind you, tried to buy a couple of times.'

'So it's only guys who live here, then?' I asked.

'Originally, yes. Sort of men's club-type thing. The mansion had a bath-house and a restaurant because the sets hadn't kitchens or bathrooms when they were constructed. All the owners had to sign a covenant declaring they wouldn't behave in an unacceptable manner, keep pets, or entertain ladies overnight in their chambers etc. It's changed a piece now, but I had to sign it when I arrived. A bit of camp, you know. Mainly to do with noise, you see.'

'Ladies,' I said, looking at Jean, who was concentrating. 'D'you mean I'd have to dress the lovely Shrimpton up as a chap?'

'No, no, but it wasn't until recently that a woman actually took up residence. Her father had no sons, so he left his set to her. She moved in. The Captain heard about it and shot along to see her, waving his deed of covenant. She glanced at the parchment and said, "That's all very well, but show me a law of England that says I can't live in my own property." Smart girl. Covenant only a bye-law, see?'

'So girls live here now?'

'Oh, yes, thin end of the wedge. Changed the whole tone. Chaps moved out, wasn't top drawer any more.'

As we were leaving, I turned to say goodbye to the host and heard myself say, 'Well, if you ever hear about a set going . . . '

'Delighted,' John interjected, 'I'll let old Geoffrey here know. All the best, now.'

A month later, Geoffrey called. Someone John knew at Sotheby's was going to New York to launch a Stateside branch. The job would take two years, but the gent, a Mr Timewell, wasn't planning on returning to England. He was retiring to Morocco. His idea was to let his chambers, furnished, for the duration of his stay in New York. If by then the tenant wanted to hold on to them, all well and good.

'He knows it's me?' I asked Geoffrey.

'Oh, yes, dear, he knows it's you. He's seen that butch photo in the supplement. Quite curious to meet you in the flesh, he is.'

I had posed for Lord Snowdon at the newspaper's studio in Holborn, one of half a dozen young British actors to be featured in the new colour supplement. Kathleen Halton, who was later to marry Ken Tynan, was writing the accompanying article and also attended the shoot. Snowdon was charming and easy going. Towards the end of the session he'd asked me if I wouldn't mind taking my shirt off. 'Snap a few beefcake poses for Kathleen,' he'd winked at me. Mind? I had my chest – what there was of it – bared before you could say knife. It was only when he looked through the camera I felt a bit self-conscious, so I folded my arms in a Rudolph Valentino pose, pushing out my biceps to make them look bigger. 'All I need is a string of pearls,' I'd said. The Lord had snapped the moment I finished speaking. He was fast. I listened to Kathleen and Snowdon whispering to one another. After the little conflab, where my table manners had obviously been discussed, I was asked to join them for lunch at St James's Palace. We had an extremely fine lunch, drank equally fine wine, and afterwards the Princess showed me their games room, where I warbled 'Alexander's Ragtime Band' and she accompanied me on the new pianola, which played like a whole orchestra. Very cheery.

The feature came out better than I'd expected, although Miss Halton hadn't made me feel at ease and I'd slipped into my barrow boy dialogue during the interview. She'd also used the old trick of referring to an unnamed director to 'quote' her opinion that actors were megalomaniacs, but Snowdon's pictures were the business.

Before moving to Piccadilly I should have changed my lifestyle, reviewed everything and discarded a few outworn attitudes. I could have taken Jean into Albany with me, equal partners, doing it together, a balance of yin and yang. I didn't. It is a big regret I have. I think it is correct to say that at the time I was possessed. I could say I was dazzled by wealth, success and fame but, actually, it was one of those occasions when I knew full well what I wanted to do, while simultaneously doing the opposite, as though my so-called free will was being overridden. My life with Jean was total, Halley's comet every day, but I behaved like a child with a full plate, reaching for more. 'Your eyes are bigger than your belly,' my dad used to say.

Bennison and I discussed the décor to be carried out at D1 – my new chambers. I had persuaded my landlord Mr Timewell that his furnishings were too valuable for me to live comfortably with, but paid him the full, two-year rent in advance, in compensation for the bother of placing his belongings in store. For his part, he assured me that, as soon as his stint in America ended, he would come to London en route to Morocco and 'fix things' with the Albany secretary, Captain Charles Adams.

I took off for Amsterdam. I'd no sooner arrived at Heathrow than I was introduced to an extremely sultry creature by a film assistant who was making sure that artists and crew scheduled to leave caught the appropriate flight.

'Terence, this is Tina; Tina Marquand, Terence Stamp.'

The mane of black straight hair was tossed aside revealing hot, dark eyes which gave me a cursory glare. She then went back to discussing her travel plans. Marquand, I knew that name. I don't think she caught the plane. I didn't see her again until she turned up on the set, playing my favourite girlfriend – Willie Garvin's, that is. This time she was as friendly as a Cavalier spaniel, which was fortunate because we were both naked for our first love scene. Ah, the vagaries of film schedules! Tina – the daughter of Maria Montez and Jean-Pierre Aumont, now newly married to Christian Marquand, actor, director and best friend of Marlon Brando – was an overall good looker as I was well placed to discover. Over a cheese *fondue* supper with a group of film folk, including my stand-in and friend, John Ketteringham, she told me about Christian and times with Brando.

'Where are you staying?' Tina asked.

'In the Doelen,' I told her. It was an ornate, old hotel overlooking the canal. I had rented myself one of the turret suites. 'It's cosy, terrific.'

'You are so lucky,' she purred in her thick French accent, 'I'm at the 'ilton.'

Doug Hayward, a chum of mine and Jimmy's who'd recently moved his handsome frame and tailoring business into a shop I'd spotted vacant in Mount Street, joined in the conversation.

'You should ask them to swap you over, if you don't like it. I don't s'pose it's any cheaper at the Hilton.'

Doug had landed the job of cutting my suits for the film, and he'd managed to get the production to fork out for a weekend in Amsterdam in case of any last-minute adjustments.

'What is this swap?' Tina wanted to know, fixing Doug with a gypsy eye.

'Change yer room, luv. I'm checking out myself, Sunday night. There'll be one vacant, for sure.'

I was only listening with half an ear. I'd turned down *Alfie* to do this and now I had *Modesty Blaise* to cope with. Monica was proving to be a pain. Shooting had been delayed for two hours on the first day because she didn't like her costumes and wouldn't leave her hotel room until ten o'clock. Richard McDonald, the designer from the Slade School of Art, had been asked by Losey to design the look of the picture. I thought his designs for *Modesty Blaise* were brilliant, catching completely the zanyness of the Sixties before any of us had realised it was a pop era.

Vitti's tantrum was only a warning. I'd never worked with a

Modesty Blaise – Willie Garvin.

temperamental star before. There was worse to come: she absolutely refused to do any profile shots. Whenever Losey lined us up facing each other, she would slide round to face front. To keep eye contact with her I wound up with my back to the camera.

Losey said, 'If she does that again, I'll nail her bloody shoes to the ground.'

Within a month Joe Losey's statement, given to the *Evening Standard* at a sparkling press conference in the Ritz, that he was delighted to be directing the Roman sex goddess, became an infuriated plea, whispered into any vacant ear, 'Do me a favour, get that fat, lazy, Italian cow off my back for five minutes, will you?'

The film moved on to Taormina in Sicily. I ignored the Swedish beauties on the beach, counting the days for Jean to arrive. I boarded in a stately hotel, an old converted monastery that I wanted to share with her. I had Jean met at the airport but the paparazzi spotted her. She happened to be wearing a pair of Scholl wooden sandals.

'Looka me plis, *Signorina*, Jinn, how are these *scarpe?*' pointing at the feet.

She smiled.

'For fashion?' asked another. Getting no response, he prostrated himself on the cobbles and aimed his camera up her skirt.

'Looka me, Jinn, smile, please.'

Jean spotted the driver holding a production board and strode out like a thoroughbred amidst a herd of asses.

'For beach,' someone added triumphantly.

Jean made it to the car.

'For orthopaedic,' she said through the window.

She arrived at the San Pietro, flushed and full of the successful banter at the airport which she obviously considered her first press conference. She was concerned, however, about the puffiness around her eyes. I could see it was only the heat, perhaps the time of the month. A well-known crimper had had surgery under his eyes to tidy them up. She hadn't considered it, but it was the current gossip of the fashion world. The roll towards surgical perfection had started. She pulled nervously at her eyelashes.

'I, I wanted to postpone coming a few days. I haven't been feeling well. I should have waited but I didn't want to disappoint . . .'

There was a tap at the door, a waiter in whites glided in with a jug of iced tea. The room was dim, the shutters drawn to keep out the heat. The high curve of the ceiling allowed the air to circulate, but it wasn't cool.

It is a peculiar constant in my life that the loveliest women I've met never believe they are. The less endowed often think they are, or are not bothered. The most beautiful all have strings of reasons to prevent them feeling so. Jean was no exception, and nothing I said seemed to convince her, although I tried at every opportunity. I felt much the same way about the puffiness, for instance, as she did about my puny shoulders. Sometimes, especially if I hadn't seen her for a few days, observing the fragility of the changing shades beneath her eyes would bring a decidedly unmasculine lump to my throat. I spent a lot of time with Jean burying those feelings of mine, convinced it was my macho side she was drawn to. I always found it difficult to reveal my deeper emotions to her face.

'You know how butch you East End boys like to think you are,' Geoffrey had said, but then his insight touched areas that I couldn't even acknowledge. When I missed her, really missed her, that first moment together always cut through me.

I held her hand chastely in the darkened stillness of the Monastero San Pietro, sensing it was tenderness not passion my friend needed.

'Before I knew you,' I began, 'I admired you from afar. I dreamed of meeting you in a lonely setting with time to get to know you, but knew I never would. My fantasies were the same as all us boys have. In my need to know you, I pored over newspaper photographs of you with a magnifying glass.' Jean closed her eyes and lay back against the heavyweight bolster that ran the width of the mahogany bedhead.

'All I could see were black dots. It's always eventually black dots.'

She smiled without opening her eyes.

'One day, Mike Caine showed me a colour picture of you holding a shrimp in your mouth but I could only look at your eyes. It was the first time I'd seen you in colour, you see. I felt such a sweet sensation deep inside me, that I began to think perhaps there was something in store for us. No matter how impossible it looked. Some kismet that would bring us together. When I eventually met you, saw how content you were with Bailey, I began to bury the feelings . . . '

I looked at her face, her breathing had slowed, I think she was asleep. I didn't withdraw my hand. I sat for an hour looking at her. The melting ice in the tea created condensation which ran down the outside of the glass jug. Undisturbed.

15

Location work on *Modesty Blaise* eventually ended. In Sicily I heard Dirk Bogarde had jokingly lifted up Monica's skirt. Whatever had actually happened, Monica was suddenly filled with hatred for Bogarde. She was an extremely touchy lady. I didn't spend much time with any of the cast when Jean was there. Dirk hung out mostly with Losey, giving him suggestions; Joe even shot a sequence where Dirk appeared in costume and make-up from *The Servant*. I lost heart. I could see Monica didn't have the spunk or physical co-ordination to play Modesty as written; Twentieth Century Fox were hoping for a female 007. She was in a world of her own, playing some kind of screwball comedy and, as ninety per cent of my action was with her, I anticipated a lot of our footage falling to the cutting-room floor. The film was slowly but surely becoming a vehicle for Dirk's camp villain.

One lunch-time, the final Saturday in Sicily, we were shooting near a beach. When we broke, Losey and I found ourselves swimming in the same stretch of water.

'Terence,' he said, floating on his back, moving only his arms to keep him in one place.

'Yes, Joe?' I attempted to do the same – I was never a good floater.

'Terence,' he repeated. 'D'you like Monica?'

'She's O K,' I said diplomatically.

'Do you know her problem?'

'Not really.'

'You could solve it for me,' he said. A few more strokes.

'I'll do what I can, Joe.'

'Give her a seeing to, would you?'

'There you have a problem,' I said.

I was as nice as I could be. Actually, the only friend she had on the film was a travelling companion, who spoke English. I kept in mind how alienated Monica must have felt and by the end of the Italian shooting we were on quite good terms. As a result, Monica arranged to make lunch for me at her apartment in Rome *en route* to London, even taking the trouble to check my favourite Italian dishes. She and Antonioni lived separately but were neighbours, their homes joined by a circular iron staircase. He put in a brief appearance at our lunch and I was introduced. He spoke a little about a film he was preparing, how he was considering a location change from Milan to London which would utilise the swinging English scene as a background. The hero was to be a fashion photographer. Was I interested at all? Sure. He would speak to me in London. *Ciao.*

Jean had returned to London from Sicily, prior to the troupe's move to Naples. I wanted to buy her something special, something she would enjoy. Rome might have been designed for a moneyed lad in love with a beautiful girlfriend. This was my first shopping trip in the Eternal City and it didn't let me down. I spotted a frock in the window of a tiny boutique at the foot of the Spanish Steps, directly opposite Babington's English Tea Rooms. I'd dallied in the quaint café, sipping cup after cup of their tarry lapsang souchong, and had amused myself by steadying my wobbly table with a combination of wooden blocks thoughtfully provided by the Italian waitresses.

Edified, I stepped out into the sunny piazza where the aroma of horses wafted by from the assembled carriages patiently plying for hire. I was contemplating how nice it would be to take Jean on a shopping trip to Rome and trot over the cobbled streets in a horse-drawn buggy, when I saw the dress – a trapeze-line cut from what appeared to be fine chiffon silk. It filled the frame, as we say in the movies. The predominant shade was red, but mixed with a pageant of bright squares that might have been stolen from the palette of Vasarély. I went in. The item was the work of designer Ken Scott.

'What colour is *la donna?*' asked an assistant with a Grecian urn figure and a perfume too heavy for a hot afternoon.

'*Non importa,*' I said, not wanting to sound like a tourist and exercising the Stamp system of Italian, which consisted of putting an O or an A on to the end of just about everything.

'*Quale misura?*' enquired the over-scented urn, obviously assuming I was a local.

It had worked the first time. I tried it again, '*Non importa, Signorina.*'

The repetition, however, brought a cloud of uncertainty over the set-to-please face.

'*Non importa,*' she said softly to herself and then something which sounded like, '*Non capisco, Signor.*'

Discarding my aloof Italian noble attitude, I mimed pulling the dress out of the window.

'Ah,' she beamed, '*questo!*'

'Exactly mento, *questo,*' I echoed, dragging the wad of Monopoly lire from the pocket of my Levi's.

'*Esattamente,*' she corrected me, reassured by the sight of the filthy lucre.

I had no doubts about the suitability of the gown. Red is always the most difficult colour to wear and match, even if you're dark, which Shrimpton certainly wasn't, and I had to guess her size in a line I didn't know, but I'd seen her in the dress the moment I glimpsed it in the window. Her image had flashed in front of me, had given me the irresistible grin, showing me how elegant she could look when she cared to. I put down the bundle of notes on the glass counter top.

'Wrappo it up, primo class, *per favore.*'

Jean stood in the middle of the drawing-room of the flat in Mount Street, facing me, holding the knitted silk dress close, her face flushed. I did buy her things, used birthdays and Christmas as an excuse to adorn her with expensive novelties, although in the main we were a couple who sought out amusing gifts, silly items which conveyed an awareness of the other's quirks. I had scoured the East End many times, finally succeeding in locating a particularly old style of sherbet dab, constructed like a firework with a soft liquorice straw to suck up the phosphorus-sugar. I appreciated her presents and I think it was mutual. She always proudly sported the Piaget wristwatch with the china-white face I'd given her, and I walked down Bond Street for years wearing the black Herbert Johnson hat that she'd designed for me. Her draughtsman's eye had extended the width of the brim to accommodate precisely the width of my head.

'I wanted to see you as a Dutch painter,' she'd said.

It was the first hat I'd owned, and I wore it as proudly as my dad had worn his pearl grey trilby. Still do.

'Let's see it on, then,' I demanded, anxious to compare my mental image with the real thing.

'But . . . ' She looked down at her shirt, jeans and Sally-Ann strap shoes.

'Don't care,' I insisted. 'Look, I'm lucky enough to live with the world's most beautiful model. I haven't seen you for weeks. I want a show. You know what boys are like, humour me.'

Jean, still flushed, repaired to the bathroom. She was gone some time. I tapped on the door.

'Five minutes, Miss Shrimpton,' I called.

'Go away, you'll have to wait. I'm doing my thing.'

I sat in the black leather chair with my back to the door, regarding my hands which I had kept in the sun for what seemed like days in an effort to get them brown. They'd resisted the effort and were still pale compared to the rest of me. They made me feel like a primate.

'You can look now,' her voice said from behind me. She'd entered silently on bare feet.

I turned. She had put on a light make-up, eyes echoing colours from the design. Her hair was up, even the fringe lifted back off her face – it was the only time she had intentionally bared her forehead. There was an intimacy about the gesture. She coolly turned a slow full circle like a catwalk mannequin. The fragile, bright silk followed, hinting at the *chute des reins*. Jean glided around me, the fullness of the line concealing her high-stepping action. She did a little namaste, closing her hands together against her chest.

'Thank you, it's lovely. How did you know the size?'

'Thank you,' I said, 'I didn't even ask. It had your name written all over it.'

'Oh, Stamp,' she squealed, 'it's beautiful. When can I wear it?'

'Don't take it off. We'll stop at your place, slip into a pair of shoes, those blue ones with the red trim'll be fine, and I'll take you to Parkes'. Table in the kitchen. You can have a Pimm's, as it's Saturday.'

Jean was a cheap date as far as alcohol was concerned. The only drink she could manage was a Pimm's cap bolstered with lots of fruit and extra lemonade; even then, one glass could make her fragile the following day.

The kitchen table at Parkes' was actually in the kitchen. Consequently, Tom Benson, the young owner, only gave it to people he didn't mind watching him cook. The menu of the restaurant was exotic: dishes came festooned in flowers or, in winter, caviar might arrive nestled in handfuls of fresh snow. It was always an occasion. We confined visits to Friday or Saturday nights for candle-lit suppers. I'd heard Orson Welles wined and dined Marlene Dietrich at the same tiny table.

'You'll make me all silly,' Jean said, anticipating the effect of the Pimm's.

'I'm not averse to a little silliness, now and then,' I said. 'You do look wonderful, you make me feel like a white gorilla,' I said, showing the backs of my hands.

'I'm not averse to the odd white gorilla,' she said. 'OK, guy, let's get out of here, shall we?'

16

Antonioni was even more secretive than I was. He came to London, asked me for a list of my 'swinging friends', and interviewed people in his suite at the Savoy. He approached Jean about playing in an opening scene of the film, modelling for the photographer I was to play. I heard Antonioni had also consulted Bailey and Donovan. Neither was too forthcoming, but the photographer acquired a convertible Roller like Terry and an attitude like Bailey, anyway.

When Jean and I talked about it, I voiced my doubts about this project as a film debut. She had never spoken of any desire to act. It wouldn't be difficult for her to get a proper part in a movie but I advised her to prepare herself. I gave it a lot of thought and suggested my old voice teacher, Kate Fleming, who would give her the low-down on acting, while building her voice. Jean took only one class. She said Kate frightened her. I tried again with Cecily Berry but again Jean went for a few classes only. She never said why she didn't persevere. Her media image was a figure so removed and mysterious that to see her actually moving and speaking, I thought, would be a big initial shock for an audience. The first exposure would be crucial. Nicholas Roeg and Donald Cammell understood this well when launching Mick Jagger in *Performance*. The Rolling Stone hadn't fared so well in his second feature, *Ned Kelly*, when less care was taken. Until now, Jean had been immune – models don't receive the kind of criticism actors regularly come in for, and I suppose I was hoping to protect her. Antonioni's offer had apparently tempted Jean to branch out. It wasn't hard to understand: being a household word hadn't made her much money. Jean didn't use a lot, she didn't have the compulsive shopping illness I had but she did like to be independent and to run her own ship. I decided to get on the case. Make her some. I consulted Jimmy Woolf.

'Who is her agent?' he asked.

'She only has a model agent, that's why she's never made any bread. She's at her peak of fame now – should be able to cash in on it.'

'Take her to John Heyman, he's fly, he'll know what to do.'

Heyman was an ambitious agent I'd met with Jimmy: he was smart, had an agent's easy-going manner. Jimmy had introduced him to Hugh French, an old-time Hollywood manager, who'd represented Richard Burton for years and who had inherited Liz Taylor when she and Richard were married. John Heyman was fixing things for Liz and Richard in no time.

I made an appointment and we went to his new offices off Grosvenor Square. He was certain and enthusiastic, with all sorts of ideas. Jean was quite taken with a small bubbly woman who worked with Heyman called Felice Gordon. Soon film commercials were flying in. Fees went up. Sponsorship deals were discussed and everything looked rosy.

Not long after, I received a call from John Heyman to come in to the office, alone. There was something to discuss. Apparently, Jean was paying him twenty-five per cent as a management fee. He wanted to give me ten per cent of it.

'What for?'

'You brought her to me, Tel, I'm grateful. You might need a new agent yourself, sometime.'

'Well, I don't need to earn money from her,' I said, feeling like a pimp. 'I want her to accumulate some dough. She can't model for ever. I think she's had a rough ride. Everybody's copped except her.'

He held up his hands in exasperation.

'My boy,' he said, smiling, 'she's agreed to the twenty-five per cent. I want you to have it. Gratis.'

'Look, John, I'm rolling in bread. Every time I accept a movie it's like I've won the pools. I'm paying 19/6d in the pound tax, as it is. Why don't you take less? Give her the ten per cent.'

'You know what these girls are like, that's why she's hard up now. Take the ten per cent, put it on deposit, make her a nestegg. Surprise her.'

I thought it was the first good idea he'd had.

'OK,' I said, 'give it to me in readies, I'll invest it for her.'

I've always been a sucker for surprising people. I pictured her face when I handed her a be-ribboned basket of money.

'Can't do cash, sorry, Tel. Sign this.'

'Why do you need a signature?'

'Only office accounting. Quarterly, keep everything kosher. Should have a nice bundle in a bit. She's such a lovely girl.'

He put the biro in my hand like the chap from the Pru and I signed the way my old mum and dad did. Something worried me, though, and I told Jimmy Woolf about the off-the-wall conversation.

'Sounds like a nice gesture to me. He's a good boy, is John, good businessman,' Jimmy said, speaking, as usual, through the wet Havana clenched between his teeth. 'What's the problem?'

'John Heyman frightens me a bit. He seems so smart, just like all those boys I went to school with, they were all so clever with money.'

'That's no reason to be frightened of anyone. It's a skill, like any other. Some people need to let you know how smart they are. Some are more secure. Remember, regarding money, it's what you use that's important, not what you have. He likes you, that's all, he'd like to represent you. We've spoken about it but I've told him that as far as I know you're satisfied with James Fraser.'

He thought for a moment, closing his eyes to prevent the cigar smoke getting to them. He inhaled deeply and then crunched it out.

'Don't worry. It's simple. You tell Jean everything, or you don't. If you want to surprise her, OK, buy her a painting, something that will increase in value. Geoffrey told me you'd already bought her a valuable old portrait, little girl with a whip, wasn't it? I'll help you choose something, if you like. I know about that. I helped Larry. He has a fine collection now. Or Geoffrey, if you prefer his taste. Ask him, but you're right to watch out for her. If you were going to marry her, it would be different. You're both young. Lots to look forward to. You're an actor, you can have a long career, if you're smart.' He gave me a dig. 'It's different for a model. Fashion changes quickly. They'll find someone thinner or younger and she could be finished in a second. It's good to interest her in other things. Painting, good stones, property, things that last. Heyman's all right – ambitious, but basically proper.'

*

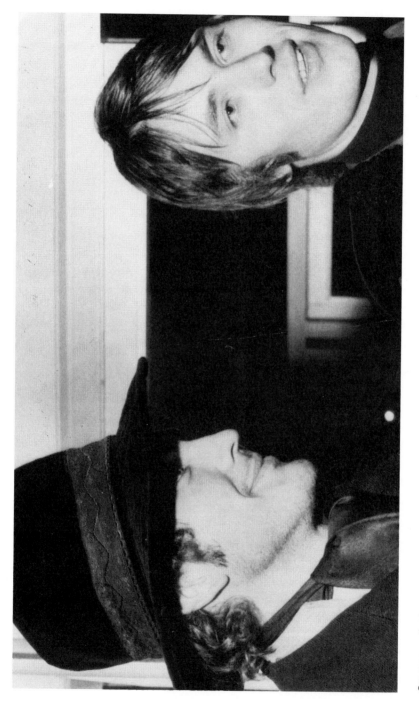

Stamps on the town.

The complaint I'd contracted in Washington – from asparagus – recurred. My brother Chris, by now making a name for himself in the pop world, was consulted. He had a head full of bizarre contacts used by the Rock and Roll Raj. He'd found a group in a pub calling themselves the High Numbers and re-christened them the Who, forming a partnership with a fellow assistant film director named Kit Lambert. They planned to form their own record company and launch their discoveries on it. Jimi Hendrix's first waxing, 'Hey Joe', went out on their label, Track Records.

Chris told me of a specialist, Doctor Harkness or Harky, as he called him.

'He's lovely. A laugh. It's not embarrassing. He likes a giggle. Go and see him.'

I did. He lived and practised at Lister House, Wimpole Street. His rooms on the first floor were musty and dusty with papers, discarded glass tubes and enough jars to fill a larder. Harky himself was old. A shrunken angel in a three-piece suit, his waistcoat buttoned tightly over his concave chest. The face was wizened, but warmth beamed out of him as we shook hands.

'Spot of trouble?' he asked.

'I'm afraid so.'

'OK,' he said, 'get your trousers off and jump up on the table.' He pointed to a high leather-topped affair that almost filled one half of his examination room.

'It's probably the old NSU,' he said, squeezing the life out of my dick in his enthusiasm to produce a smear for the glass slide. Delighted by his efforts, he fixed the glass under his microscope and squinted into the eye piece.

'The bloke in the States needed twenty-four hours to get it analysed.'

'Oh, had it before, have you?'

I nodded glumly. 'In Washington, last year.'

'Yes, but this is my field. I discovered this.'

'What?'

'The non-gonococcal variety. Yep, that's the fella,' he said proudly, pointing to his 'scope. 'Wanna have a look?'

'No thanks, things like that make me faint.'

'Do they? Interesting.'

I got the impression lots of things were interesting to Harky.

'I might have been a surgeon, otherwise. I felt the calling.'

'Oh, you should have persevered, you'd have overcome it. Now, let's have a sample, fill that up.'

He passed me an enormous flask, large enough to display hydrangeas.

'Fill it up?'

'Well, do the best you can.'

'Is there a loo?'

'There is, but you're peeing into the jar, not the lavatory. We all pass water the same, you know.'

I located my traumatised organ and managed a sample.

'That do?'

'Yep, that's fine.'

He held the gallon container up to his eye as though viewing a rare amontillado.

'Wrong side of the hill?' I asked.

He turned his head like a turkey, without moving the sample.

'Oh yes,' he giggled. 'D'you drink?'

'Not much. I like a glass of wine with dinner.'

'Oh, what d'you like?'

'I'm into Gévrey Chambertin at the moment.'

I could see what my brov liked about the visits.

'Where d'you come from?' I asked.

'South Africa, came over with the rugger team before the war. Loved it. I stayed on and qualified here.'

'International rugby cap, eh?'

'Oh yeah, I was good, twinkle toes.'

'I bet.'

'Look at these threads, that's the bacteria. I'll put you on these.' He rummaged around a desk drawer. 'Save you buying them.' He produced the ubiquitous antibiotics. 'Cheaper than John Bell & Croydon.'

'Good ole Fleming, eh?'

'Well, it was the other chaps who did the work, but Fleming received all the credit. Now you know the drill, every six hours. Come and see me in a week. Come Monday at,' he looked at his diary, 'nine o'clock; don't relieve your bladder till you get here.'

'What?'

'Don't have a pee before you arrive.'

'OK. How long?'

'You chaps are all the same. All you want to know is when you can start with the nooky again. The old chaps, on the other hand, want to know how soon they can have a whisky.'

'Doc,' I said, 'don't lie to me, now. I know I was better before I was cleared in Washington. My girlfriend turned up in tasselled knee socks. Bloody sadist, that doctor.'

'He was only doing you a favour. I get lots of them in here – oversexed pop groups, demon lovers all, just like you. I lay them off an extra couple of weeks. Give 'em a rest.'

'Don't do me extra favours, Doc.'

'Cat around, do you?'

'Eh?'

'Put it about, lots of ladies?'

'No, only the one. Special. Never felt like this.'

'Hmmm.'

'Can't seem to leave her alone . . . '

'Well, you're young; I got into masturbation early, myself. Saved me a lot of heartache.'

' . . . every time I look at her. It's not only lust; there's something else peering over my shoulder.'

'Listen,' he said, 'have you a few minutes?'

'Sure, my time's my own, no good me rushing home, is it?'

I shook the capsules, they looked like relatives of Jimmy Woolf's Tuinols. Harky pulled out a twenty-pack of Senior Service and offered me one. No filters here – a man after my own heart. He strolled next door into his sitting-room where curvy Forties armchairs waited on either side of an electric fire. He clicked on a bar.

'Feel the chill at my age,' he said, luxuriating in a serious inhalation of his Senior. He stretched back in the easy chair.

'I'm only qualified to treat venereal disease and I'm a bachelor, but I'm an old codger, nearer ninety than eighty, and I've done a bit, seen a lot.' He grinned. 'This is where all the big nobs hang out.' I could see he'd cracked the joke more than once. I laughed.

'Sex is mostly psychological, don't you see? The body is constructed for reproduction, but like the rest of Nature, it's abundant. The healthy male has over 5,000 ejaculations in his lifetime, totalling roughly four gallons of sperm. That's what Kinsey reported, you follow?' I nodded. 'The average healthy semen spent

Terry O'Neal posed Chris and me like gangsters.

during intercourse contains between 200,000,000 to 500,000,000 separate cells, any one of which can fertilise a female egg. Your Terence Junior' (now recovering modestly in my corduroys) 'could, by itself, fertilise five hundred million female eggs. So there's no shortage. You see what I mean?'

I was impressed. I didn't comment.

'That's what the male body is equipped to do. Actually, the planet doesn't need re-populating at present, although you could technically generate enough sperm to do it single-handedly. You follow?'

'Hmmm.' I mused on this addition to my fantasy list.

'Women are more powerful than men because they are passive. They cannot be exhausted. From a biological standpoint you can't even satiate them as they don't have a penis that collapses after ejaculation. That's a frightening prospect for a man. Any man. But it is a male psychosis. Women do not *need* to be overwhelmed sexually, they derive satisfaction from all kinds of things. Sex is only the glue that holds it all together. Your girl doesn't love you more because you're virile, but because you love her. You complete her, as she completes you. You be yourself, Terence. It's all right. Now, go and think about it. Talk to her about how she feels, really feels. Stop damaging yourself. Don't drink any alcohol for a bit, and don't empty your bladder on Monday, until you arrive here. You have strain. Now rest. Or next time I'll give you a prostate massage.' He wagged a menacing long middle finger at me.

'I have a condom tailored for the job with a pot of particularly chilly Vaseline. It'll hurt you more than it will hurt me. You won't like it. So take it easy. OK?'

'OK, Harky. Thanks. Cash all right, save you billing me?'

I pulled out some tenners. His eyes twinkled. I'd pegged him for a cash man.

17

I went along with Antonioni's intrigue for eight months. It was my own fault. My snobbery provided the film maker with a button he could keep pushing. At the time I didn't mind, although Jimmy Woolf nagged me to get a paper, a letter, anything. I trusted the director. After all, his mum had christened him Michelangelo, he must be a Renaissance man. I travelled to Rome for conferences, taking Jean with me for long weekends. We hired small cars and drove to the coast to lark around in the sea. We dined at Mastino's on the beach in Fregene, eating *rughetta* salad spread out on wood-fire toasted country bread. We were served blackened sea bass pulled biblically from the sea by the restaurant owner's seven fishermen sons who brought them to the rough wooden tables where they peeled the flesh from the bone like surgeons of their trade. Hot nights, hot afternoons and hot mornings followed without regard for my new, old friend's advice. We'd siesta in the shuttered rooms of the Hotel Raphael, listening to the sounds of the fountain in Piazza Navone and drink the red blood of oranges at dawn; visit the Caravaggio painting on the dim chapel wall, a stone's throw away in the church with the unfathomable opening times. We'd lick the famous Tre Scalini, bitter-sweet chocolate ices, as we lazed in heavy wicker chairs set out on the cobbled street, gazing wistfully at the terracotta walls of penthouses whose spacious terraces overlooked the ancient square. Having a good time. Being in love.

I often used to think that if I died today, this moment, I would have had more than my fair share. No man could have asked for more.

We extended those trips, combing jewellery shops on narrow streets, adding to Jean's modest collection of enamel serpent trinkets and Greek wedding rings made of varying shades of

intertwining gold. 'A wedding ring you bought her, Stamp?' I hear you say. It crossed my mind a lot in Rome. As we became more sure of foreign travel, we would take the train to Naples or ride the *aliscafo* to Ischia, the less fashionable younger sister of Capri. Open air, all-night discos. Long evenings, long nights. I learned to water ski in Ischia.

'You flash sod,' she said, as though in envy of my East End determination to get up first time. She was joking. She repeated my feat immediately afterwards. That night she wrapped my burnt Anglo-Saxon skin in cream and lay down beside me carefully.

'It'll stop you burning up,' she said.

'Burn up? Me?' That'll be the day, I thought, laying my hot cheek on the cool nape of her neck. I was thinking about death, but planning to live for ever: progeny from the Stamp half billion cells matched equally by the long, rangy matrix of the double Scorpio beside me. Not only that, hadn't Chinese astrologers since ancient times agreed that those born in the Year of the Horse become the best friends with the big-pawed Tiger? Ask her. She can only say no. She might even say yes.

With the earnings from the new work that she was doing, Jean bought herself a small house in Knightsbridge. Helped by Felice Gordon, her new agent with lots of business acumen, she did a deal with assorted gas and electrical companies to re-fit the basement with a splendid modern kitchen. Jean sought advice from decorators and antique dealers she knew and, while Geoffrey was finishing my new chambers at Albany, she was transforming the bijou town house into a dream nest of her own, filling odd spaces with period painted rocking horses and tables draped to the floor in felt, scattered with an assortment of blue and white porcelain. My only contribution was the midnight blue bathroom tiles despatched from Rome to match the Victorian flowered pedestals that Jean had chosen for the water closets.

Jimmy Fraser and Jimmy Woolf had succeeded in completing a deal for me on the Antonioni film which was to be financed by Metro Goldwyn Mayer and entitled *Blow Up*. The terms were finalised at a meeting in Jimmy Woolf's apartment with Fraser and MGM's attorney, Lee Steiner, present. I was having a steam bath in the men's club at Les Ambassadeurs that afternoon when Jimmy

Woolf telephoned to lay out the terms and get my approval. I was delighted, and agreed immediately – shooting was to start soon. Before the deal was settled verbally and the headings of agreement noted by Fraser, Jimmy Woolf had asked Lee Steiner, 'Do you have the authorisation of MGM to complete this matter?'

The big US lawyer assured him he did, although he was later to deny this, despite giving his assurance before the two Jimmys. I continued to practise my impersonation of a photographer with the camera Jean had given me. There was considerable publicity about the fact that I would be working with the Italian director on his first English-speaking project. An assistant director named Claud Watson, who had worked on *Billy Budd*, rang me and expressed his enthusiasm about working with Michelangelo. I told the Maestro, and Claud was taken on as his first assistant. One of Antonioni's peculiarities, aside from an uncontrollable twitch of the mouth, was his need to keep the second half of the film a secret. During all of our meetings the story line was only discussed up to a certain point. I must admit that I was curious to receive my copy of the mysterious script, but it wasn't forthcoming. Joanna Shimkus, an actress friend of Antony Norris, my old photographer chum who was coaching me, had been seen repeatedly by Antonioni and had been told by him that she would be playing the enigmatic female lead. I was happy for her. It was a good break and she was a talented, beautiful girl to play opposite. There was to be considerable nudity in the action.

I celebrated the start of *Blow Up* by moving into my Shangri-La. The set at Albany was finally finished. Bennison and his workforce had stripped the place to its bones, replacing all the floors (which were filthy and disintegrating) and all of the wiring.

'It looked like it hadn't been overhauled for a hundred years,' Geoffrey said. He'd done a phenomenal job and, although I'd been consulted at every turn, the finished effect was beyond my expectations. He was proud of it, too. I wasn't aware of it at the time, but doing up the chambers represented a triumph over a huge emotional block for him, and he arranged for the décor to be photographed and featured in *Homes and Gardens*, as though announcing his comeback.

That first afternoon I rolled around on the carpet in front of the fireplace, hugging myself in reassurance it was true. Geoffrey had painted the floorboards of the two main adjoining rooms white;

apparently, he'd rubbed the paint into the boards with his own hands to achieve the effect he wanted before varnishing. The wood looked as though it had been embalmed in clover honey. In the bedroom the floorboards led the eye over a polar bear skin to an Empire bed shaped like a boat, but severe in line. Geoffrey had overseen the widening of the piece of furniture to accommodate two people comfortably. Only an expert who knew that beds of this style and period were constructed solely as singles would have guessed it had been altered. When not in use it was covered by a black, biscuit and cream overlay, with matching sausage bolsters at each end so that it resembled an oversized day bed. On the floor next to the boat of dreams was a Goan ebony chest inlaid with ivory flowers and scroll clouds, containing a patchwork of drawers, sixteen in all. It served as a bedside table supporting a black angle-poise lamp and telephone. Like a chemist, I was badging odds and ends away into the different compartments when the telephone rang. It was Claud Watson, Antonioni's new assistant. As it was Saturday evening and the picture set to start shooting within the next fortnight, I had been anticipating a call to wardrobe for days.

'Hi, Claud,' I replied, squatting back on my haunches and lowering myself to a sitting position on the polar bear's back. It was fortunate I did.

'Terence,' Claud said slowly, as though thinking of how to frame his words, 'it looks as if David Hemmings is doing the part.'

'Part? Which part, Claud?' I wanted to know.

'Your part in, er, *Blow Up*,' he said hesitantly.

You could have knocked me down with a feather.

'Who's David Hemmings, when he's out?' I enquired, in shock.

'He's, he's an actor. An unknown. Michelangelo saw him in a play. I'm sorry.'

There was a long, awkward pause as I gathered my wits.

'O K, Claud, thanks. Goodnight.'

No good venting my rage on him. It wasn't Claud's fault. He was a chum, used by Antonioni as an oily rag. I'd recommended him, that was the irony. He'd sounded as sick as a parrot. It was spineless of the director not to ring himself, though. He might have treated me to a *cappuccino* and told me to my face, but then he wasn't the other Michelangelo. I caught sight of myself in the mirrored doors of the corner cupboard – I looked like something that had been thrown away.

My shock was offset when Joseph Janni approached me about acting in his forthcoming production of Thomas Hardy's *Far From the Madding Crowd*. It was set for the autumn and was to be directed by John Schlesinger who'd helped my old friend Julie Christie win an Oscar in *Darling*. Naturally, I was enthusiastic, but still bitterly disappointed. I could have handled both.

Jimmy Woolf advised me to issue writs on Antonioni, MGM and Carlo Ponti, the producer, for breach of contract, defamation of reputation, etc. I did. I won, of course, but settled for half the fee and *Madding Crowd* instead. Joe Janni had wanted me, anyway, but Metro, who were backing Joe's picture as well, dictated their terms to him. He could use me only on the understanding it was in substitution for the role in *Blow Up*. This was the less glamorous aspect of movie making, although Jimmy Woolf relished all the two-faced cut and thrust and knew well the philosophy 'If you kick 'em in the balls first, the heart will follow instantly.'

With Mr Jimmy by my side I could have taken them to the cleaner's. All of them. But Jimmy died in a bungalow at the Beverly Hills Hotel in May. The book found open on his pale chest was *The Valley of the Dolls*, the eye-catching dust jacket illustrated with a selection of barbiturates or dolls, as they were calling them in Los Angeles in 1966. James Woolf, a remarkable man who couldn't sleep.

I missed Jimmy more than I ever thought I would. My friendship with him was different from other mates – he'd been older, a bachelor, childless. Although his influence on me wasn't always positive, I'm sure he saw a glint he'd have appreciated in a son: a bit of a loner, a bit eccentric, interested in going against the stream, if only to see what happened. Not unlike himself. After his burial at Willesden cemetery, Jean drove me to Rose Hill Farm. Her folks were away and she took care of me, comforted me as one would a child. She was the only woman, save my mum, I'd allowed myself to be a kid with. She hadn't offered to mother me before – it was unexpectedly calming and beautiful, another texture added to how I felt for her. My twenty-four-year-old mother. This caring continued, becoming a gentle undercurrent, never verbalised, mutually valued. We went out less and she started cooking more, at first receiving hints, then taking instruction from Tom Benson at Parkes'. She shopped with him in Harrods Food Hall, excited by her increasing skills. She was pleased that I appreciated her choice of food, her talent with a contra fillet and growing mastery of the elusive salad dressing. My sixth-former was growing up, and I liked it. I sought her companionship more and more, hurrying home from my Saturday football matches with the boys or, on weekdays, arriving before she came in from work, waiting, excited but content, for her steps. The part of me that I'd been frightened to give, to commit to another person was unfolding.

Then John Heyman made his move, after which the relationship I had with Jean was never to be the same. I didn't even have Jimmy Woolf to turn to for advice. In any event, considering Jimmy's experience in showbiz he may well have shrugged off Heyman's behaviour with the adage 'business is business', as though commerce was somehow separate from life.

The agent had achieved his lifelong ambition and got a film of his own off the ground. He'd secured the services of a young director called Peter Watkins who had made an impressive debut with a film shown on television called *Culloden*, a low-budget black and white epic. Heyman had him signed to direct a futuristic tale of a mega pop star. He'd spoken with me about it a lot, with the pop lead in mind. As the hero needed to be able to sing 'Ave Maria' at the climax of the story, I declined. You can only wing it so far. I had turned down the part of King Arthur for the great Josh Logan in his production of *Camelot* for the same reason. Undaunted, Heyman approached Shrimpton – a smart idea to cash in on her fame and beauty. For him. I advised Jean against it. I suppose my protective attitude towards her could be seen as possessive, but it didn't feel like it at the time. I knew what it took to make movies and I also knew how fragile she was – heard it in her voice. I counselled caution. Heyman had a pep talk with her. I don't know exactly what was said but he convinced Jean I was taking a kickback, and he showed her the paper I'd signed as proof. He'd never paid me anything, incidentally, but he persuaded her she could no longer trust me or my judgement.

She left me. I couldn't find her and I was desperate. I took to waiting outside the place in Eton Villas she was sharing with a friend. Finally, she turned up. I didn't know what was wrong. She, sobbing, confronted me with the accusations.

I must confess I am a guy with a few problems and more than a few faults, but making money out of loved ones isn't one of them and, actually facing me, I think Jean realised she'd been duped. After all, if I'd been promoting her to line my own pocket I'd have hustled her into the film. She apologised. I forgave her. In a loving reunion I took her off to the Old Guildford Hotel in the Bay of Sandwich. I'd walked by it so often as a boy and sworn one day I would visit there with the love of my life. Now the time had arrived.

In many ways the languid weekend was idyllic, enlightening. We fitted, slotted easily together. I saw there was no reason to artificially distance myself from her, making tension that, when released, intensified the coming together. For her there had never been a need. The rift had hurt us both; we were pleased to be reunited. Relaxed, we indulged in juvenile excursions. We went to Ramsgate and played the penny arcades, ate twirls of Rossi's ice-cream from cornets and rediscovered the seafront stalls of cockles and whelks. Mundane things spiced by our togetherness.

Together, that was the answer. I finally saw the simplicity of it all in Sandwich. During our first weekend together in an English resort we lay in the high old-fashioned bed listening to the waves, or strolled hand-in-hand along the beaches as fine and even as table salt – sand I'd moulded as a boy in summer camp castle-building competitions when I'd looked out to sea and dreamt my dreams. Now I'd completed my circle and realised my dream. Or had I? Something untoward had occurred, had happened inside me. At first I didn't notice or wouldn't look – wonderfully distracted by rediscovering Jean and the depth of my affection for her. Her affection for me. Although we were distanced by miles from the threatening environment of showbiz, there *was* something, a harbinger, and, when we left the mysterious healing given off by sea and sand, I had to confront it.

Jean agreed to play in Heyman's film. She refused to withdraw, intended, in fact, to keep her word, even though it meant going against my advice. I went along with it, I had no choice. I hoped I would be wrong about the outcome. I'd said my piece, expressed my misgivings, but I had no great desire to be right this time.

Something else that I'd been unable to put my finger on came to me in a flash. I recalled the conversation with nightmarish clarity.

Buzzing through the Garden of England towards the Kent coast in Jean's beloved EUU 633 C with me at the wheel, I'd made detours to old haunts, showed her the oblong Marlow Theatre I'd played in Canterbury and stopped for a drink at the Olive Branch pub, where I'd been adopted by the publicans and been boarded in their grown-up son's old room. We strolled in the grounds of the cathedral. When we returned to the car, I'd tuned to Radio Caroline. The pirate station was airing 'Black is Black'. I kept enquiring every few minutes whether she was all right. Jean, exasperated, finally drew attention to it.

'Please don't keep asking me. I've said I am.'

Her words had silenced the chattering in my brain. I came to. I'd not been aware I'd been asking until she asked me to stop. When I reflected later on the fear her remark had brought to the surface, I realised I was terrified. I had experienced life without her and knew, now, what she could do to me. I thought I had finally found a person I could give myself to without fear of rebuff, without the fear of pain. I'd tossed myself into the void, made myself vulnerable. I'd come a long way in my own little way but when the body blow came I couldn't take it. 'Are you all right?' I'd asked. Am I all right is what I'd meant. I saw my past like a map before me with conditioning, concepts and special neuroses all clearly marked. My feelings were intensified, having tasted the loneliness of life without her. Grounded as I was in insecurity, I hoped I could, by some superhuman strength, pull it all together, and start anew, but somewhere deep in me I knew I'd blown it. The oneness I'd experienced with her began surely and inextricably to evaporate. As her independence emerged, so did the sense of alienation I feared so. The fear deepened the alienation. A vicious circle. Unable to contemplate life without her, I pushed her away. I tried others – many others – in an effort to replace the lost magic. I discovered that that old angel Harky – old Harky, who was with them now – had been right, all along. Too late, I heard. Too late, as always.

'What a piece of work is Man,' the poet wrote. What he chooses to do with himself is nobody's business.

18

Dr Harkness had passed away. The loss, I felt, was the price I always paid for the luxury of having older chums. Harky and I had become firm friends. Apart from my official visits for strain – there was a lot of strain about in the Sixties – I made it a point to drop in on him whenever I was passing. Sometimes he would be with a patient and I would wait downstairs to see one of pop's satined peacocks in Cuban heels emerge from the surgery a bit white around the gills, no doubt having experienced, at first hand, one of Harky's infamous prostate massages. He always had his nurse rustle up a cuppa between appointments and he seemed to enjoy our chats. It was during one of these he had expanded his view on the man–woman conundrum.

'You know, Terence,' he would always begin, grabbing a pack of Seniors and flipping one into his mouth with deft abandon, 'when you serve your time in the medical profession – although today it's mainly drug peddling, nothing to do with Hippocrates any longer, I'm afraid – you do get an insight into the absolute perfection of the human body. I'm not a religious man at all, can't stand all that parsimonious clap-trap in God's name. Anyone at university who couldn't cut the mustard took a theology degree. Anyway, you can't ignore the intelligence with which it is all put together. There are no mistakes, and you can't improve it. For example, the Jews and Muslims have been slicing off bits of foreskin for as long as they've had knives – God knows what trauma it creates – haven't made a dent on the design of old John Thomas have they? You'd think after a few thousand years Nature would get the picture and start turning out new models.'

'It's really brutal,' I added. 'I saw a tribe in the Atlas mountains, mass-circumcising their sons. The screams were terrible. I've never believed that guff about being too young to remember it.'

'I won't make your pad too camp,' Bennison said.

Harky blew a smoke ring. I returned a few samples of my small series.

'I've heard that originally it was done at puberty to discourage self-abuse,' Harky said.

'Bit drastic, don't you think?'

'Some Arab sects amputate the woman's clitoris.'

'That's barbaric.'

'Well, we mustn't get too far into that topic.'

'It's bringing tears to my eyes, as it is; what were we talking about, Doc?'

'The man–woman structure.' I poured us another cuppa. 'You can understand why they used to call man a half-angel. He's only part complete until you put him together with a woman.'

I wondered who had called man a half-angel, but he was in full flow.

'The sexes so balance one another physically, you'd have to be a real dolt not to think about potential on other levels. I've often thought about an exchange of energy during sex. There's a mixing of fluid, lots of different fluids, actually, but after ejaculation one feels let down. I'm sure it's to do with this attitude of the man overpowering or conquering the submissive woman. Actually, the man is throwing off much more energy than the woman during intercourse – there must be a way of complementing each other, a superior use of energy while it's flowing strongly. It goes soon enough.' Harky grimaced. 'It's been a few . . .'

'Harky, don't tell me you haven't had it up this week.'

'Oh,' he giggled, 'let me tell you about this old patient of mine, wealthy chap, English but lives abroad. He's getting on a bit. Eighty last time I saw him. He comes to London in the spring for his suits, shoes, that sort of thing, and always pops in to me. I give him a check-up, make sure his prostate's in order.'

'Still at it, is he?'

'Well, that's the point, last time he was here, us being gentlemen of a certain age, I said, "Now look here, young man, actually how active are you?", thought he might have some tips, you see. He said, "Well, I still have that mistress, you know, she lives in my house, so it's a pretty regular sort of arrangement. I usually make love to her once a year but, just between you and me, last year I was unfaithful." What do you think of that, then? Dirty old beast.'

'You know, Harky, it's hard to think about it all just ending. It seems so pointless if you stop and think. There has to be more than eating, sleeping, getting laid, having kids. I don't know about afterlife. I only know about now! Sometimes, when I'm making love to my girl, everything stops, I just fall. It's like I . . . there's . . . this watching, as if a mirror is looking into a mirror. I don't know if I'm her or me, who's reflecting who. It is sort of motionless. Timeless. Afterwards, when I think about it, I can't seem to recapture the sensation, but it's somehow more real, nearer. It worries me. Not when it occurs, later. It only happens when I'm with her, you see. It makes me so dependent. If she left me I . . . I know I'll never meet anyone like her . . . but . . . it doesn't feel right to be dependent on something, someone outside yourself, to be happy. Everything changes. People, everything, it's all so dreamlike, I don't know.'

Harky looked at his watch. He was obviously expecting a client.

I blew one of my grand series smoke rings while I waited for his reply. It drifted solemnly over his head, momentarily giving him a halo.

'The sexes, the difference, that's why we feel so helpless. We keep trying to adjust, refine, but it's like trying to change the shape of . . . ' He looked around. There was a vase filled with bluebells brought from his country cottage on the table next to him. The sunny window behind his chair threw a shadow of the vase on to the oak table-top. Harky reached out his hand and made to grip the shadow. Naturally, it didn't move. He looked at me, then his nurse knocked on the door and came in.

'Doctor,' she said, 'there is a gentleman who says his name is Spyder, to see you.'

'Tell Mr Spyder to go through to the surgery and remove his strides . . . er, trousers.'

She left, leaving the door open.

'We'll talk about it next time,' Harky said.

'I'll come by soon,' I assured him. I passed an anxious Hell's Angel on the stairs. The next time I called Harky had other things on his mind. He'd been diagnosed terminally ill with cancer. Both lungs.

After the initial shock, Harky was philosophical. He didn't even stop smoking, although he encouraged me to. He had his medication and he assured me that he wasn't in pain. I discovered he loved a curry and brought by some aromatic chilli powder a friend had sent me from the spice bazaar in Durban. His house-keeper made us one up. I recall that visit with some poignancy. Not because of what he said, although later on his remarks had even greater impact, but because it was to be the last time I sat opposite him, his body shrunken, diminished by the armchair.

He was visibly weakened and spoke of the cancers as though they were uninvited temporary guests to be put up with.

'They don't affect . . . me,' he said, pointing a waxy forefinger towards his sternum.

'Have you been sleeping all right?' I asked.

'Oh, yes, but I never needed a lot of sleep, and I'd rather be awake now . . . in case he comes round.'

'He?'

I assumed he meant his doctor.

'Yes, he comes at the oddest times, never comes in. Stands by the door.'

A wave of something passed over his face. He tipped a large capsule from a container and popped it into his mouth followed by a gulp of milky coffee. 'Opiates,' he said with a wave of his hand. 'The specialist didn't want to prescribe too many,' he giggled. 'Said I might get addicted, can you imagine? Good stuff, though, distracts the brain much less than the pain, and that's important, right now.'

'Is that why he drops by, with your prescription?'

'Oh, him, no, he doesn't visit. I'm talking about my guest, he looks in to see if I'm ready. Never comes right in, mind you, waits by the door. He's nice and clean – never seen such a clean fella. Smart, too. Sharp brown suit, well-trimmed black beard. He'd be fun to go on a trip with.'

He smiled and drifted off, his head falling gently into his chest. He didn't rouse himself. I waited a bit and then quietly made my exit.

The next time I dropped in, he'd gone. I missed him. I commem-orated his passing by planting a Harkness rose in my parents' garden. It did well in warm summers and its unique perfume brought his sweet nature to mind. Magically, my non-specific cleared up permanently. Maybe he and his friend fixed it. Perhaps I was growing up. I didn't have cause to think about Harky's immaculate stranger until many years later when Herbert Kretzmer, the lyricist/journalist, who'd been a friend since he came to interview me in Ebury Street for the *Daily Express*, told me a story.

Herbie, or Haqq, as I call him, and myself, are typical of people bereft of extra-sensory abilities, and we mull over the happenings of others at length. It was Haqq who told me the story that brought to mind my last chat with Harky so vividly. Oddly enough, it also centred around a gentleman who had signed the Hippocratic oath.

Herbie had been suffering from a foot infection and had visited his local chemist on Old Church Street several times to purchase the ointment and dusting powders recommended. The problem persisted, however. Mr Kretzmer, by nature persevering, went into the chemist's shop a third time.

'It's still here,' said Herbie, indicating his heel.

'Right.' The man in the white coat reached behind him to a wall telephone and dialled a number. A few words were exchanged.

'Can you see the doctor now? He's in Harley Street, name of Meyer.'

'I can be there in fifteen minutes,' replied the limping lyric writer.

He was ushered into the rooms of a doctor in late middle age. As he gave his particulars, the medical man looked up.

'Meg's boy, are you?' he asked.

Herbie was stunned, speechless.

'Krunstaat, wasn't it? Outside Jo'burg?'

'My God,' said Herbie, 'how d'ya know?'

'Brought you into the world, young fella. Delivered you myself.'

It was the start of a long and friendly association. He fixed up the foot in no time and, later, when Herbie's wife Lynnie fell pregnant, he delivered both their children.

Eventually, it was the elderly South African doctor's time to depart. Herbie used to go and see his old friend in hospital.

'How are you feeling, Doc?'

'I'm not too bad,' he said, 'tried something new a few days ago.'

'What's that?'

'That stuff all the young people smoke, pot.'

'You didn't – how d'you get it?' asked Herbie.

'I asked a young intern, said he didn't know what I was talking about at first, but I insisted. He brought some by.'

'Did you enjoy it?'

'It was nice, soothing, but it made me sleep and that's not what I need right now.' He smiled. 'You know?'

'I guess so.'

Herbie admits he doesn't know what made him ask but he said, 'Anything else?'

A distant smile came over the dying man's face. After a moment, he said quietly, 'There's a man who comes to see me.'

'Is there?' said Herbie. 'What's he like?'

'He's clean, immaculate. Stands by the door, there.'

'Doesn't come in?'

'No, no, waits by the door, smiling. He has a neatly shaped black beard. He always dresses in brown, all brown.'

'Does he say anything?'

'No, he just smiles – he has a most beautiful smile. I'd go anywhere with him.'

He passed over two days later. Accompanied by his black-bearded friend, no doubt.

19

Jean bought me a horse for Christmas, a mare. I called her Modesty – my Christmas morning surprise. I was learning to ride properly for my part in *Madding Crowd*. Now, at weekends, we roamed the countryside astride our own mounts. I was also mastering the military sabre, a heavy, unwieldy beast used by mounted soldiers in the 1860s. John Schlesinger, who was set to direct Thomas Hardy's epic, had been informed that during that period only right-handed soldiers were accepted into cavalry divisions. He insisted I learn to use the sword with my right hand. The first few weeks of my new discipline were murder, as I hardly used my right hand for anything other than cutlery. My legs were like jelly from the daily riding at Mill Hill and my right arm the same during the afternoon ritual with the Master of Sword, Ian McKay, who came to me at Albany. We cut, thrust and parried back and forth across my drawing-room, the blows ringing out into the covered rope-walk. It must have been quite like old times for the spirits of the blades in the neighbourhood. Eventually, I went off to Dorset to commence shooting. Jean stayed in town, with me commuting most weekends. I'm sure Jean was apprehensive about my co-star Julie Christie and me playing Hardy's romantic twosome. She needn't have been. The lovely Dragon lady had a special place in my heart, but she was also happily settled at the time with a painter. Passion was confined to the celluloid. As Bathsheba and Troy, Julie and Terry were inspiring lyrics, however – the Kinks songster, Ray Davies, included our names in his 'Waterloo Sunset'.

1966 should have been a good year for me: I was involved in the project of the season alongside Peter Finch and Alan Bates, to say nothing of the Rep, an assortment of actors so talented and creative they floated hilarious productions of their own in Weymouth, to pass time. Nicholas Roeg, probably the greatest of the

Far from the Madding.

English directors of colour photography, was lighting his last masterwork before starting to direct films himself.

It all looked so good. Not to be. During the reading on the first day Schlesinger, hearing the diverse accents of his cast (some of us had worked out Dorset accents, others hadn't), decided the principals would do without. It was a crushing blow for me. I'd learned the part thoroughly in dialect – I had it all in my mouth – and I felt it a major setback to have to re-do it. I failed to understand why an Army sergeant, native to the country, wouldn't speak with a local burr. It was to be the first in a long series of differences between the director and myself that rankled us both.

I'd heard that Schlesinger had wanted to cast someone else as Troy but Joseph Janni, the producer, and MGM had foisted me on to him. We saw eye to eye on hardly anything; it wasn't a happy movie for me. I would rush home to Jean at weekends in a frenzy of need, driving my new Silver Cloud II Rolls Royce from Weymouth like a maniac. I was putting a big load on her shoulders without confiding my problems, but then I still felt it wasn't manly to worry the women with your troubles. I expected an awful lot of reassurance from those slim arms. I came home one Saturday to the house in Montpelier Place, flushed and exhausted from driving near the edge for two hours, to find a small lunch party she was giving in progress. It threw me into a mood I couldn't disguise, and I must have given off such a bad vibe, her guests cleared the house in minutes. I was ashamed. My behaviour was completely irrational. On the way up, I'd been listening to the Beach Boys' pop opus, 'Good Vibrations', so filled with love in anticipation of seeing her, so proud to consider myself part of the new generation that believed in good vibes and intent on overcoming baser characteristics; yet here I was behaving worse than my ole dad did when he came home and discovered my mum chatting to a neighbour over the garden fence. Except it wasn't even my house. I hadn't contributed a penny.

I think it was at this time that Jean must have started considering moving on. Nicholas Roeg drew my attention to an article Jean had given to a daily newspaper about the new house. I believe it was part of her deal on the kitchen to secure publicity and she had also made some ambivalent statements concerning her bedroom décor.

Bathsheba and Troy.

Nick chuckled. 'I'd keep an eye on her,' he said, 'seems she's on the look-out.'

I dismissed the remark as part of Nick's wicked sense of humour. The film finished. I was happy it was over. Glad to be back in town. Jean had completed her work on *Privilege* and we resumed our life together. One night we were eating in a small restaurant in the Hollywood Road when Jean drew my attention to a group at a nearby table.

'That's Jordan,' she said, 'Socolsky's friend from New York.'

I assumed it was someone in the fashion game. I looked and saw an extremely dark-complexioned man, like an Indian or Mexican with thick black hair. Nothing special, I thought.

'He's with . . .' so and so, she named a model Bailey had photographed and escorted briefly, 'I suppose the agency's fixed him up.'

She sounded piqued. I didn't give the incident much thought. A few days later, preparing supper in her small basement kitchen, she asked me, 'Stamp, what exactly is circumcision?'

It was such an off-the-wall question, I laughed.

'Well, you know, they cut the end of your John Thomas off. It's a Semitic ritual.'

'But what does it do?'

'Well, I imagine it hurts a lot, for one thing, and I've always supposed it makes the guy's cock less sensitive.'

'Why?'

'Well, when the tip of the foreskin is cut off so there isn't enough flesh to cover the end, the policeman's helmet is permanently exposed.'

'What does it look like?'

I obliged by unzipping the pants of my new bottle-green corduroy suit to illustrate the point. I found the demonstration curiously erotic. Supper was late that evening.

Shortly after, we took off for New York. No professional reason: shopping, or so I thought. Silvio Narizzano, the Canadian director, rang me. He'd heard I was in town and wanted to take me for tea. I liked Silvio – there had been some talk about me playing in his comedy film, *Georgie Girl*, but it hadn't come to anything. Alan Bates had played the part. At tea he spoke about a Western he was about to start for Paramount in Utah. It was to star Robert Redford and called *Blue*.

'That's a wonderful title, now, why didn't you offer me that?' I asked.

Silvio grinned, 'You're so fussy, don't like to offer you anything,' he replied.

Two days later I received a call from him. Redford had withdrawn. Did I think I'd like to play the part? A cockney scrubber born in Bow starring in a Western and named *Blue*. I didn't even read the script, which maybe was rash. Well, what the hell! The chance to play a cowboy.

There was a proviso: I would have to socialise a little. Dinner was arranged with Charles Bludorn, the tycoon whose company had just purchased Paramount, and his newly-appointed West Coast studio head, Robert Evans. Jimmy Woolf had always told me two things: don't mistake bustle with business and if you want to get the measure of a man, look at his shoes. Bludorn's shoes didn't make it, and Evans was into bustle. It wasn't a nice evening, with me having to jump like a poodle to impress the owner of Gulf and Western who knew less about movie making than he did about footwear.

After the meal, Jean said, 'I don't want to go to any more of those kind of dinners.'

I was taken for the part, and had to leave for the coast almost immediately to brush up a Texan accent (most English artists playing Americans are encouraged to speak in a deep Southern drawl) and to get the hang of fast-drawing pistols with both hands.

Jean had a few things to do in New York. I would go on ahead and find a house for us to stay in. She would follow in a week. I was looking forward to it, being back in Hollywood where it had all started for us.

A man named Pete Kameron, a New Yorker who was managing my business affairs, was also expected in LA to finalise the deal on *Blue*. I'd asked him to look over a contract that Felice Gordon had negotiated for Jean with Yardley. When Jean had first been approached I had insisted to Felice that she should have her own perfume, even her own Yardley range, it was a natural. As it would be a one-time deal for Jean, she needed to be in on it and to have a percentage. The deal entailed Jean going out on the road with the product, attending functions and speaking in public. In fact, all things that Jean had found stressful.

Felice had assured me, 'They can't give her a perfume,' (I would have withdrawn, then), 'but I've done a good deal.' When I saw the deal I knew it was flaky so I asked Kameron to talk to Yardley. The executive he spoke with slid open a drawer and drew out the contract, signed by Jean. Within a year Candice Bergen and Lauren Hutton were doing deals with cosmetic companies that netted them millions. Jean had trail-blazed for peanuts. I'd taken her to John Heyman and introduced her to Felice, and I didn't feel good about it, I can tell you.

Pete Kameron arrived in Los Angeles to break the news that Jean had sold herself down the river.

'I saw her in the Palm,' he said, naming a New York eating house with sawdust on the floor and bottles of shmaltz (chicken fat) on the tables, 'she was with a guy.'

'Really,' I said, 'what was he like?'

'Jewish, naturally,' he said with a smile, 'a listener, she was doing all the rapping.'

'Naturally,' I said.

'Why do you say that?' asked Pete.

'It's the only way you Jewish boys know how to get laid. You listen 'em into bed.'

Pete laughed. 'You could be right.'

'So, what did he look like?'

'Oh, he was one of those dark Jews, you know, like my cousin Bert. Had a nice smile, though.'

'Those are the kind you have to be careful with,' I said. 'I'll ask her who he is when she arrives.'

I'd found a cute house above Sunset on Kings Road and moved in with Pete and my brother Chris, who was on his way to a pop festival in Monterey and needed a bed for a few days. The house had plenty of room.

Everybody I met was smoking marijuana that summer. My mum had always been fearful of drugs, but I thought I'd give it a try. I bought some from a muso who came to the house. It turned out to be exceptionally good grass and, by the time Jean arrived, the house was permeated with the acrid fumes. She was withdrawn and thoughtful. I assumed the reality of the deal with Yardley had hit her so I didn't ask her why she had signed the contract or about the mysterious dark stranger she'd had dinner with. We spent the next day at the pool. Chris had permed his hair to resemble his mate Jimi Hendrix, and the results made Jean smile. We worked at making her giggle, cheering her up. After Chris left to go to an appointment, I invited her to try some of the grass. She wasn't sure.

'It's OK,' I reassured her, 'it's not like a real drug, it's nice, a laugh! Makes you feel mellow.'

I showed her how by inhaling deeply. She took a few puffs and coughed a lot. We sat quietly. We were by the tiny swimming pool in the garden with the hot midday sun shining directly down on us. Neither of us spoke. I was almost as new to the scene as she was: waiting for it to take, to see what would happen this time. I hadn't ingested this much before. I looked across at her. She looked incredible, fine, a silvery unworldly sheen to her face. I felt an upsurge of feeling for her. It was like nothing I'd experienced before. I was about to move, speak, as I couldn't contain it, but then a rush hit that stopped me cold. If it lasts a moment longer I'll die, I thought, but I wanted it never to end. The marijuana was loosening my emotions, whole strata of inhibitions were falling away. As I looked at her, I knew beyond all doubt that this was the woman destined for me. It wouldn't happen to me again. Not like this. I knew I was in an altered state, knew I was profoundly high, but at the same time I knew it to be right and in keeping with the best part of me. I saw clearly the nature of my boyhood longing, fantasies that had guided me to her. I understood why it was called falling in love – the fall was from concepts one held of oneself, fear of what would have to be given up. It was clear, suddenly simple. Everything. That's all. Everything had to be given up. Not even had to. Happy to. It was the loss of self in the beloved. I didn't know how time was passing. One of the characteristics of good grass is the loss of the sense of time and space. All I know is I sat there looking at her, appreciating her in a way I'd never known. It was the single most blissful moment of my life.

She lifted her eyes to me. Somewhere in my mind I'd expected the pupils to be dilated, black, large, drawing me. It was a shock to see they were the opposite. Her eyes were almost all blue, startlingly blue in the strong sunlight, with pinpoint pupils. It was then my vision began to change. My sensitivity to her loveliness remained open, but the nature of what I felt went into a Möbius curve as the idealised face in front of me changed texture. The silvery astral quality became snow-like, then marble. I was looking at a Greek goddess, but a sculpture, as terrifyingly chilling as the previous vision had been comely. A great fear gripped my heart. I knew what was to happen.

Within the hour she had left the house, to stay with Felice whose husband was in town writing a script. I had watched her pack. Tried to console her about her puffy eyes, swollen from tears.

'It's easy for you to talk,' she'd said bitterly, 'you're a natural beauty,' running her hand across my face like a razor. I didn't feel it, both stoned and grounded by the shock but not yet level.

'It was the stuff, the grass, I wouldn't have been able to tell you, otherwise,' she'd said in the sunlight. She rinsed through some underwear I'd discarded. I watched, as if from a distance.

'I'd like to make love to you, before you go,' I'd said.

Her 'Oh, just do it, then,' had rendered me instantly desireless.

Felice Gordon rang me. She thought it a good idea for Jean and me to have an intimate dinner. Talk things over. I accepted. I'd have accepted any straw thrown my way. Felice recommended a restaurant by the sea, saying it was nice. It wasn't.

We had an awkward dinner.

I believe Felice half-expected me to propose. I didn't. Jean said she had met another man and wanted to spend some time with him. If it didn't work she would come back to me.

'But you wouldn't have me, would you?' she asked bitingly, looking me straight in the eye. I didn't know what to say. I couldn't believe it was happening. My mind kept wandering, trying to retreat. Was it all some bizarre joke? She would smile in a moment, explain why she'd played this trick on me and we'd go home.

All Scorpio archetypes are said to have a sting in their tails: some, in their haste to use it, sting themselves. I'd never seen it in Jean, but here it was. Directed at my heart.

AN END

AND

A BEGINNING

20

Those of us who have been stung by a scorpion and have lived to tell the tale know the initial effect to be one of numbness: Nature's little bounty before the real paralysis sets in. Three days after Jean left the little house above Sunset and me, I had to start a film. I remember waking those first few mornings in a miasma of misery, second only to the hurt of retiring alone at night. I indulged increasingly to take myself away from the pain of reality: smoking my last reefer of the evening, I would take the precaution of wrapping another to be close at hand when consciousness returned. While it is true to say that marijuana does not blot out reality, the zigzag path you travel when stoned doesn't allow you to sink too deeply into any single aspect of your life. Flashes of realisation of what I had done with the love of my life, were alternated with rushes of insight enabling me to glimpse a purpose behind this present tragedy. Or so it seemed. As the start date of the picture loomed, my mood swings intensified, and I cried unashamedly one minute, giggled hopelessly the next, generally in the company of sympathetic Pete Kameron and a girl I hardly knew whom he'd fetched home to stay. My brother, God bless him, had thankfully departed for the pop festival in Monterey and didn't have to witness this childish behaviour of mine.

'Whatever am I going to do?' I bleated in a moment of sanity. 'I have to start a picture.'

Pete observed, 'Well, you've done OK so far, with the grass. Why don't you do the picture behind it?'

'I can't do a movie stoned,' I yelled. 'I can't act wasted out of my brain, you pillock.'

'Look, the worst is in the mornings, waking up, right?'

'I guess so.'

'You have a few tokes to get you on the road. Once you're

performing you should be OK. When you finish you smoke a numero to cool yourself out for the evening.'

'Do you think I could handle it? I'm supposed to ride John Wayne's palomino.' The mention of riding revived memories of the horse Jean had bought me and the last happy Christmas with her. I fell instantly into black depression.

'I think you'd better score some grass before you head out to Moab – that's Mormon territory, no telling what it will be like. Better supplied than sorry.'

'I know a man,' piped up the girl, 'who has some lovely stuff for sale.'

'How much is it?' asked Pete.

'A thousand dollars a key,' she replied.

'What's a key?' I asked.

'It's a kilo.'

'That's a lot,' said Pete.

The marijuana plant is harvested late in the season after it has been pollinated and is heavy with resin and, consequently, seeds. The kilo I purchased was a solid block, dried and condensed under pressure and containing whole plants complete with seeds, twigs, everything. Most smokers of grass clean theirs as they need it. Unaccustomed as I was to turning on, and having no knowledge nor anyone to enlighten me as to the various methods of retaining the herb's potency, I cleaned my grass, all of it, the night I took delivery. I used the task therapeutically, much as inmates of institutions are encouraged to do needle-point. My painstaking efforts filled a shoebox of squeaky-clean Acapulco Gold. 1967 was the year the gold came in from the state of Guerrero, and I happened to be on hand to purchase some, not knowing it was the heads' equivalent of 1906 cognac. To me, it was just grass: it smelled exotic, had a yellowy tint and left a stain on my hands, not unlike the mark left by the hops I'd helped to harvest as a boy in Kent.

The evening after Jean and I had taken what was to be our last meal together, I was invited to a full-moon party. I was supposed to escort a young English actress who had arrived in Hollywood that day and didn't know anyone. Although I didn't feel up to the party – to be held in the Malibu home of Roman Polanski and

Sharon Tate – I felt too terrible staying in my house alone. So I lit up like the man in the Strand advert and, feeling all-one, went off to pick up the new girl in town, Jacqueline Bisset. Poor Jacqueline, what an introduction to L A life I must have been. She had also started out as a model, working for my chum Terence Donovan, and something about her innocence, her beauty, her Englishness, made me feel worse. I drove her to the beach house and virtually abandoned her until it was time to leave. Not that she was short of admirers.

People tell me there is a down-side to getting high, although it never affected me enough to make me quit. Things can change fast, however: one minute you're sitting comfortably sipping tea and the next you're hanging in space, clinging to the table which is upside down over your head. If you have any set ideas about areas you don't want to go to, or bits of yourself you'd rather not look at, I can imagine it might become a bit freaky. That gathering at the beach was the nearest I ever came to having the tennis ball turned inside out without breaking its surface.

On entering the front door I found myself at the start of a long passageway which ran the full length of the house. That particular night it was dark, the only light coming from the room at the far end and the cross shafts that raked from side-doors as they were opened.

Pot and the smokers of it were relatively new to showbiz – heads hailed mainly from the jazz world. It wasn't yet considered a social ritual and, although the straight people were probably in a serious minority, those of us who indulged went into empty rooms or took a turn outside on the sand by the sea. The cosmic swing into Aquarius had happened but *Hair* was yet to be launched; so nobody except the most serious stargazer was aware of the change. I retrieved the newly-rolled joint from my sock (I hadn't mastered the art of hand-rolling and was still using a machine which was too bulky to carry around) and fired up, looking at the moonlight on the waves, when a man who resembled a famous singer joined me.

'Don't bug that joint, pal.'

I looked around. As I was the only person on the beach I assumed he was talking to me. He relieved me of my travelling New York slim.

'Huuu,' he murmured, sucking in through pursed lips and

trapping the smoke in his lungs. He took a follow-up gasp of sea air and intoned on the in-breath, 'Now it all gets very funny.'

We finished the number between us. He ambled off and I rejoined the do.

In spite of the grass, I was hurting that night, scalded on the inside. I kept thinking about Jean, imagining she'd arrive to take me home. 'Come on, Stamp,' she'd say with a grin, 'time boys like you were tucked up in bed.' At one point, glancing up the long hall from the main party area, I saw her. I went stumbling along the half-lit passage towards her. She'd come back. My ordeal was over. When I came closer, I saw it was Michelle Phillips from the Mamas and Papas pop group. Michelle was wearing a pair of heavy silk pyjamas, luminous, between silver and grey. She did look lovely, but the wrong face, as they say in the song.

I continued to look around, not staying in any one place long enough to be drawn into conversation. I had my work cut out not making a fool of myself. I wandered from one end of the house to the other and back again, keeping a vague eye on Miss Bisset, ready to split as soon as she gave me the nod. She didn't. Perhaps she was feeling nervous about being driven by me again. I wasn't too steady on my feet.

Then I saw a fairy. She floated across the hall from room to opposite room. Something from *Les Sylphides*. How strange, I thought, distracted, and made my way into the room she'd entered. It was dim and appeared empty: I looked around, seeking another exit. There wasn't one. I looked up the chimney and then sat on the floor. Perhaps this is what was meant by hallucinating. I'd overheard someone say of Acapulco Gold, 'It's so good, you can actually hallucinate behind it.' Maybe I was. Interesting. I leaned my back against the wall and closed my eyes a moment. When I opened them the fairy was standing in the door. The light was shining in from behind so her face was in shade, but I knew it was her. Her dress was long, almost to the ankles, the skirt flared, the bodice tight, lacy, high at the neck; the whole ensemble white, with stockings and flat pumps on her feet to match. Yeah, Sylphide, I thought groggily. She was speaking to me in a hesitant voice. It wasn't an obvious stammer, but being an expert I zoned in on it.

'Ar . . . Are you feeling all right?' she asked.

'How did you do that?' I wanted to know.

'Do wwhat?'

'Come into this room, not leave, but not be here, when I look.'

She came closer, tentatively, like a child intrigued by an unfamiliar dog. The back light fell on her straight hair, which contained an extraordinary number of shades, blonde on blonde on blonde. She looked at me askew. I guess she could see my face although I couldn't see hers.

'You're ssso stoned,' she said. It wasn't critical: the opposite, almost in awe.

'Are you a fairy?'

'Oh, you're so stoned,' she repeated, more slowly, more emphatically.

'Can you wave a magic wand and make it all right?'

She didn't reply, but crouched down in front of me, her dress falling around her like spilled cream.

'Could you teach me how to fly away?'

'Don't do that,' she said without rancour, dropping the end of her sentence.

'What?'

'Be so strange.'

'Am I being strange?'

'You know you are,' she said. 'And you're so stoned.'

'I'm just high.'

She looked into my eyes which felt prickly.

'No,' she said, shaking her head gravely, 'stoned.' It sounded the definitive opinion.

I could have sat there all night listening to the gentle, quavering voice, slowly piecing together in my mind the impossibly pretty face – the lip that trembled before she spoke, and the way she used her voice to let you know she wasn't quite serious. She wasn't Tinkerbell. I'd been wrong about that. This was Wendy, who healed boys everywhere. Unknown to me at that moment, she'd been cast to play in *Blue* and came with us to Moab. She was to become a lasting friend.

The evening before I took the plane to Salt Lake City I found myself at someone's flat in a tall block on Doheny Drive. It was fashionably dim, with scarves of Indian silk hung on the lampshades muting the beams. An extremely slowed-down version of a Supremes' standard by Vanilla Fudge was being played on the tape deck. I kept drifting off, transporting myself to the first weeks in Albany: Jean and I lounging on the Empire bed watching *Top of the Pops* on the television that had been set into the diagonal corner cupboard by Bennison – real playboy stuff, I winding her up by pretending to swoon over Diana Ross, she retaliating with Georgie Fame. It was now all heady fragments of memory. Vanilla Fudge kept hanging on. A young guy sitting next to me was saying something. I withdrew myself from the memory of Jean's calves, glacial in the reflected light of the black and white screen.

'You're Terence, aren't you? You're about to start *Blue*?'

'Yeah, that's right, man – go to location tomorrow.'

'Yeah, I read for a part in that movie.'

'Which one?'

My attention was dividing itself again; it was difficult to concentrate on the conversation.

'The assassin – it's small but effective.'

I turned my face to his in an effort to focus. I'd have to stop thinking about her some time; every day I didn't hear made her return less likely. I'd sent her a postcard, a riddle like the ones we'd indulged in when it all started. 'What weighs a ton and goes around stamping out forest fires?' She hadn't answered.

The would-be actor by my side was good-looking, swarthy. He looked like a Mexican bandit, good casting for the assassin, as it happened. I wondered if Silvio had seen him personally.

'I thought if perhaps you could speak to someone? I could really use the work.'

'Sure, man, tell me your name. I'll find out if it's cast.'

'I'm Julio, Julio Rosso.'

It sounded like a chianti. He introduced me to a girl, olive-skinned like him, whose name I didn't catch. The assassin moved off; she moved closer. I looked at her straight on, trying to get a fix on her without disturbing the soft-edged look the grass gave. In the half-light I could see she was something.

'D'you act?'

'I do all sorts of things,' she said, curling a wide lip in an enigmatic grin.

'Really?' I said. 'Sounds fun.'

'Do you want to go somewhere for a drink? You look wasted.'

'I could use the air, but you'll have to drive. I . . . I don't have a car.' The pain suddenly. A memory of the first night Jean had

come to L A: our nervous two-car caravan, my Lark, her Chevy.
Everything ahead of us.

'How d'you get here?'

'I'm not sure. I must have walked. I walk a great deal in London.
Mike Caine taught me. It's good for you, saves money. We wore
Clark's desert boots with cardboard . . . '

'I'm sure it does,' she said, taking my arm and steering me
towards the door.

In the lift I saw the face properly. I had been right, she was a
looker. Circe with a forehead. Her car was parked in front of the
block. A black Thunderbird convertible. I'd always loved the look
of them but had never been in one. She opened the door on the
driver's side and climbed in. I saw she had the developed legs of
a dancer – the kind I'd liked before I'd become strung out on
Shrimpton's.

'Get in,' she said, 'the door's not locked. D'you want the top
down?'

'Sounds fine to me.'

'Where d'you want to go?'

'Don't care, you decide.'

We took off. Up, up into the hills above Hollywood, the wind
blowing my hair over my face like a scarecrow.

She pulled the T-bird on to a kind of promontory, I think on
Mulholland Drive. The electric ordnance map twinkled below us.
I couldn't figure why they twinkled so. Every time I fixed on any
one light it stayed constant.

'Are you going to get Julio the part he wants?'

'I'm gonna ask.'

'You'll tell them you want him?'

'It doesn't work quite like that, but I'll do what I can.'

'Good.'

'Are you his girl?'

'I'm a friend, a good friend.'

'What's your name, friend?'

'Mercedes.' She pronounced it Merchedes.

'Julio and Mercedes?'

'That's right. Hoolio and Merchedes.'

'Like the car?'

'Like the car. You're beautiful,' she said, leaning across me and
then drawing the back of her hand across my groin.

'A natural beauty,' I sniggered.

'Yes,' she agreed, missing my bitterness. 'A natural beauty.' The palm of her hand was now dusting the denim of my 501s.

I felt no response: no rush of blood; to put it bluntly, no erection. I didn't register immediately, engrossed as I was by the array of lights stretched out in front of me. When I did turn to look at her, she had hitched her skirt and drawn her legs up on to the bench seat, the knees smooth, like persimmons. I saw the superfine traces of hair on her thighs, goldened by the Californian sun. That usually did it, although usually I didn't have to think about what did it.

Mercedes, responding to my hand caressing the tight skin above her knee, flipped open the metal buttons of my Levi's and gently slid her fingers across the Egyptian cotton smoothness of the boxer shorts Jean had selected and purchased for me in Rome. There was nothing. Not a flicker of interest. I looked down at her hand, concealed now inside my strides. She wore a small watch similar to the first one my mum had bought me for Christmas with her club money at the Co-op. My first watch. I thought of the watch I'd bought Jean: china-white face, black roman numerals, and a sapphire set in the winder. Little glinting . . . God! I'm impotent . . . stone.

I suppose the central fear of a Jack the lad or leaper, as they say in the East End, is having his genitals clasped and finding the wherewithal absent. I'd heard many stories of the lengths that supposed cocksmen went to to avoid this ultimate humiliation. Caine told me the best one, about an English box-office idol who had periodical lapses on the hard-on front. One night in Malta, Caine had assured me, the star had set his bed sheets on fire to distract his partner from the fact that he wasn't rising to the performance.

'*Hombre*,' said my golden companion in a husky voice. 'You're not with me.'

'I'm sorry,' I said. 'I'm a little wasted, you said so yourself.'

'I've never met anyone that wasted.'

'You have now.'

'Does it upset you, if I progress you a little?'

I thought about it. I didn't feel anything. I wasn't even embarrassed.

'No harm in trying – it's a beautiful night.'

Mercedes leaned over to me, the soft wide lips touched my ear;

she whispered something in Spanish then slid her head slowly down the front of my paisley shirt. I laid my head back on the seat, looking up at the clear night sky.

'Stars,' Jimmy Woolf had said. 'Stars, my dear Terence, only shine at night.'

That's true, Jim, certainly tonight, I thought, as I felt Mercedes's warm breath reach my lap. The fear of the fact is often greater than the fact itself. It was something I'd first heard at Method acting school, of all places, as the teacher tried to prepare us for our stage debut, but it could be applied to almost any life experience. Certainly, the warm wetness of Mercedes was nothing to be frightened of. Warm, wet, not unloving.

My calmness was the unexpected factor. It had always stunned me how freshly castrated animals calmly licked their wound and went on with their new life. Now I knew. It wasn't bad: the trick was not desiring it to be different. The pain was in the space between how it was and how you wanted it to be. I gasped at the truth of it. If I came through this in one piece I should try to remember that. Mercedes mistook my acknowledgement of insight. She lifted her head.

'I'm sorry,' she said with a delightful smile. 'No vitamins for Mercedes tonight.'

21

Blue was aptly named, rising as it did like a phoenix from the ashes of confusion and despair, and the storyline with its allegorical qualities appealed to me. Early in the colonisation of the West an English family arrive by covered wagon and make a homestead close to the Mexican border. They have a son. During one of the frequent attacks by Mexican bandits who cross the border to raid the settlers, the boy's family is killed, their cabin burned. The gang leader, played by Ricardo Montalban, spares the young child and takes him back over the border where the boy grows up almost like a son – but not quite. Traumatised by witnessing his parents' death, he loses, or decides not to use, his power of speech. Others, including Ricardo's natural progeny, are jealous of the fair-skinned boy's standing in the gang, but are wary of his bursts of ferocity and ruthless use of knives and guns. He is known as Azul, or Blue, because of the colour of his eyes, and his blond hair is usually concealed beneath a bandana. After a border raid the wounded Blue is left on a settler's property. The settler is a widower, Karl Malden, whose daughter, played by Joanna Pettet, nurses Blue back to health. At the climax of the film Ricardo and his men return to find Blue who has to decide between the two cultures.

Silvio Narizzano, the director, wanted Blue to have a dark beard along with his blond head of hair. This was dual-purposed: at first Blue passes as a Mexican, albeit with light eyes, because he never speaks and because his hair is concealed. This enhances the moment when Joanna and her father undress Blue and realise he is a gringo. Silvio also hoped it would suggest a physical manifestation of Blue's schizophrenia. I'd remembered a fellow student of mine at the Webber Douglas Drama School, Stuart Anderson, who'd returned one term from a skiing holiday, his normally dark

Silvio and me as seen by Larry Schiller.

hair almost white-blond. I assumed the change had come from a bottle but he insisted it hadn't.

'It always goes like this in the sun,' he assured me.

The incident had stuck in my mind and I used it to justify my odd appearance. Silvio played up the split in the character's personality to parallel a generation gap that was becoming increasingly apparent. We all held high hopes for the project, although we who came to the red-rocked landscape were a curious bunch, clutching our few travelling accessories like comforters. As our stories unravelled and friendships grew, many personal tragedies were revealed.

Silvio had cast Mike Nader as the assassin, calling him Dream City, and he was: built with wide shoulders which hung over a shallow rib cage and a stomach that was cut on the concave. His was a natural grace and he carried himself like a swordsman. Had he been born this side of the Atlantic his brooding looks would have been put to good use in the classics. When Nader finished his part – he was killed off in the opening of the film – production wouldn't extend his *per diem* and I discovered him packing his case.

'I'd love to stay here in Moab,' he said. 'I've no great reason to return to LA but I can't afford to pay for the room myself.'

'Well, Mike,' I said, 'you're welcome to crash on my sofa; it's big enough for half a dozen.'

(I'd felt so lonely at the house offered to me, I'd moved into the motel where the other artists and crew were holed up.) Michael's dark eyes lit up.

'That's terrific, but,' he added after a thoughtful moment, 'you know what everyone is going to think. Somebody is bound to say we're having a scene.'

I laughed. 'Oh, man, people have been saying that I've been screwing everything that walked for years. I've done with fretting about what people say. If it's not a problem for you, it sure isn't for me.' So Mike moved in and Joanna Pettet became his next-door neighbour as well as mine.

Joanna had a body uncannily like Jean's. One day she mentioned that her birthday fell in Scorpio and I realised the resemblance was archetypal. She was also feeling tender, only recently having ended a long-term relationship.

'I need sympathy at the moment, but everyone in Hollywood wants to get into my pants.'

'Very elegant pants they are too,' observed Nader, giving the extra long legs a once-over.

Joanna looked at me, 'How about you, neighbour?'

'I'm in need of healing myself. I've done with romance.'

'Too much of a good thing, eh?' quipped the assassin.

'I really dig your boots,' Joanna said to me, with an approving nod to my hide cowboy boots.

'They're costume,' I replied. 'I wear them all the time to feel comfy in them. I've never worn heels. I know it's bad for yer feet, but I'm nervous of the Duke's horse; it looks superb but it's a real git. One word from me and it does exactly what it likes. I have trouble keeping my stirrups sometimes.'

'It's nice to wear your costume, though,' Joanna agreed. 'I'd like to wear mine all the time, it's lovely. I feel I'm a real settler sometimes.'

'That Anthony, the costumier, he did a great job. I think I'll ask him if I *can* wear my outfit all the time,' I said.

'I'm sure he wouldn't mind, if you ask him nicely.' Then she smiled and as the large lips stretched her face changed completely.

'What?' I asked, questioning her smile.

'I was thinking about you jumping that horse off the bank into the river. You took it so slow, I wondered if you were going to make it.'

She was referring to a shot in which all the bandits cross a wide yellow river on horseback, swimming their mounts across the border. I pointed out that the other guys were all stunt wranglers – Yakima's boys. (Yakima Canutt was the best second-unit action director in the business; he'd shot the chariot race sequence in *Ben Hur* for Wyler. Wyler was envious and had wanted to shoot it all again to prove he could do it better, but had finally settled for Yak's footage. Wyler had confessed to me that he couldn't improve a frame.)

We were lounging in my rooms at the Motel. Silvio's assistant had been killed in his car that morning. We had broken early. Everybody was down. Silvio was such a pussy cat and we all felt wretched for him, but the director wanted to spend some time alone. We didn't know when we would shoot or who would direct us.

Peggy Lipton.

'What's that strange smell?' Joanna asked.

'Oh, yeah, it's me,' I said.

I showed her the small dark bottle of oil I'd purchased from a shop named Aphrodisia.

'From Brazil.'

I unscrewed the bottle. Gave her a whiff.

'That's a serious smell,' Jo said. 'What's it called?'

'Patchouli. Isn't it strange? I've never smelled anything like it. The front is murky like a tuber rose or a lily, but then it gets serious, musky, almost like you smell when you've been riding a steaming horse. And the back, that's *heavy*, it's like . . . '

'Falling,' said Mike.

'Or dying,' I added.

'D'ya wear it often? I haven't smelled it on you.'

'First time today. Building up the old courage. I'm going to – it's going to be my password.'

'Password?' asked Joanna. 'For what?'

'To let all the freaks out there know.'

The following evening I ran into Peggy, the fairy from Malibu. I'd been driven home from location, and on the way to my little suite I'd glimpsed a forlorn figure kneeling by the pool in her floor-length film costume.

'Hi,' I said, uncertain for a second that she hadn't been beamed down.

'Hello,' she replied with a smile. 'You're the lost boy, aren't you?'

'And you're Wendy, come to take care of us guys.'

She smiled.

'You look sad today.'

'I'm nnnnot sad. I'm just rescuing bees from the swimming pool. They come for a drink and some get their wings wet. If you put your hand into the water and, keeping your brain very quiet so as not to frighten them, bring it gently up under them they dry off quite happily and fly away.'

'Just like Peter Pan.'

'Peter Pan didn't have wings; he just knew how to fly,' she said matter of factly.

'Were you shooting today?'

'Oh . . . nno I . . . ' she looked down at her dress. 'I'm having a wardrobe fitting . . . over there.' She pointed to an open door. It was a room the wardrobe had commandeered for their costumes.

'You on yer own?'

'My brother Bobby is on the film. He's one of the bandits.'

'Wanna have a bite tonight?'

'If, if we can go out. I don't like the food in the . . . ' She pointed to the coffee shop of the motel.

'It's a deal. Seven o'clock OK?'

It was the first of a lot of times I spent with the fascinating Miss Lipton.

Peggy, I soon realised, was what might be called an unwitting medium. At least, that was my conclusion when I thought over our conversations. One evening we were slumped in a red leather booth of the motel drugstore – neither of us liked it at first, but it was the only place in Moab to hang out and be able to watch the local scene or the Movie, as Peggy and I entitled it. We were indulging in just this, observing the local stars and their reactions to our outlandish clothes and unusual side orders (fetching our own pot of honey for our herb teas and the like), when Peggy started expounding about the Aquarian Age, its causes and implications.

'You do feel it, don't you, Terence, the new vibrations?'

As previously we had been discussing the pros and cons of feeding exhausted bees and butterflies on sugar or honey, I was a little taken aback.

'The what, Peg?'

'The new vibrations resulting from the shift of the Earth's polar axis.' Ignoring the blank look on my face, she went on.

'The North Pole is now pointing to a different set of stars and, as you know, the North Pole has always been looked upon as the entrance which enables cosmic energy to flow to Earth. I felt sure you would have been aware of the change in quality of the emanations.'

'Well, Peg, I have been feeling a bit different of late but I'm not sure it's down to cosmic fallout.'

'Oh, you're much softer than when I met you. Don't you feel the right side of your brain functioning, the receptive half? I see it everywhere. The music, the colours, appreciation of different aspects. Boys growing their hair, becoming aware of their own inner beauty, the beads – it's the result of an inner appreciation, not the cause. Anyway, as it's happening to you, I wondered how conscious you were of it.'

'I figured I was going through a chick phase,' I said. Actually, I felt it was a side-effect of my emotional crisis, something I hadn't owned up to with Peggy or anyone else, as it happened. My ego was wasted enough, as it was.

'Well, you are, although it is not a nice way to put it, or even think of it like that.'

'How should I think about it?'

'You should see yourself as a new breed. A bridge-builder into a different age. An androgyne who is developing his emotional intuitive faculties as well as his masculine attributes. A person who regards every creature as a part of himself, not a separate entity.'

'Is all not one, eh Peg?' I quipped.

'It is, but no one lives it. Don't be frightened to refuse to be what you are. Don't pretend to be what you're not.'

'But Peggy, it's easy to say it's all one, and I understand what you're saying, but is it? Do we really know? I get closer to it when I'm stoned. The thing I like most about the high is that it eases the sense of separation, as though you fall closer to oneness. It takes away the sharp edges of feeling fragmented and individual, with all the problems or responsibilities we associate with those things. I believe you. Intellectually, I understand, but I don't feel it often. That's the truth.'

Peggy stirred some honey into her tea.

'That's why you're nurturing your female half. It's your craving for the female to complete yourself, to make you feel whole. But the need is only reflected out: the real communion is inner.'

'Prove to me the oneness, Peg.'

'Coincidence is proof of oneness.' She gave a little giggle of a laugh. 'Thththat's all the proof you're getting tonight, anyway.'

'Could I squeeze you, Miss Lipton?'

She gave me one of her old-fashioned looks. I was momentarily unsure.

'I, I meant a cuddle. In England a cuddle can have implications,' I said, getting in more of a mess.

Peg's smile widened.

'What I meant was, I'm a bit fragile at present. You know? Under normal circumstances, I'd be . . . '

'I know what you mmeant, Terence. I'm flattered, but what's normal? My feeling is the nat is nicer than the norm.'

'The nat?'

'The natural. Your nature at the moment is fragile. I prefer it. I like the chick side of you. I know you're a guy, but it's OK to be less than macho. We have these lovely girly natters. Come over here, I'll give you a cuddle. You can shout for help if you're in trouble.'

I talked a bit to Nader about the gist of the talk I'd had with Peggy.

'Did Peg actually say that about the polar gate receiving cosmic energy? I wonder where she heard that,' said Nader.

'It's no use asking her. I've already tried to recap a few things – she says she doesn't remember.'

We were sitting under an awning which had been erected by the catering department. Mike looked saturnine in the shadows of the canvas. He'd been taking sun regularly at the motel pool.

'What d'ya think?' I asked.

'About what?'

'This female side.'

'I'm not incriminating myself.'

'I, er, sometimes feel . . . I used to feel, when I was with this girlfriend of mine, an English girl, that, well, I, this real passive thing would come over me, and I . . . ' Mike couldn't stop grinning at my discomfort. ' . . . sort of would have preferred her to do everything.'

'Be taken, you mean?'

'Er, well yeah, taken. Perhaps I should have . . . '

'Been more yourself?' said Mike. 'Did she ever dress you up, put make-up on you?'

'No.'

'Only asking.'

Mike laughed, leaned back in his metal stacking chair and continued giggling.

'Nader,' I said, 'I'm trying to explain – I didn't . . . '

'It's OK, man. I don't mean to laugh, but you're so damn English sometimes.'

'Uptight, you mean?'

'I didn't say that, but as you . . . ' He started to laugh again.

Giving Mike's mystical twist a try.

Silvio came into the shade of the awning, his face red with a white stripe across his forehead where he'd tied a kerchief, Silvio who'd been happily married for years and who'd one day upped and left home and returned to bachelor life. He waved to the assistant who was queuing up to order his lunch for him.

'I'm over here,' he said, 'with the butch numeros. Now, what's all the merriment?' he enquired. 'Comparing girls, are we?'

Mike gave me a low look under his dark lashes and then swivelled in his seat. I knew he was about to wind me up.

'It's funny you should ask,' he said. Another sidelong glance at me. 'Because I was just about to make Terence here an offer he couldn't refuse, make him see life a lot differently.' He paused, working the moment. 'Change his outlook, teach him a mystical twist.'

22

Blue was the last film I made on which special photographers were used. By the Seventies, accountants were increasingly important in the studio hierarchy, and the cost of two photographers – one to take stills and another for media layouts – was questioned. As the stills man was normally under contract and drawing weekly wages anyway, the tradition of the expensive freelance chap from Magnum or Black Star died. That's primarily the reason why the stills auctioned today, the ones that fetch big money, are usually older. The 'special photographer' was one of those artists squeezed out in the new breed of executives' headlong rush to reduce budgets. Today people often remark that they don't make movies in Hollywood any more, only budgets: it's true, it started in the Seventies – after *Blue* was dead and buried.

Lawrence Schiller burst into our lives in the rock desert like a roadrunner from *Loony Tunes*. It was odd that he had more energy than any two of us put together – unless you equated energy with kilowatts per kilo.

I became aware of Schiller's bulk the first day he arrived on location. Seasoned as I was by Sanford Roth, to say nothing of Donovan and Bailey, I recognised a good smudger when I saw one. Schiller was light on his feet, his movement beside the camera and amongst the lights reminding me of Ustinov, but the speed of his hands put me in mind of a boxer. I could see the savvy of an athlete functioning in the outsize frame. Later, when he showed me his series on sportsmen, I realised he was a text-book case. Larry was younger than he looked. His face had the set of a son who'd taken on familial responsibilities a little too early in life. He was also straight, very straight.

'What are we going to do with Larry?' enquired Mike one day.

'Do with him?' asked Peg.

'Loosen him up,' I said. 'I think our beads make him uncomfortable.'

'No,' said Peg, 'we are doing our thing, doing the best we can to feel good, get by. If he feels uncomfortable, he feels uncomfortable.'

'You make yourself uptight. No one does it to you,' Sally Kirkland pointed out. Sally was a formidable Method actress from New York recovering from a love affair and an attempt at suicide which had momentarily rendered her brain-dead.

'He's only tense sometimes. Work turns him into a dancer – maybe he's holding a lot down, can't risk letting go,' I said.

'It's his affair; everyone is different,' Sally added. The chiselled features of Sally's face set hard. She was obviously consulting some inner oracle. We were lazing in my sitting-room, our regular congregation spot after sundown, before deciding if we were going to bowl or eat.

Joanna peeked in at the door – she'd taken longer than the rest of us to shower off the day's dust. Her expressive mouth smiled. 'Safe to come in?' she asked.

'Couldn't quite get clean today, hmm, Jo?' Nader enquired.

We were all a bit obsessive when it came to showering after work.

'You're one to talk,' she replied.

'I, er, heard the ultimate clean-freak story. You wanna hear it?' I said, knowing I had a captive audience. 'Might be a little close to the bone. Some of you may recognise yourselves.'

'Oh, come on, Terence,' said Peggy, feigning exasperation. 'Tell us the joke.'

'It's not a joke, Peg, it's true. It's a true story, that's what makes it so great.'

Sally, whose mother was an editor of *Life* magazine, said, 'You tell us the story and we'll tell you how great it is.'

I took up the glove.

'This is about a flute-playing clean-freak in a jazz band on a tour of America. On the evening this particular event went down the band had played two sets at a local jazz club. One of the impressed customers invited the whole band to a party she was giving that night. All the musos made off to the ball directly from the club, but the flute player . . . '

Mike Nader with Peggy.

'Being a clean-freak went home to shower and change first, right?' interjected Joanna.

'Right! Couldn't go to a nice all-night party with a shirt damp under the arms, could he?'

Chorus of Oh, no, oh, disgusting etc. I continued.

'Immaculately clean, talcum-powdered toes and armpits, change of socks and quick brush of the suede shoes – he was off. It was midnight before he arrived. The joint, a mansion house in its own grounds, was jumping. People spilled out of the front door on to the lawn. Our flute player, a little apprehensive about venturing into such crushed, perspiration-inducing confines, but drawn by the promise of excitement and perhaps romance, carefully squeezed through the crowd into the hall and made it to the main room where music was being played and dancing was in progress. He found himself a little place against the wall, near enough to an open window and a draught that would prevent him getting sweaty too quickly. However, he had only been observing events and enjoying the music a moment when he saw a wonderful girl: a cool-looking creature, with long silky hair and a delightful softly-curved body. She was wearing a flowered dress of the lightest weight cotton which hung crisply over her slim hips. She was, of course, like him, as clean as a whistle. He had to meet her. He delayed his approach waiting for a nice slow tune to dance to. When the right waltz tune was struck he asked her to dance. She accepted and melted coolly and cleanly into his arms as he confidently led her to the rhythm.

'"I'm a musician," he said.

'"I can tell," she answered, looking up at him: a match made in waltz-time heaven. The dance ended, but another started up immediately. He was calm, his hands cool, one lightly holding hers, the other resting on the sensuous indentation of her back. They stayed on the floor and he ventured further into the middle of the crush, allowing the mass of other bodies to press her closer into his arms. Suddenly, almost without warning, he needed to go to the loo.'

Peggy put in, 'Oh, no, he couldn't wait.'

Mike added, 'He was peeing in his pants.'

'Worse.'

Joanna's face, held still by the tale, fell. 'Oh, no.'

'Oh, yes,' I continued, 'he stuck it out as long as he could but I'm afraid seconds were becoming crucial. He felt his hand becoming moist, wetting the back of the lightly starched frock of his dancing partner. Unable to make it until the end of the dance, squeezing the cheeks of his bottom together, he hissed, "Excuse me, please, urgent, be right back," and keeping his buttocks clenched he pushed his way to the door of the big room, where a waiter stood with a tray of drinks.

'"Where is the men's room?" he gasped.

'"Upstairs, the second . . . "

'"Stairs, God. Nearer, one nearer?"

'"There is one in the hall, sir, third door on the right. Unfortunately, the light switch is broken."

'"Thanks."

'He was off. He made it. As he opened the door he sighted the vague outline of the pedestal in the overspill of light from the hall before slamming the door closed, ripping down his trousers and hurling himself on to the darkened john.' I paused.

'But . . . ' Squeals of anticipation from fellow clean-freaks around the room. I waited. A hush.

'His sighs of relief were curtailed by the realisation that he hadn't lifted the seat cover. When the full awareness of what he'd done overcame him he vomited and passed out.'

'Oh, God!' gasped Peggy.

Joanna was speechless, her mouth a little open.

'And that's a true story?' asked Sally.

'True as I'm standing here.'

'Well,' said Nader, 'I bet the poor guy was in the shower for days.'

Joanna said, 'More likely at the fire station getting hosed down.'

'Pulitzer-winning stuff,' said Sally with a twinkle, 'good delivery, though.'

'Would I get into the Actor's Studio, Sal?'

'As an observer, maybe.'

'Right,' I said, 'who wants to use the bathroom before we eat?'

'Oooh, I feel sick,' said Peggy.

Joanna snuggled close to me and said, 'What were you all saying about Larry when I came in?'

Mike said, 'Only his two personas. The artist and the business man.'

'He'd make a great creative producer, actually, and that's rare,'

Action!

Cut!

Stepping out with Joanna – Moab style.

I said. 'This could be a crossroads for him. We were thinking of ways to loosen him up.'

'I like him,' Joanna said. 'He's cuddly, a big teddy. I think we should just appreciate him.'

That's what made Miss Pettet so lovely. She didn't mess about, just went straight in. As it turned out we wound up following her lead.

Someone located a diner at the end of town and we changed our *modus operandi*, lingering over tasty Western omelettes and looking out over Moab's main street. Our togetherness off-camera paid off in front of it: there were some subtle nuances when my character was launched into the town society, but in spite of the charm and reassurance of my new friends, my inner turmoil persisted. Held in abeyance during the day by a patchwork of distractions, the repressed emotions surfaced at night. Sometimes too down to socialise, I would forgo supper and stay in my rooms writing odd little verses and things as if my life depended on it. One evening, my fingers too stiff to continue, I fell into an unhappy sleep. I became aware I was floating, attached by a single shining thread to what appeared to be a reclining chair with an indistinct figure sunbathing far, far below me. I wasn't ill at ease; the dream was somehow familiar, my balloon dream. I heard a crack, delicate but profound, like the snapping of a tulip stalk. It had been my silvery ground line. I was drifting untethered although I continued to look down towards the figure who was looking up at me – suddenly in intense focus. Tears ran down her face as she beckoned me to her, but as I floated further and further away she began to wave goodbye. I was awakened by Nader, kneeling by the sofa and gripping my arm to stifle my cries. The room was dark, save for the perfumed candle lit to keep me company. The flame flickered on one side of his face, accentuating his anxiety.

'What's up, man?' he asked quietly. 'You don't have to be so blue to play this part, you know.'

I tried to smile, but the concern in his voice cut through my attempt at stoicism. I felt that lump in my throat, tears filling my eyes. He rubbed my forearm as though reassuring a hurt child.

'You don't have to take this alone. You can share it, you know.'

'It's . . . it's such a drag, boring . . .'

'Hey, you're not on your own. I've a demon too. My X factor.'

'You have?'

'Sure, that's why I ride the tiger. To keep my demon occupied.'

'I ride a tiger.'

'I know.' Mike gave me an encouraging grin. 'All scoundrels do.'

'I lost my girl.'

'Was she wonderful?' Mike could have pulled teeth without gas if he'd wanted.

'Yeah. I should have taken care of her. I did stop telling her I loved her, but only because my feelings seemed to die when I put them into words. She must have thought I was keeping it like tea time. Life is so meaningless without her. I can't think how I'll pass the time. When a double Scorpio zaps you with that lightning sting, you feel it all right.'

'Double Scorpio, eh? You sure pick 'em.'

'When I first met her she said . . . she said, "I know what you're like with girls. I don't care." She did say she didn't care.'

'And you were?'

'Yes, she said . . . '

'It doesn't matter what women *say*. It's best to assume what they want is their man to themselves. After all, this feeling you had was mutual, wasn't it?'

'I thought so. I'm not so sure now.'

'Had to be. Couldn't be otherwise. One and one making six – wasn't you on your own.'

'I did screw up, though. I keep thinking how I could have made it different.'

'Did she ask you to behave differently?'

'No, I could see she was unhappy . . . but I . . . '

'Did you talk about it? You both did it, like you both made it special. If she's a Scorpio she doesn't like being led. So don't take all the blame. She is not blaming you, she's getting on with her life.'

'I know. I can't seem to get up. I feel I've lost my arms and legs. It's such a dumb feeling.'

'Are you sleeping O K?'

'I wasn't too bad last night, dropped off early. 'Bout midnight the phone rang. "Hello, that Terry Stamp? I'm calling from London, *Daily Express*; didn't wake you up, did I? Oh, well, sorry, listen Tel, I hear the Shrimp's left you. How d'ya feel?" I suppose they figure I'm fair game. Nothing like having your ego smashed on a public anvil – the flip side of fame.'

'Listen, you want to stay up? We can make some coffee. You been writing?'

'Yeah, writing down some of the things Peggy said, trying to put it into verse, it . . . stops me thinking, feeling sorry for myself.'

'Hey, I saw a card in an Indian shop today. It was a saying of a medicine man. You know, the dudes who eat the peyote.'

'Peyote?'

'Cactus buds. I guess it's hallucinogenic. It's reserved for special rituals, for giving chosen braves a glimpse behind the curtain.'

'What was the saying?'

'You want I make some coffee?'

'No, I'm first up tomorrow. I should try to get some sleep. What you scribbling?' I pulled off my boots.

'This quotation I saw, perhaps we can go by the store. Buy a copy.'

He pressed the scrap of paper into my shirt pocket. I was dead on my feet. I didn't think about it until later.

The next day word came: she had gone for ever. That evening she was seen in Colorado with 'a dark-haired man with a limp'. He had nice ways, no doubt. Antidote, I thought. Now it was my turn to experience pain. No medicine for me, only the baking sun and the pungent evening fumes of the gold from Acapulco.

On the way to work I saw a couple of figures walking by the roadside, trying to hitch a ride. I said to my driver, 'Let's give these people a lift.'

'They're Indians,' he replied flatly without prejudice, just letting me know.

'It's OK,' I said. 'Let's offer.'

They climbed into the back seats silent and dignified – the first Indians I'd seen in the flesh. It seemed indelicate to turn round and look but their presence sure filled the automobile. I glanced out at the rocky landscape, maroon in the early light, feeling my peroxided hair to be silly, superfluous: the chiselled heads in the back blended in far better than the head in the front. That's when I recalled Mike's note. I took it out. It read 'Sometimes I go about pitying myself and all the time I am being carried on great winds across the sky.'

*

253

Back to Hollywood with Mike and Joanna.

Larry and I had become attached: I appreciated his work and went along with his ideas for layouts he had above and beyond the call of shooting hours. I'll never forget how proud he was the night before we left Moab when he rigged up his magic lantern and projected his colour slides on the wall of my lounge. All the group was present, cheering as one after another of his illuminated images hit the whitewash.

Joanna said, aware that the on-set shots utilised our camera director Stanley Cortez's light plan, 'If the film is as beautiful as your photos, Larry, we're in good shape.'

Larry beamed – energy shot out of every pore.

Like the rest of us he had his crisis, too. After a call from home with obvious bad tidings I had missed him, had searched for him, eventually finding him in a terrible state. Although nobody pried, we gathered round him taking turns to see that he wasn't alone too long and staying close to him through the next days. Then his stills arrived back from the lab, and he became his old self again.

Six weeks' location in Moab ended. We celebrated like Pilgrim Fathers reaching the New World, finding our way to the magical oasis of Schofields, a spot in the middle of wilderness that a man and wife (with the help of a couple of discarded railway carriages and a lot of loving care) had transformed into one of the truly original restaurants in the world. After the candlelit farewell dinner, the wife read our palms. When my turn came, she gave my hands a cursory glance and then looked into my eyes.

'It is dark now for you. You are standing in your own light. It won't always be so.'

How long, how long! my mind screamed. And can I hold out?

She didn't answer, but moved on to Peggy sitting to my right. I heard her say, 'Ah, a seer,' before my mind took up the conundrum.

How did you stand in your own light? More importantly, how did you get out of the way?

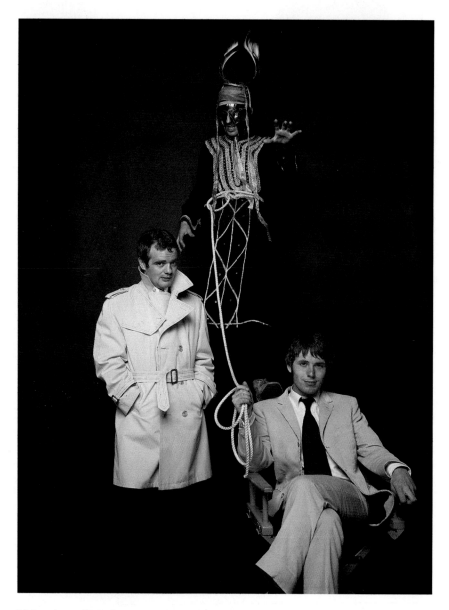

Kit Lambert, Chris Stamp, with new signing Arthur Brown.

23

We were all sad about leaving the haven we'd created and returning to face LA where I, for one, felt my life had started and ended. When we arrived at the Paramount Studios on Melrose in Hollywood, Judd Bernard, our producer, purchased bicycles which we rode around the lot, racing one another to see who could get to the set first. I was allocated Elvis Presley's dressing-room: a maze of open spaces and passages all painted an unlikely red and linked by a curious intercom system that extended even to the lavatories – it appeared the King liked to know what was going on *all* the time. Checking in at seven a.m. every morning was a bit like entering a blood clot, but whoever was shooting congregated in Elvis's suite, the door temporarily altered to bear two names – his and mine. Our group didn't form a circle and hold hands or anything like that, but we stayed as close as we could, hoping our collective energy would carry us through. Our secret our strength. We didn't try to convert anyone or change anything. Only ourselves.

One morning Nader and I were indulging in a bit of homespun psychotherapy: self-evaporation, we called it, owning up to things that made us uptight, people we had problems with. Larry was hanging out, observing, as usual.

'I hate do-gooders,' I stated, stretched out on the King's giant sofa, a plate of tuna salad from the commissary at hand and a frozen pad of witch hazel – a trick I'd learned from Larry Harvey – over my puffy eyes.

'Dylan said don't hate anything except hatred,' Mike piped in.

'Yeah, perhaps hate's too strong a word. I do have a hard time with them, though.' I also had a hard time keeping in mind our reasoning that any form of hatred was a subjective involvement which bound one to the hated object. Chastened, I said, 'Something rubs me the wrong way. If you think about it, there is no authority whatsoever given to anyone to set anyone else right.'

Schiller, bent on one knee by the low table in front of the couch, said, 'I know what gets up your nose. It's people in glass houses throwing stones.'

I'd awoken that morning with a sentence unravelling in my head, but it had slipped away as I opened my eyes. Larry's remark broke my dream and I recalled the line: he who accuses with authority proves he has the fault in the same proportion. There was a click from Larry's camera; I heard Mike saying, 'You're right, you know, Larry. I'm sure it wouldn't rankle if Buddha, Moses or the Naz laid a bit of sound on yer, but . . . '

Larry was grinning behind his camera. 'What's the difference between doing good and being a do-gooder?' he asked.

Mike, sitting on the floor, drew his knees up and put his arms around them. He furrowed his forehead.

'If you're asked to do something, a good turn, you do it. No question, but . . . '

I said, 'If a blind man knocks into you and asks to be taken across the road, you do it, but if you see someone with a white stick happily walking the other way, and run after him insisting on helping him across the freeway, you've a problem.'

Schiller summed up our meanderings, 'You're saying the do-gooder shields behind righteousness, as a subtle postponement of putting his own house in order.'

Mike clapped his hands together.

I said, 'Right on, Larry. I couldn't have put it better myself.'

In the Sixties there was a place at Kitty Corner, where Sunset Boulevard going east splits into Holloway, known as a head shop. It sold all the accoutrements of dope without selling the stuff itself and was, therefore, within the law. One of the people who ran this establishment also made leather wear. I had ordered a multi-coloured jerkin with a phoenix depicted on the chest and, as this article needed several fittings, I became quite familiar with the place and its owners. (I also spent a long time studying a paparazzi photograph that was pinned on their notice board. It showed Marilyn Monroe getting out of a low limousine and confirmed once and for all the rumour that she didn't wear underwear.)

On the day I picked up my completed leather shirt its maker was singing the praises of an ingenious new water pipe. We were joined by a young girl with skin akin to milk chocolate. Although she looked as though butter wouldn't melt in her mouth, she knew all about the pipe.

'It really makes hash a cool smoke. My name is Devon. I'm a groupie,' she added with such aplomb that for a moment I thought it was an exclusive doctorate. I hadn't graduated to hashish, which was reputed to be considerably stronger than grass. I told her I was only into marijuana and, as it happened, I was getting rather low.

'What have you been smoking?' she wanted to know.

'Everybody calls it Acapulco Gold. It's good. I haven't smoked anything else. I started late in life.'

Her spicy eyes lit up.

'Well, you're lucky, and spoilt. Chances are there won't be another batch of anything like that for years. Grass is like wine, you know, every crop is different.'

I realised the implications. I smoked grass like housewives chewed Valium – I hadn't considered that my first score might well prove to be a one-off.

'I gave away most of my grass. I thought a lot of people were hitting on me for the odd joint, but I was sharing. You know, what's mine to give is not mine to withhold, sort of thing. No wonder I was so popular, I might just as well have been giving away bottles of Yquem 45.'

'Getting low, huh?'

'Well, yeah.'

'I've heard about a head honcho, claims to have invented a new hybrid. Let me see if I can put you in touch with him.'

'Where is he?'

'I don't know, he's a careful sort. It's understandable if he's growing the weed himself.'

'I'll give you my number, if you make contact with him . . .'

'OK. No problem – listen, if you're doing a lot of grass I'd take some mega-doses of vitamin C on a regular basis. Three or four grams a day, orange juice won't do it, you know.'

'Thanks. What d'ya think of the phoenix – turned out great, eh?'

She laughed. 'Fancy yourself rising out of the ashes, huh?' I grimaced. She went on, 'Adversity only bends a great man. An old Chinese told me that.'

'Did he say how?'

'By drawing on the deepest stratum of your being, this alone is superior to fate,' she quoted. 'Don't forget I'm Devon. I'm the best,' she added unselfconsciously.

'Are you?' I said. 'I'm Terence.'

'Yep, I know. I don't forget a face. I saw you at Ondines – the Doors' first New York gig, but you were with someone. You're groovy. I'll check you out.'

It took her less than an hour to make contact with the inventor. It seemed he was intrigued to meet the actor who'd played *The Collector*.

Three days later my phone rang, and a baritone voice said, 'Good morning, I'm Jim. I grow things.' There was a deep chuckle on the other end of the receiver in response to my audible confusion.

'You'd like to meet to discuss my high breeds,' he said.

'Oh, yeah, when, where?'

'You working today?' Jim asked.

'Yep, finish at six, here by six-thirty. I can come anywhere that's local.'

'I'll pick you up, if that's agreeable?'

'Yep, that's fine.' I gave him the address.

'See you at seven,' Jim said. 'By the way, that was some movie, *The Collector*.'

'Well, it was a Wyler movie, you know.'

'It was a Stamp movie as well; don't be so modest. It's not good for your esters.'

'Esters?'

'Your spirit, buddy, your spirit. See you at seven.' He hung up.

It was my turn to be intrigued, and I spent all day trying to put a face, a body to the deep voice. I finally settled on a huge-framed guy, mid-forties, with a beard, like the sailor on the Player's packet. I couldn't have been more wrong.

I heard the deep-throated roar of a car engine at seven on the dot followed by a burst of toots. I emerged from my house to discover a shiny black AC Cobra with chromium trim sitting outside. At the wheel was a tow-headed young man with the wind-blown complexion of a surfer who could have been my own age. His flaxen hair had even lighter streaks; I'd heard beach boys rubbed their hair with lemons to achieve this effect. I assumed Jim had sent a driver. Perhaps Jim was gay. Lots of wealthy older homosexuals allowed themselves and their expensive cars to be chauffeured by young paramours.

As soon as the driver spoke, however, I knew this was the man himself. I'd never heard such a deep voice from such a slight frame.

'How do you feel about seat belts?' Jim enquired, as I climbed over the low passenger door and lowered myself on to the rich leather seat.

'Well, generally, I regard them as a sissy, but . . . '

'But is right,' agreed Jim. 'Shelby put a lot of poke under this hood.'

I buckled up a formidable triangle of belt, like that of a helicopter.

'I used to design ads for A C when I was a boy,' I said, thinking of my train trips out to the factory when I was in advertising.

'Yep, the A C Company sure made the most beautiful car but it took Shelby to spot it: he leaned on Ford's to build him a worthy engine. You never had a ride in one?'

'A Cs and Acecas, yes, but not a Cobra.'

'O K, let's go for a spin.'

The sports car shot off like a demon that had been trapped inside a bottle too long. Jim knew his Hollywood hills. He could also drive. Racing through the canyons, toeing and heeling around the bends, he gave me a thrilling ride before zigzagging back into Hollywood where he stopped the car outside a modest, detached, one-storey house in one of the still tree-lined avenues south of Fountain called, appropriately, Meteor Street.

'Fancy a beer?' he asked.

The dwelling wasn't his home. It was owned by a blind osteopath from whom Jim rented a room and a garage with his own entrance at the back. The studio resembled a habitat that students the world over use in transit: a poster of El Cordobes fixed to the wall, a refrigerator from which Jim extracted two Mexican beers, a settee, an armchair and a low table. On the table was an encyclopaedic work on the rose and a copy of a pharmacopoeia. I sank into the sofa. Jim squatted on the floor.

'Got any dope?' he enquired.

I pulled a joint from the concealed pocket of my leather shirt.

The twisted ends protruded out of both sides of a Beverly Hills Hotel book of matches.

'It's Acapulco Gold,' I said, hoping to excuse the travel-worn condition.

'Is it?' Jim questioned warily.

He split the joint open with a long thumbnail, gathering the contents into a sizeable pinch before sniffing at it.

'Hmm,' he said knowledgeably. 'It's a good yella, fella.' He pulled a drawer towards him that was set in the middle of the table and extracted a packet of liquorice cigarette papers. Sticking two of the dark brown skins together he expertly reassembled the joint.

'Only polite to let quality grass breathe a little,' he said by way of explanation.

From the same drawer he took a swathe of incense and an amber bead, like a boiled sweet with a hole in the middle. He lit one of the sticks of incense with a Zippo and placed it into the centre hole of the bead. The odour was heavy and cloying, the kind present in Indian bazaars the world over.

'I know it's not nice, but it's strong,' said Jim. 'The neighbours, you know.'

He fired up the grass, inhaled like a pro and handed it to me. Before Jim had re-rolled my joint he'd extracted two seeds I had missed and laid them carefully on his rose book. While I was busy ingesting my share of the smoke, Jim picked up the pair of seeds and held them in his right palm. He didn't speak for a while and, as I didn't try, the room fell silent. The burning spot at the top of the joss stick went into slow motion and individual specks of scented wood dust sparkled as they fuelled the fire. I felt that shift into what I thought of as the olfactory equivalent of clairvoyance, when my nasal sensory channels dilated. I could trace the different perfumes blended in the incense: the sweet of the rose, the dryness of the sandalwood. Into the silence came Jim's voice, low, vibrating.

'It's funny to think it all started with these,' he said, regarding the seeds in his hand, bigger than poppy, smaller than raisins. 'When the Spanish invaded Mexico they brought Moors with them as servants, and in the pockets of their boudoir pants the Moors brought their seed. Of course, as soon as the Conquistadors subjugated the local Indians and put their blacks, the Moors, to work on the gardening, the Indians became the blacks of the blacks. The Moors handed the Indians their seed from home and instructed them to get on with it. An industry was born.'

'Is that how it happened?'

'Sure did.'

'And you, you're a bit of a gardener yourself?'

'I dabble in lots of things. Since you're curious, I'll show you something,' Jim said. He went over to the fridge, opened it and took from the salad drawer at the bottom what looked like a large cucumber wrapped in tin foil. When the silver skin was peeled off, an oblong cedar box was revealed, like a classy cigar container which had been simply, but ingeniously, concealed.

'Shazam,' said Jim, sliding the top off as though it contained pencils. He tilted the open box towards me: inside were four dried samples not unlike the seed pod of a magnolia.

'Behold the fruit of my labours,' Jim whispered dramatically. 'Can you discern the colours in the colas?' he added.

I studied the contents. The colas, as he'd called them, resembled small lilac blooms but each moss-brown mass bore its identity colour threaded throughout: purple, red, green and yellow.

'What are they?' I asked.

'Them's is colitas. Small colas of sinsemilla.'

'Sinsemilla?'

'Translated as Sin – without, semilla seeds. You are looking, my dear friend, at the first ever line-bred marijuana. How about a glass of juice? I'm becoming a little dry in the throat.'

Jim raided the fridge again and brought out a medium-sized jug of what looked like orange juice. It was more delicate.

'To compensate for the incense,' he said.

The glass container held the juice of freshly squeezed mandarins. Jim re-lit the dog-end of my joint; we took a couple of tokes each.

'Where d'you do your horticulture, Jim? If I may be so bold?'

Jim smiled enigmatically, 'In them there hills.'

'In Mexico?'

He chuckled, 'No, dummy, Beverly Hills.'

'Wot?' In shock, my old cockney glottal stop reared its ugly head. 'You've got bottle, Jim, I'll say that.'

'I'd agree if I knew what it meant.'

'Guts, man, guts. Bottle and glass: arse. It means you don't crap in your pants easily.'

'It's true.'

'Under glass, eh? Camouflaged?'

'No can do.'

'Not in the open?'

'Yep.'

'I don't believe it.'

'You'd better. If you're only interested in getting wasted you can grow it hydroponically – but it won't get you high.'

'What's hydroponic?'

'Without earth, using chemicals under artificial light. It can be done in a fairly contained area. Growers using that method utilise a light that was developed for night work on building sites. Some smartarse noticed all the surrounding weeds were doing unusually well.'

'So, why not use that method? Sounds safer.'

'It is. It is, but the esters. It's basically for the esters.'

'You mentioned that on the phone.'

'When I was studying, preparing to try to grow the stuff, I heard this famous gardener giving a series of master classes on the radio. At the end of each programme, listeners could phone in with questions. A couple of guys tried to draw him out on cultivation of grass but he implied that it was an illegal substance and he couldn't comment. I figured I could only get the info I wanted by asking the right question. I gave the matter some thought.'

'What did you ask him?'

'I asked him why roses weren't grown under glass.'

'And?'

'He said because of the esters. It's the esters in the roses, twenty-three or twenty-four of them that give the bloom its perfume. These esters are dependent on, or even symbiotic with, the rays of the sun, movement of the wind, prana in the air, etc. That's why hot-house roses don't smell.'

'Wow.'

'It didn't take me long to figure it was these famous esters that give the marijuana its mimetic psycho-active compounds – what you think of as those mind-changing qualities we all know and love. As soon as I understood that, I knew why some grass only gets you stoned while others get you high. Getting high was my aim, you see?'

'I do.'

'After that it was a simple case of studying the chronicles of Mendel the Monk on line-breeding genetics and acquiring the best seed.'

'Was that easy?'

'No – I had to hike all over Mexico. I'm glad I did it, though, when I did.'

'Which was when?'

'Basically, before they built too many roads. When I arrived there shopping for seed, families were still growing in isolated communities. As these were mostly too far apart for haphazard pollination, I was able to score my yellow (what you call Acapulco Gold) in the State of Guerrero; the black, or purple, as I call it, from Jalisco; the red on the southern slopes of the Popocatepetl Volcano and the green in Michoacan. Shortly afterwards the tarmac roads were laid and that made it almost impossible to locate the pure seed-lines I need. The differing shades and varying states of high bear no resemblance to street grass which is just a mish-mash. It's like blending high-grown Darjeeling with poor-quality leaves from Kenya. Not the best cup of tea.'

'I've only smoked this stuff, I'm new to it all, as it were.'

'You were lucky. This is a fine grass. I could grow a stately yellow from these two seeds.'

'I bet.'

'Would you like to see my plantation?'

'I'd be honoured, James.'

'OK, let's make a deal. Why did you start getting high, anyway?'

'Oh, it's, er, my girl left me. I'm finding life a bit thin. I can't seem to get above it.'

'A touch of the feathers, as they say in the old country.'

'Ireland?'

'Precisely. I don't mean to pry, it's just that I'd like you to clean out for a few days before I show you my garden and let you sample the wares. It's a conceit on my part, but it's how I get off. So you fully appreciate what I'm doing.'

'Since you put it like that, I'm sure I can manage it.'

'I'll call for you, Saturday, around four-thirty, OK?'

'OK.'

24

I was looking forward to the excursion, but all the next day I held this damn thought in my head, like a tune I couldn't stop, that Jean would be coming back to me on the Friday evening flight. The notion became an obsession – so much so that as soon as I finished work at the studio I climbed into my car and took off for the airport. I used the same route as on the two previous wonderful occasions, sticking to it fastidiously as though the least deviation would jar my premonition. I made it on time and took my customary parking space on the red line. I sat in the car a long time, but when I saw passengers arriving I couldn't bear it – I rushed into the terminal, hanging about until all the passengers had left. Somebody had stuck a parking violation under my windscreen wiper. It was the last straw. I felt suicidal. I could hardly breath and it took a while to start the car and get moving. My eyes were misty; I couldn't see properly, couldn't stop thinking of the last time: my own rainbow next to me, her perfumeless aroma filling my nostrils. Her soft hand resting on my thigh. She had worn a perfume later. I wanted to buy a bottle, smell it when I missed her, but I couldn't for the life of me recall the name. I put on the radio mechanically. 'You're tuned to K Earth 101, and now from across the pond, Frank Ifield.' 'I Remember You' filled the airwaves. I'd seen Frank perform the song the week it had hit the number one slot, in Brighton, I think; he'd been way down a bill topped by Billy Fury. 'And when the angels ask me to recall the thrill of them all . . .' I switched off.

At the entrance to the freeway were stood a couple of bedraggled hippies in an assortment of black leather and ankhs. One of them had a hand up in a limp peace sign. My heart opened: company to help me back home, I thought. I stopped the car. The smaller of the two, who turned out to be a girl, slid in next to me. She had

rings on all her grimy nail-bitten fingers. Her friend opened the back door and climbed in behind. They both smelt strongly of the Patchouli oil I'd been wearing. The girl kept turning around and looking at her companion. I gave him a red-eyed once-over in the driving mirror: he was grubby, unshaven. He saw me cruising him and gave a weak grin, showing a set of soiled, broken teeth. Then he drew a gun.

'OK, brother,' he said, 'let's have your dough.'

It was so third-rate Bogey that if I hadn't felt so dejected, I would have laughed. As it was, I continued driving like nothing had happened.

The waif said, almost reassuringly, I thought, 'He's got a shooter.'

'I can see that,' I replied.

'Well, hand over,' she said, waving her hands. I became preoccupied by her jewellery – even her short thumbs were encircled by toy-shop silver. Now, if it is a fact that outer adornments compensate for lack of inner treasure, I mused to myself, I can't expect any luminous depth from this little number.

'Listen, guys,' I said. 'I've been waiting for you two clutzes. Just don't mess it up, OK? Put the pistol right on the base of my bonce, and make sure you get it right.' I could hear my voice, low, even, but authoritative.

The girl, becoming hysterical, shouted, 'Give us the dough.'

'Pull the trigger, asshole, or piss off,' I shouted, all control going out of the window.

'Stop the car, stop the car,' bellowed the gunman.

'Do it, man, come on, do it,' I yelled.

'Stop the fucking car,' he yelled back.

I took no notice, driving recklessly through the early evening traffic. The waif grabbed at the key and turned it, and the car slithered to a halt in the fast lane. Traffic weaved around us hooting angrily, as though infected by the tension inside the vehicle.

'It's not real,' gasped the girl, staring intently at my face. The boy in the back jumped out trying, ineptly, to breach the aluminium divide in the middle of the road.

'The gun's not real, it's not real, d'you hea . . . say, aren't you . . . '

The boy was screaming to her, 'Get over here, get the fuck outta there!'

She scrambled out of the passenger door, narrowly missing being sideswiped by a Mack truck, whose driver bellowed, 'Hippy assholes,' from his high window. Running in front of the car and looking at me through the window she shouted, 'Dez, it's, it's that guy.'

'What?' screamed Dez.

'It's that guy, the crazy from the butterfly film. It's him.'

'Let's get outta here, for Christ's sake.'

'But it's him, the crazy . . . '

'He's fucking crazy, all right.'

I put the car into neutral and switched the ignition on. As I drove away I watched in my mirror the two small beetle-like figures clambering away looking for something to crawl under, she plucking his arm as if trying to convince him of something. I could feel sweat running down my back. It was cold. Not my Friday for prayers answered, I guess.

My friend Jim picked me up, as arranged. On the dot. His glamorous Cobra had been replaced by a humble VW bug.

'Few people notice these,' he said, his blond-streaked hair tucked demurely under a baseball cap. We drove up to the top of Laurel Canyon and turned left, meandering within the speed limit, up a curved pass on to a small unmarked side-road where we stopped in front of a pair of open wrought-iron gates. As soon as Jim was clear of the car, a meaty white Staffordshire bull terrier, with a mahogany brindle patch over one eye, started a run at him. There was a line painted across the drive where its gates would align if closed. I saw that Jim placed his feet this side of the strip of weathered paint. About ten feet from him the dog leapt into the air, travelling like a bullet. It was only when his length of chain ran out and the dog was jerked to a mid-air halt, I realised it was a game.

'Meet Commander Whitehead,' grinned Jim. 'That's his favourite trick at the moment.'

'I bet he scares the postman,' I said.

'You can say that again. They stopped delivering when they realised it was only junk mail.

'Hi, Commander. He's rather territorial, I'm afraid. Commander, this is Terence. He's a friend.' Jim let the big American

Staffordshire off his chain. 'He's a pussy cat when he's not on duty.'

I smiled at the Commander. He smiled back. I patted his muscle-bound shoulders.

He jumped on the bonnet as we drove the beetle through the gates and parked in front of a small, elegant house. Jim gave his dog a snack and looked over the long glasshouses that could have been modelled on Kew Gardens. The wooden frames were the colour of the Commander's mahogany eye patch.

'Did you build these?' I asked when Jim joined me.

'No, no, that's the beauty of this place. It was like this when I found it. An old English fella had it built to cultivate orchids.'

'I thought you didn't grow under glass?' I said.

'Strictly speaking, I don't, but it's handy to have them seed indoors. I keep them here until I'm able to sex them.'

'Sex them?'

'It's the first stage of my cultivation programme. Come, I'll show you my beds. You're fit, you can handle a climb.'

Climb it was. The garden was landscaped to include a steep natural ravine which ran through the property. On the floor of the crater were neat lines of Jim's sinsemilla. One line of each colour. It was still hot, a natural suntrap.

'I need the heat. This stuff is accustomed to being between 9–12,000 feet above sea-level. Good lookers, aren't they?' He brushed his hand over the nearest cluster, gently, the way one would caress a baby. I thought of the years of patient tending the Persians must have spent developing their wild rose.

'This is a seedless purple. She's a grandchild of my first success.'

I could see the main stem of the damsel was already almost black.

'I don't want you to divulge your secrets,' I said, 'but . . . '

'It's no secret; as a matter of fact, I'm trying to dream up a way of telling the world. It's not my living. I've made a lot of bread out of it, 'tis true, but I've always had bread. I charge a lot for my crop, but only so buyers appreciate what they're smoking. These folks around here, they hate to get something for nothing. They love a bargain but like to pay for it.'

'How much d'you charge?'

'I'll tell you later. Now, let me explain. What is usually smoked is the female. It's always the female, actually, that's why there are

271

so many seeds. What I have done is to create a hybrid female. As soon as the plants choose a sex, they start to show different characteristics. That's when I destroy the males. All the males. The female doesn't notice at first, she's like a young girl. However, when she is ready to pollinate, she enters a period of florescence. She then senses there is no male pollen to create the union – to restore the somatic chromosome balance – so she tries harder, producing more blooms, pumping resin into herself in the hope of catching that one speck of pollen. Her key to infinity. In the final weeks when she is heavy with resin I halve the water and prune away the sun leaves, leaving just the laden flowers. I only grow the plants I can tend myself. No more, no less. It's gruelling work, climbing up and down this ravine all day in high September, but it's worth it. When I fire up my first beauty, it's like smoking a fucking nun, man!'

Jim shielded his eyes and glanced at the sun.

'Not a Libran, are you?' he enquired.

'Why?'

'Supposed to be a natural meditation for Librans, watching the sunset. Thought you might have a little balance in there, some-where. Across the eyes, perhaps.'

'Don't know.'

'Let's watch the sun go down, anyway.'

We clambered up the hot steep hillside, I following carefully in Jim's footsteps. The front of the house which faced the setting path of the sun had a first-floor verandah. It ran the length of the building, resembling the widow's walk galleries of Suffolk coast houses. Jim pointed at it as we neared the house.

'That's my sundown spot,' he said. 'I'll pick up something to drink first.'

The house may have been styled Victorian country English, but the kitchen was all-American: refrigerator, a freezer of grocer shop proportions, waste disposal, juicer, water softener, the works.

'I figured to make us some tea. I know how you English feel about a cuppa. Had a dude here from Ceylon last year, a Muslim, they're only allowed to leave Ceylon once, to do the *hadj* to Mecca. He and his missis used the opportunity to go around the world. Gentle fella, manager of a tea plantation in Kandy. He'd been let down by the tea in England. All his life he'd been sending the cream of his crop to London but when he finally arrived he discovered there wasn't a good cuppa to be had for love nor money, as he put it. All blended with inferior grey leaves from somewhere else to give bulk.

'Any rate, I sent him off with a little stash of "red'll run you right across town" and he posted me two pounds of his finest high-grown, delicate top leaves, picked only by teenage virgins, he wrote me. First-class bouncy tea.'

'Dammit, James, you're a man after my own heart,' I exclaimed.

'Thought that might grab you.' He filled a kettle with spring water, warmed a china teapot and drew the lid off his branded box of tea, easing aside the heavy tin foil lining to show me the tiny tea leaves picked with loving tenderness.

'Now, honey? Let's see. I'm making this strong to cut the munchies. Too many heads give in to appetite, and scarf ice-cream. It wastes the high, in my opinion so, yeah, this should blend nicely.' He lowered a jar of Desert Sage honey from a selection in an overhead cupboard.

'My grass is for getting high. It hits quick, so it's good to plan a little beforehand, make a strategy. Often it takes the mood you're in and intensifies it, so understand that. If there is a girlfriend aboard, it's OK to be feeling sensuous,' he said smiling. 'It is strong medicine. Can make you feel hungry. I've had people smoking sinsemilla the first time spend all evening in the kitchen going through the book, one spoonful after another. The oddest combination – ice-cream, pickles, syrup, biscuits, peanut butter, toppings, chutney, even spoons of Tabasco on toast.'

'Sounds like a kid let loose in a shop. I know the feeling.'

'Right, let's you take this tray upstairs and pour a couple of cuppas. I'll fetch the herb.'

I placed the tea tray on the planked floor of the verandah and did the honours, stirring a generous teaspoonful of the dusky honey into each. The tea had already brewed itself strong. Jim arrived with a flask of boiling water for the second pot, which he preferred, and a cedar wood oblong container similar but smaller to the one that had contained his four shaded samples.

'Have you decided what colour you're going to initiate me with?' I asked.

'Yep, but I want you to inhale this, unlit, first.' He passed me a 'Mexican thick' joint with both ends untwisted. 'Just suck in.'

I did. A strong flavour hit the roof of my mouth. It was not unlike the Wintergreen my mum had rubbed on my chest as a boy.

'That must be the . . . green,' I said. 'Profound but delicate.'

'Exactly.' He looked pleased. 'After you've smoked my ganja a few times you should be able to grade the quality by squeezing a bud under your nose. Can't go sampling everything as smoke – too heavy on the vocals.' He rubbed his Adam's apple. 'Like coffee buyers. They only need bite the bean to know the strength.'

He slid the top section free of the box. Inside was a single bloom. 'What d'you see?' Jim asked.

'Well, the wood is near black, but the threads of colour in the flowers are . . . red.'

'So?'

'You've crossed two lines. A hybrid hybrid.'

'I have, and it is. We are about to become the first to smoke it. I cut this cola on the last full moon. I've been growing one early as a show bloom to photograph for my catalogue. That was a laugh. I had to scour LA for a straight photographer. "What's this?" said the assistant, posing with the purple, "it smells real strong." "It's a herb," I told him, "good for glaucoma." Would you like to roll?'

'No, no, I defer to the young master.'

'Breathe,' he said, gently squeezing the single floret he'd separated from the cola under my nose.

I inhaled, long, slow. The smell was rich, spicy. The front resinous like my Acapulco, but the end reminding me of heliotrope snuff. There was something else – an aroma I knew from a long way back. I couldn't place it. I kept trying. Early, from my childhood. What was it? Hops! It reminded me of hops. The residue that permeated everything, adding the unasked-for oniony flavour to cheese sandwiches, sliced cake from the Sally Army, everything you touched. The nuisance every new hopper complained about for a day or two and never mentioned again, content to remove the dark layers by mouth.

'It's hops,' I shouted triumphantly. 'The end is hops.'

'You have an elegant nose, my friend. Cannabis, a derivation of hemp, the botanical cousin of the vine *Humulus lupulus*, which gives us the bitter catkin that flavours real beer all over the world.' He held up the cluster. 'Remind you of anything?'

'It's a giant-dried hop.'

Jim wagged his head like an Indian porter. 'Ah cha.'

'You mean, all my hop-picking ancestors were stoned out of their brains every September?'

'Hop-heads all, no less.'

'I was probably conceived in a stoned frenzy.'

Jim held up the slim one-skin roll. No seeds, only blossom.

'Welcome home, babe.'

Jim smoked a full half of the number. He wasn't being greedy or forgetful. He was ensuring that he was the leader of the trip, albeit by only a minute or two. Perhaps not. The effect might get to me, uninitiated as I was, even quicker. Either way, I need not have worried.

'Vaporise some of this into you,' he offered. I did. Jim had said the high hit fast. He'd made no comment on the smoothness of the lift-off. After three substantial tokes, Jim relieved me of the roach – the strong section into which he'd inserted a carefully rolled piece of book-match cover to serve as a filter. Sucking up the last fragments of smouldering ingredients, he blew the pungent smoke into the air in front of him and casually tossed the butt sideways over the rail of the balcony. I watched the glowing end of paper lift, pitch and then roll as it descended in its slow motion death throes. After what seemed an extremely long moment it landed on the lawn beneath, a single spark marking its demise.

'You wouldn't get me up in one of those,' said Jim, lifting the precise words from my head. We chuckled at the synchronisation of our thoughts as well as the metaphor. My brain had that slightly expanded feel. I was as high as a kite. I looked at my watch. Jim had lit the purple red two minutes before. I already felt sure I'd been on the verandah for hours. The orange tree adjacent to us shook with presence and a feathery squirrel surfaced amongst the leaves, holding the fruit it had chosen and squirting juice into its face as it went to work. Perfume of orange filled the verandah.

The sun fell slowly that day. As it finally disappeared beneath the rim of our horizon I glimpsed a flash of lovat-green move across the setting aurora. I looked towards Jim. He confirmed with a wink that he'd also seen the strange ray.

'Did you get a buzz?' he asked.

'I think I did. Marijuana is marijuana, but this is . . . this.'

'And *this* is against the law,' he stated.

*

275

I learned a lot about Jim that first sinsemilla high we took together. His father had been a prop man at Universal and knew Jimmy Stewart and Garbo – perhaps more intimately than his own son. Jim had rejected his dad's suggestion to follow him into the studio. Hit by the new influx of energy of the Sixties, he had his own ideas. He invented one of the first pop-out polystyrene surfboards, bringing the surfing craze within financial reach of a whole generation of toehangers, but he sold early when the market was cornered. He learned to fly and bought a light plane, hopping modest cargoes of top-quality marijuana across the border and burying his stash in the desert outside Los Angeles before landing officially at the Santa Barbara airstrip.

'It wasn't the big business it is today,' Jim said of those early years. Nonetheless, a couple of hundred grand a year, tax-free, was fine, and he invested wisely in blue-chip stock. He made friends on his travels, mainly Indians who lived and cultivated at 10,000 feet and the dusty wanderers who drifted through the California deserts. Jim paid attention. His steady eyes didn't miss much. He also had ears that heard like a bat. On one trip, climbing high to an outlying village on the Istasiuatl mountain – shaped like a reclining woman – in search of a pure strain of his beloved purple, Jim overheard a tale of a magic strain of grass that had been found by a wandering Moor on an abandoned finca. Jim brushed aside the folklore that the garden had been shaped like the hand of Allah written in Kufic script and concentrated on learning what little was recalled of the botanical characteristics. It was from these fragments he flashed upon a lonely female, seeded in a remote spot from the droppings of an animal or bird, growing to maturity in ideal conditions but deprived of a mate. He went to Persia where he rented an estate in Tabriz with a high-walled garden, reading *The Conference of the Birds* and producing in legal peace his own strain of Persian purple seedless. He confessed he even contemplated registering the brandname officially when Jack Kennedy sat in Camelot and there was talk of legalising grass in order to sever the link it formed with harder drugs. After 1963 Jim set up shop growing 'orchids' in the last place anyone would think to look for large-scale cultivation, the hills of Beverly.

I confessed to Jim my fear of returning to London where the host of memories might burn me up; and he offered me a position in his own walled garden as his oily rag. I'd water, prune and learn the mysteries of tenderly bringing his ladies to full heat.

'Have a think about it. A dude like you can't go on showing his arse in public for ever.'

The notion held great attraction for the romantic in me. I said I was honoured and promised to consider it.

'I'd like to set up a trip for you,' he said.

'A trip?'

'Two trips, actually. One into the desert and one into another desert. Dream clearing, it's called by the braves. I'd love to sell you my produce; it's great to grow for someone who appreciates the crop, but my colitas are not for forgetting, they are more for recalling. It may not be the way for you. At 250 dollars an ounce I don't want you to make a mistake.'

'250 dollars an ounce?'

'Yep, not negotiable.'

'My key of Gold cost me a thousand.'

'Counting the weight of seed in your key, that makes my grass about twice the price of yours, right?'

'That's about it.'

'You don't compare a log fire to an electric one.'

'You don't.'

'It's a question of *kaif*.' Jim anticipated my query by raising his hand. 'A term I picked up in Persia. When an experience which is trivial gives one a sense of uplift this may be *kaif*. A gent named Barik Ali said of it, "If it is not there, true enjoyment is not there."'

'I guess you're right. You've thought about it.'

'I have. Let me set up a meet with my chum, Great Elk, who I would call *kaif* master. You may not need to invest a dime. Let the Beverly hillbillies, with their hot film green-backs, pay for my experiments.'

'OK. Whatever you have in mind.'

'Something in those orbs of yours. They say there is more fire in blue eyes. Maybe it's a hunch. You might be ripe for some proper medicine. I'll fix it up.'

'Sounds mysterious, but I'm a sucker for intrigue.'

'So am I. Oh, one thing. No need to tell you, probably. Not a word of this location to anyone. OK? Unless I buy the farm before you.'

'Buy the farm?'

'Yeah, a flyer's expression for crashing your plane.'

25

Blue finished main-unit filming the next Friday; apart from one or two pick-up shots at the studio the following week, I was free. Larry Schiller opened his home to us for an end-of-film celebration. It was a big do: all the cast came with escorts, favourite stunt men, crew, loved ones. Ricardo Montalban brought his wife, Georgina, the lovely sister of Loretta Young. When Nader spotted her timidly tapping her foot to some Who music (Keith Moon, the Who drummer, was in town and had brought along the latest pressings), he persuaded her on to the floor for a dance.

I bopped until I dropped with everyone who'd have me: Peggy, Joanne, Sally, Keith. By myself. Larry asked me if I was OK. I assured him I was.

'When you going home?' he asked.

'Home? Ah. Don't know. Don't care.'

'When you decide, let me know – I'd like to come with you. Finish my layouts. Tie everything together.'

'Only work, eh, Lol?'

'No. I'd like to keep you company. See you safely back on to home ground.'

I relayed the conversation to Nader. He said, 'Looks like Joanne was right. He's a prince.'

'Looks like it.'

Jim came through. Before sun-up Sunday morning, having followed Jim's explicit instructions to fast on Saturday and drink only spring water, I was heading east on Interstate Highway 10 into the high desert for a rendezvous with an old medicine man known as Great Elk. I carried one of Jim's hand-rolls in my moccasin.

'In case you become nervous before blast-off,' Jim had assured me, 'go for it, man: close a few old doors, open a few older ones.'

The car was doing what it was built to do, racing smoothly over the wide empty tarmac. 'She wears an Egyptian ring,' Dylan was telling me, 'she's an artist, she don't look back.' HIGHWAY 62 ... YUCCA VALLEY ... IDYLWILD ... TWO BUNCH PALMS ... JOSHUA TREE ... TWENTY-NINE PALMS ... Time to start looking for a man by the roadside.

'He'll wave you down. He has your number.'

The distant hills look indigo. There he is wearing a faded tartan shirt, Rob Roy red. He waves to me. I stop. He climbs in looking like everyone's grandfather.

'Howdy,' he says in a voice that could pop corn. 'Take this turning here.' We drive slowly along an almost invisible dirt track, the rocks on each side of us growing larger, yet more surreal. We come to a halt at the end of the track: we're in a moonscape.

'We walk. You follow me, walk in my steps. Lots of snakes here. If you see one, stop, don't move. I will speak to him.'

He gives me a phrase – breathe in, 'The Great Wind is the light of my blood', breathe out, 'My blood is the light of the Great Wind'. I ask him how far we will walk but he doesn't answer. Jim had suggested I take the flute which I had started to teach myself to play in Moab, a simple bamboo instrument.

'Bring the flute,' says Great Elk.

I retrieve it from the passenger seat and follow him, breathing in and out my phrase. The sun is still below the hills but only just. My moccasins, made-to-measure at the shop in the valley, actually work – the stony path passes underfoot soundlessly. Great Elk stops dead ahead of me. 'Snake,' he whispers, 'to the left: rattler.' I look but don't see anything, then it rattles: a chilling sound. It's on the road, coiled at the bottom of a boulder. I freeze. Great Elk is speaking to the snake, his tone conciliatory, as though to a younger brother or sister.

'I know how shy you are. We are sorry to disturb you on your ground. We pass in friendship. I am going to reach down and lift some Mother Earth, sprinkle it near you so you can move.'

He kneels, picks up a handful of earth, removes a few pebbles and scatters it cautiously, close by the snake. It stays motionless. Great Elk takes a step forward, the rattler uncoils, moves back. The snake slides forward, the man back. This see-saw goes on a few times until Great Elk says to me, 'It is no danger: he is lonely. He is playing. Breathe the words, move on.'

I walk behind him and wait while he says goodbye to the snake. He passes me without speaking. We move off again.

By sun-up we reach a circular log cabin protected on one side by a sheer rock face perhaps a hundred feet high. The cabin is primitively constructed and hardly noticeable in a dell between mounds of boulders. It is empty save for a spent fire in the middle. He closes the wooden door behind us and, as my eyes adjust to the sparse light from the circular hole cut in the roof above the ashes, I see a cloth, like a tea towel on the floor. Beside it is a beaker filled with what looks like tea.

'Undress,' says Great Elk. I hesitate. 'Save shoes.'

He is undressing. I do the same. He picks up the tea towels, carefully unfolding them and extracting a fistful of what appear to be loden overcoat buttons. He opens his right hand and cups the palm slightly to form a hollow, before tipping the buttons into it and scraping a few off to leave a level handful from the heel to the fingertips.

'This is good measure. Would normally measure in own hand. But because you are not a brave, exactly . . . '

'Not exactly,' I giggle, embarrassed by my nudity. I feel like a skinny Donatello caught without the wings and clad only in my moccasins.

He continues, ' . . . I have made you cup of tea. Our friend says English like tea.'

He places the buttons on his tartan shirt which is laid on the floor and picks up the beaker.

'You drink this,' he says. 'It is bitter. It is more bitter than anything you have tasted, or will ever taste. You must swallow. Try not to sick up. You will never forget this taste. It will stay with you always. The taste is the juice of Mother Earth. If you do sick, it will be only excess to make your measure perfect. Do not clean or try to clean mouth. Nice taste will follow after bad medicine leaves. These are the ripe, peyote button. They have sung to me. I will eat these. You will drink tea.'

He peels the two tea towels apart, wrapping one round his midriff like a loin cloth and, handing me the other, motions me to do the same. I feel all right: as though I'm at the Saturday morning Turkish baths in East Ham. He offers me the beaker – the smell is woody like a potion concocted from roots, maybe burdock or ginseng. The taste isn't. It is revolting – how I imagine hemlock to taste – the most disgusting thing I've ever put into my mouth. At the first taste I gag but breathe in slowly through my nose. I recall a record sleeve of a Noel Coward long-playing 33. It shows the master standing in the desert near Las Vegas, bedecked in a Savile Row suit and buttonhole and taking a sip of tea from a bone china cup and saucer. I'm an Englishman. This is my drink, an unusual cuppa, that's all. Juice of Mother Earth, from Jackson's.

I slowly, carefully, swallow the whole draught. The sensation of wanting to throw up starts. It doesn't stop. I reach for the joint in my moccasin.

'What for?' asks Great Elk.

'I, er, while I wait,' I answer lamely.

'No point,' he says, 'different hamburger.'

I wonder what he means. He opens the door allowing early sunlight to flood the space.

'Flute comes too,' he says. I take up the bamboo stick.

As we walk, I start saying the phrase, breathing deeply to allay the nauseousness. The rhythmic walking helps me – I'm very aware of my body. My right nostril feels closed. I'm breathing mostly through my left. We enter a clearing which is carpeted with delicate yellow flowers, packed close together. A rug from Samarkand. Elk slows and walks so carefully across the flowers they spring up as his foot moves on, as though he is as light as air. I notice the distinct upside down V in the centre back of his calf muscle. He's done a few walks, old Elk. Skirting yet another cluster of rocks, we come into a secluded hollow filled with mauve flowers, again packed tight like a mat. Great Elk halts, rounding on me.

'You will stay here, this good place. Kind spirits here.'

'It does feel nice.' My voice seems to be coming from a loft.

'We call this place the nest. You sit. Play music. I go, but not far away.'

He pops another emerald button in his mouth and chews on it like it's bubble gum before wandering away. I shudder. The taste of Earth juice is still filling my throat. I try to lie on the mauve counterpane but the nauseous sensation doesn't like it, so I sit up and try to analyse how I feel. My sense, the sense that I'm here, seems to have contracted: a kernel observing not only what I'm seeing but what my mind is thinking, too. It's odd. I can't recall having experienced this sensation before, although it isn't unfamiliar but subtle, as if the eye of the mind has found an easy chair to watch from. It feels precarious yet it is held there. Held *there* by a reminder factor like an alarm clock. This timepiece stops me doing anything that will dislodge the balance of awareness, and the alarm is the feeling of nausea!

I gasp at the refinement of it. My insight unravelled this. I feel that my intelligence, usually dispersed, is being collected in an anti-clockwise spin, then condensed, stepped down, like electricity from a cloud to a one-pointed needle. The feeling of being near to vomiting is what is overseeing the spin. How uncanny. Somehow, I understand that the queasiness is an integral part of the experience, and I welcome the sensation. It's holding me on course, showing the way. I feel a light breeze on my cheek ruffling the hairs on my neck. I unwrap my loin cloth and it slips to the ground, allowing the flurry of air to caress my whole body. I pick up the flute, take a deep breath, adjust my embouchure and try my low C note. As I blow I sense the oneness of the note with the wind. The breeze picks up, whistles through the rocks taking my note with it: a wave afloat on the ocean of air. My breath is running out, but I can't fail the note, can't stop while the breeze is still blowing: I have to complete the tone I started; I hear it riding high, at one with the wind. Although I am out of breath I keep blowing from somewhere. My bladder opens: urine runs out of me and this release gives me extra air. The wind that was on my body rolls over me, drops – the note rattles to its end in the hollow bamboo. I gasp for air as, in the next valley, coyotes howl a response to the call from my pipe.

The soft sickness moves to the front of my head, above and between my eyes. I notice I'm now breathing predominantly through my right nostril. Time to move. I decide to investigate, to look for other inmates of my domain.

In the rocks to the left of the now violet dell I see the start of a path. I follow it, losing track of time. The sun is high. I find a pine tree growing. It's had a hard life and its straggly branches and grey-green needles are not at all like the lush specimens of Britain. I take a closer look and see that its bark is splitting and sticky lozenges of resin are protruding: if this tree were submerged in water for a few million years, it would be encased in amber. I hear a low hum. At first, I think it's a telegraph wire, then I see, suspended from a higher branch of the tree, a swarm of bees. I am drawn to them, carefully climbing a few of the lowest, stronger branches, getting to the bees' eye level. My hands come up to my face. There appears to be a flickering pale blue light glowing from my fingertips; I position my feet so as to free my other hand. It's true – the same light. I close my fingertips together, as if about to pray, and the light jumps across, becomes stronger. I move them apart, together, apart, as though squeezing a concertina. The intensity of colour builds. Is my sight perception expanding to the blue-violet end of the spectrum? Am I starting to see the blue end of my own aura? I stretch my right hand towards the seething mass of bees, resting the blue light of my fingertips close to them. I can feel the warmth of their buzzing bodies, yet the presence of my hand doesn't disturb their mood. I lower my hand on to them, feel the vibrating softness of their wings on my skin. I let my left hand go through the same routine, finally placing my palm flat on the other side, as though holding up a vase. I feel my heart beating, the pulsating rhythm coursing into each hand through the buzzing sponge, the live sponge beating as one with me. I hold this communion until I hear Great Elk calling me down.

His face looks finer, his skin tighter: I can see stature in the wide-set eyes, intelligence in the high, broad forehead. It occurs to me that, with the help of a little insight, it shouldn't be too hard to see the influence of the animal kingdom in everyone. I should keep a look out. He walks ahead of me and I observe him from the armchair behind my eyes, seeing how he plumps his feet flat down, accentuating the weight on his heels. I hadn't noticed *en route* from the car, but he walks like an elk: I imitate him, falling into step behind, feeling my spine shift into alignment. Energy seems to gather in my feet and rise through my spine to the centre of my head, but it's a long walk.

We slowly climb one of the larger rocks near the wooden cabin and sit watching the sun. Has the whole day gone? Great Elk is motionless, his eyes open but still. I stand up as the sun drops. A tiny shimmering humming bird stops in mid-air a few inches from my nose, its wings invisible with speed, its body a sparkling mass of bottle-green. We eye each other steadily. Hello. I breathe in, drawing him to me, opening my mouth and inviting him closer. He comes. For a second I feel that if I offer my tongue, he will rest his curious long beak on it.

'You ready now,' I hear the Chief observe behind me.

He starts the climb down. In the middle of the hut, Great Elk has built a fire: it flickers a welcome as he opens the door. We dress and sit either side of the flames. The room smells rich with burning wood. Elk places a small drum between his thighs but doesn't beat it, instead, begins a story, the resonance uneven but hypnotic, as though his whole being is embodied in his voice. From time to time I place a log on the fire and he positions it with a stick which periodically catches fire. In the soft glow his outline fades into the shadows, leaving only his voice, like Mesmer.

'When I was a young brave, we had in our settlement a great medicine man, the envy of many tribes. My father encouraged me to sit with him whenever I could. Life was exciting for a young man in our territory but I sat with the man to honour my father's wishes. A medicine man is a doctor and a priest . . . '

'But they have to bear witness to their skill.'

'Exactly. Once every year at least our man must prove he still has big medicine. He does this at the summer moon festival when he dances with snakes. Different tribes have different ritual but our people do this. As I grow up the medicine man teaches me many things: he burn red sage to ward off the bad spirits from my heart; make me talisman with herbs, stones and feathers to carry on journeys; instruct me what plants good to fix sickness; but he never speak about his power with snake although I ask him many times. All he say is serpent highly intelligent, perhaps most clever of animal kingdom. Very timid with man because understand man is also smart, but can be ugly. Snake is smart because of all creation he most perfect channel for air, for divine breath.'

He draws his fingers apart, tracing a straight line in the air.

'Snake is highly evolved in animal domain, because patient. No temper. No anger. Can draw what he needs to him by power of breath. Even living food brings to him by breath. Some snakes have light in the head. Can shine in the dark. Light made by perfect channelling of two-energy breath. If you want to dance with snake must have great respect first. First step.

'One year our medicine man is bitten by snake. He not die because he treat quick with medicine. Nobody say nothing but everyone is shocked. Me too. Next year come time for dance everyone curious. I am playing drum.' He taps the skin with his middle finger. 'I am very happy, proud, but near end of dance

285

medicine man bitten again. Fix him up with antidote. Now is serious. Once, nobody speak. Twice. OK to ask. Chief come to tepee of medicine man. Sit down. I go to leave but Chief motion me to stay. He wait, hold up one finger then two, and wait. Medicine man say, "I'm sorry. I see this coming for some years." That is when he begin to teach me dance.'

'What did he mean when he said he'd seen this coming?' I ask.

'You must understand a little how snake is sensitive. He take breath as vehicle instead of his body. He is most in harmony with all around him. He do this by being empty. Empty tube. Air flow in. Air flow out. When medicine man is also empty nice for the snake to dance. Like caress or massage. If man thinking about what to eat for dinner, or what to do with wife later, those thoughts hurt snake. He bite, let you know he is uncomfortable.'

Great Elk begins to tap his drum softly, pushing the embers with the stick in his free hand to make a glowing heap. I realise that the pulsation of my heart is being manipulated, falling into sync with the drum beat. Great Elk closes his eyes: I feel the drum go through me as if my body were glass, know it is beating in rhythm with his own heart. He slows the drum beat: my heartbeat slows. The drumming stops. Now, only the sound of my glass heart beating slowly in time with his. He opens his eyes very slowly, his fingers heavy with awareness as he reaches to a round wicker box by his side and opens it. A small snake slithers out on to the floor, coiling near the heat of the fire. It has a patterned triangular head, it rattles. Elk resumes drumming, slowing my heartbeat again to the rhythm. The snake skirts the outside rim of the firelight, moving closer to where I sit cross-legged, coming to rest in front of me. I look into the eyes which have no eyelids. The rattle stops.

Great Elk, keeping my heart steady with the drum beat, seems to fill my head with the words, 'He is your little brother. He is young. He knows only love for you. He will be happy to have you touch him. Have you appreciate his scaled body. Touch his fine beauty. If you are in harmony with him, you are in harmony with nature.'

At that moment both nostrils seem to pop open. I can feel two distinct streams of air entering my nose and sense a lightness in my forehead, where the two plumes of air meet. It feels as though a remnant of a primal eye used long ago to see in the dark has opened. I angle my forehead to see him in the new light. As my hand lifts I see the blue shimmer coming from my fingertips in the darkness. I rest the glow on him. The little serpent is being drawn to my hand. There is a moment before I touch him when I have the distinct feeling we are not separate at all, that feeling separate and afraid is unnatural. Then my fingers enclose him, feel the uncold, shiny scales, lift him up like a fragile necklet. I move my other hand to him, stroke his smooth body, and return him gently to the ground where he'd coiled in front of me; tell him he can stay with us or leave. Only the flames move. A long moment passes before he slides rhythmically away from us and disappears under the door.

The drum beat stops. I look at the fire. Great Elk has raked the embers into a likeness – an eagle poised for flight.

Larry Schiller lounged uneasily in the wide first-class seat next to me on the polar flight to London. Between spurts of conversation and strolls through the plane to stretch his legs, I went over in my mind my last few days in California. I had been apprehensive about coming home: all I saw would contain a past event, everything I touched a remembrance. Friends to be divided. Places to be avoided. At least Jean had decided to live in New York, no doubt moving in with her new beau. I would be spared actually coming upon the happy couple. Then a cable had arrived from MGM. The film company were giving a junket for the international press in Bath to launch *Far From the Madding Crowd*. Was I available to attend? I showed the telegram to Mike who advised attendance. Larry, to whom I'd also mentioned it, organised everything in a flash. I threw my belongings and acquisitions into two black wardrobe trunks Paramount Pictures had given me and, almost without knowing it, I was whisked off.

The banks of cloud beneath me brought to mind the final conversation with Great Elk. While still dark we had climbed back to the top of the rock where I'd gathered a bunch of twigs and lit a fire in a circle of stones atop the boulder. We watched the sun rise together. First the rocky moonscape was washed in pink, the Joshua trees bent low in supplication to the new dawn. Then the arc light of the desert hit, its rays of warmth illuminating, transforming the barren landscape into a teeming plenum. Beams of orange, mauve and rose lit the sky; desert sounds filled the space. I felt increasingly fragile – then a moment when I wasn't there at all, only the witnessing and my heart beating in tune with it all. Everything synergistic: sounds, light, aromas, no separation. Not a dreamed figure in a dream, but the dreamer and the dream. During the trek back to the car, our heads held high like pharaohs, Great Elk paused by a particularly striking Joshua tree, its trunk bent double over leaves that speared the ground. He stared at the tree and the sculptured shadow it threw.

'We believe where we are at any moment is the centre of the Universe. You understand?'

'All I need is a daily supply of those buttons,' I giggled, I guess light-headed from lack of food and sleep. He didn't appear to hear the frivolity I'd intended.

'Not work like that. Too hard on body. Only necessary to eat once. Open door.' He pointed at the shady earth beside the Joshua tree. 'The shadow cannot be there without the substance – but the shadow is not the substance.'

We shook hands formally. I was about to thank him, but he put his finger to his lips, motioning me to stop, as though he wanted my full attention on what he'd told me.

I had seen a sign advertising a shop, Hadley's, and pulled off the highway. The place sold fresh dates, in every combination imaginable. I had ordered a date milk shake and chosen a bunch whose fruits were as long as my middle finger. Was that a delicious snack. Here I was, the centre of the Universe, eating desert food in the desert. The trick would be keeping the fact in mind.

Our jet made a stop in Shannon. Schiller, never still for a second, found a map and realised we were nearer our destination than if we continued to Heathrow. Running late for the scheduled press lunch, Larry, fired by any challenge, charmed the airline into unloading our luggage. While I sat with it on the tarmac he made a few telephone calls, and in no time at all the sole helicopter in Ireland – property of the Irish Water Board – was wafting us to a sensational landing practically in the centre of Bath. Larry grinned at me wolfishly as the chopper began losing height and we saw the world's press scurrying along the lanes that led to our drop spot.

'Hover a bit. Give them time to get their cameras loaded,' he said to the Water Board pilot, who was happy to be our accomplice and on a wedge, to boot. Turning to me, the grin still on his chops, he said, 'Don't see why the native shouldn't return in style!'

Restaurateur with chef and his dog.

Catherine Deneuve, David Bailey, wed, August 1965.

Purple damsel.

I laughed. I felt nervous as I clasped my string of beads and bell to my chest. Return of the native as what? I asked myself. I had promised Peggy I would continue to wear the necklet we'd purchased on Haight-Ashbury 'in stodgy England'. I was trying to be a man of my word, nowadays.

26

The first night on my own at Albany was hard. I drifted off to sleep all right (having stayed awake all day with the reporters in Bath, it was eleven p.m. when I reached home and I was fit to drop, having missed a whole night's rest), but sometime around three or four a.m. I woke up, realised I was on my own in our bed and felt inconsolable. I searched my dressing-room for the only article of hers I possessed, the famous lavender jumper with the snag on the shoulder. She'd worn it when we first met and during our first photo session together. It had been given to me as a model for part of an outfit I'd worn in *Modesty Blaise*. I found the sweater, now paper-thin, rolled it into a ball and held it beside me on the pillow. In the blackness, that moment when the spirit is at its lowest ebb, I inhaled the faint memory, imagining her astral body lying beside me. In the morning I was ashamed and buried the woolly at the bottom of my chest of drawers, but neither it nor I was allowed to sleep in peace.

A few nights later, afraid of another long evening alone, I accepted an invitation to a party on Cheyne Walk. When I arrived the gracious rooms overlooking the Thames were crowded with the English hippy chapter, the new aristocrats, as the media had labelled them. The atmosphere was thick with the fumes of incense and hashish. I accepted the offer of an outsize 'prison spliff' constructed from over a dozen Rizla skins: it was my first experience of the hash compound. This particular joint was a mixture of dark Gitane tobacco and a buff, dusty substance from Lebanon – the first toke hit my cranium like a croquet ball. I had to sit absolutely still for the wave of nausea to drop without passing out. It seemed to take for ever to subside. When it eventually did, I realised I was still holding the smoking spliff. Unable to move my head for fear the room would roll over I nevertheless became worried about

dropping ash on the delicate silk carpet. With stoned lateral thinking keeping my head absolutely level, I peeked around the room,
seeking the nearest depository, eventually spotting an upturned
toadstool on a wooden stand. In stoned calm I got to my feet and
with the deliberation of a Tai Chi dancer, my head held steady by
cotton from the ceiling, I negotiated the crowded room, holding
my over-spilling spliff unobtrusively low by my side, like a roman
candle. It took an aeon to reach my destination but, when I lowered
the errant joint into the tray, I realised that it had hardly burned
down at all. The rim of ash was minuscule, the outline complete.
Time squeezed into an oblong. Since I hadn't been chastised for
bugging that joint, I located a comfortable space by the window,
taking the ashtray with me. Keeping the small of my back flat
against the wall and recalling Churchill's wartime speeches to
reassure myself I wasn't made of straw, I smoked the lot.

Some hours later when I could move my legs, I left the party.
Still too stoned to drive, I patted my Roller goodnight on the
Embankment and flagged a taxi in Beaufort Street.

'Ain't you Terry Stamp?' asked the driver in an unmistakable
East End accent.

'Plaistow, ain't it, Tel? Your ole stamping ground?'

'Near the Lido,' I managed to mumble. (I was coping for the
first time with the sensation of an exploding tongue some hash
gives. There seemed to be too little room in my mouth. I kept
thinking that if I could see my tongue in a mirror, it would resemble
the sort my mum boiled in salt at Christmas.)

'I'm a big fan of yours, Tel. I've got to tell ya.'

'Great, man.'

'Funny fing, me being born just round the corner to you in
Custom House. Someone to look up to, you know, sort of hero,
like, for me and the lads. You know . . . incentive, like. If you can
do it, get out, I mean, we can, an' all.'

'True.' I'd make it home if I kept it monosyllabic.

'Why didn't you marry that Shrimp, Tel? Lovely gel. Too many
others giving you the glad eye, I bet, eh?' He laughed, looking at
me in his mirror. 'She was a cracker, though, a blinder. Wot's it
like having a bird that's beautiful? Sorry, don't mean to pry. Where
you bin, Tel, out on the razzle? Cor, must be triffic: birds, money,
in the films, eh? Not boring you, am I, Tel?'

'Well . . .'

'You keep it up, mate, sets an example. Give a lotta people a lift, you do.'

I stumbled out of the cab and for a moment I thought he might have an autograph book. He didn't. I gave him a ten bob tip. We shook hands.

'Goodnight, John,' I said.

'God bless you, Tel. Keep up the good work, eh?'

He spun his cab round and waved goodbye as he turned right back into Piccadilly. Back off to Chelsea, I thought. I stood, punch drunk against the rope handrail on the front steps. Lordling of all I surveyed, except myself. The cab ride had brought me down, made me aware of the difference between the public image and my reality. I was touched but depressed. I let myself into the silent, dark chambers and dropping my clothes in the dressing-room went into the warm, cosy bathroom. There was my teak-enclosed bath and thunder box, Bennison's two tondos set into the bright yellow gloss wall, the comforting muted Turkey carpet under my bare feet. Brushing my teeth I happened to glance in the mirrored cabinet Geoffrey had had made for me, and couldn't miss seeing myself. Getting stoned in America and knowing the effect that marijuana had on the eyes, I had been at pains to shove in a few drops of chemical whiteness before lighting up, a way of not looking at the harm I was doing my body. Tonight, having been clean for almost a fortnight, I'd abandoned the ritual. Now I was seeing the effect of the hash in full Technicolor: my eyes were like slices of blood orange. Almost without thinking, I reached for the eye dropper but paused a moment, thinking that the damage for tonight had already been done. I read the very small print of listed ingredients; they looked poisonously synthetic. The eye: the radiant item of the apparatus, the window of the soul, some said. A fine state my soul must be in, looking out through this lot. I was ashamed to have given in to drugs once more. Was I so weak – unable to face discomfort or rejection without reaching for some substance that would take it away, blot it out, enable me not to look? Yeah, I guess I was. That's the bottom line. You might as well be dead, my son, I thought. The notion grabbed me instantly – it was the best idea I'd had in months. I would end it all, tonight.

I went into the drawing-room. Galvanised into action, I stirred the ashes in the grate, threw on some kindling and blew the fire to life. I'd never had much nerve about cutting my own body, or anyone else's, for that matter, so a slashing of the wrists was definitely out and I was much too vain to be found with my head in an oven. I recalled a recently-read essay about an oriental who'd sent cards to all his friends announcing the date of his demise and who on that day had simply lain down and died. I would do the same. I didn't possess a kimono, so I selected my favourite dressing-gown, one Jean had chosen for me in the Beverly Hills Custom Shop. A blue tender as the morning sky. I put it on and dashed off a few notes. One to my mum and dad, leaving them what little fortune I had after tax and advising them to invest it in a nice house. One to my Aunt Maude who had become my secretary and who would no doubt find me the following day, and one to Jean. I fetched a pillow from my bed, placed it on the carpet in front of the fire and lay down on my back. I told myself I wished to die. I breathed in deeply picturing my loved ones in my mind's eye, and on the out-breath sent them the most loving wishes I could think of. Then I shut down my consciousness. The last thing I remember before my eyes closed was looking up at the flickering shadows on the ceiling and thinking how like my old front bedroom in Chadwin Road it seemed, at Christmas or if I was poorly when Mum would light a coal fire in the bedroom grate. Happy, safe, contented moments dropping into sleep under the friendly shapes playing above me. There was a soft click, like my mother closing the sitting-room door below.

I must have had a dreamless sleep. I was awakened by the phone ringing. Somewhere in a deep tunnel, awareness stirred. My hand automatically reached for the mask of the oxygen tank, placed strategically by my bed to start the day with happy hormones. My hand met no resistance. I suddenly had no idea where I was. I opened my eyes to see blackness. As they adjusted to the threads of light perforating the gaps in the heavy, drawn curtains I made out the room, the shapes of familiar objects. A split second later the whole world of reality flooded into that atomic touch of con-sciousness. How wondrous, I thought. This mere speck contains and projects an entire universe. The phone stopped jangling. Damn, I thought in the silence, I'm still bloody well alive. The telephone bell started again and I managed to stumble to it and lift the receiver. Jimmy Fraser's cheery agent voice greeted me.

'Hellooo. Hellooo there.' His normality seemed unworldly. 'Have a surprise for you, are ye sitting down?'

'I guess.' I slumped on to the long-suffering polar bear's head.

'Fellini's sent to London for the most decadent young actors we've got. He wants you to go to Rome. Can ye travel today? I believe James Fox is going too. D'you fancy a trip to Rome? It's first class.'

Later that day I heard Jean was in London with her new friend. That put my back up. I felt as though someone had peed through my letter box and was knocking to find out how far it had gone up the passage. I rang Celia Hammond, a model I knew Jean admired, then went to Rome and clinched the job. While there I bought Ken Scott's newest silk evening gown for Celia to wear as my date for the Royal Première of *Madding Crowd* at the Marble Arch Odeon.

As I had made a hash of my suicide attempt, and it was on the cards I would, subject to deal, be working with Europe's most exciting director, I knew I would have to clean up my act. Fellini had been taken with me and I had fallen head over heels for him. The driver, one of the great Federico's entourage, Eaolo, who looked more like a Mafia hit-man than an Italian teamster, told me I had the job when he drove me back to the Leonardo da Vinci airport to catch my flight home.

'Theees other,' (he meant Fox) 'hee too much *Inglese*, too gentleman for Federico, you, 'ee like, *decadente*, yes?'

I was happy to hear the news, although I secretly begged to differ. I could understand the Italian maestro being taken by my dyed hair, dark roots and chest ornamented with enough odds and ends to deck a Christmas tree but, in my opinion, James merely concealed his decadence, played against it, whereas I wore mine like a label.

Fellini and I swapped stories. I told him how Antonioni had let me down by choosing to pay both David Hemmings and myself rather than have me play the role he'd written with me in mind. I gambled on Fellini having more balls than his contemporary. I was right. Later, during shooting, Fellini would delight in telling me stories of how he'd come upon Antonioni at the barber's shop.

'He ask me 'ow is your shooting, Federico? I explain 'im it's a good, it's a very good. But theese actor, this *francobollo*, 'ee is incredible. I think this artist's a *genio. Fine del mondo*.'

*

Première Royal with Celia Hammond.

Whilst awaiting the call from Rome for costume and make-up tests, I returned to Los Angeles to re-dub *Blue* a third time. Robert Evans, who had suggested I speak with a Texan dialect in the first place, now thought it out of place: as everyone else had spoken their Bronx, Midwest, California or normal accents, I stuck out like Brighton Pier. A nice Gregory Peck-vocal-type had been hired to re-voice me, which, of course, couldn't be done contractually; hence my visit.

I met a girl in Hollywood at a typical stoned gathering with gate crashers smelling the fumes emitting from the windows and wandering in off the street. During the first rush of good grass everything and everybody can appear to be sprinkled with gold-dust, although I wasn't sure if it was a boy or a girl at first: the head was androgynous, with hair cut short like an early Buñuel heroine. Until I saw the legs I thought perhaps my lack of confidence was leading me into AC/DC territory.

During my post-syncing at Paramount, however, I heard that my chum with principal boy legs had been committed to Camarillo, a mental asylum near Los Angeles, with a condition diagnosed as chronic paranoid schizophrenia. I went to visit her. During the bizarre encounter, locked in a padded cell together, we exchanged shirts. It was no robbery: her silk long-sleeved striped T-shirt became an instant fave rave. When I finally went to Rome to meet the *costumista* who turned out to be the one and only Piero Tosi – a costume designer to equal the great Hollywood wardrobe artists of the Thirties and Forties – I arrived at the Hotel Raphael carrying only my passport and a handful of lire and wearing a pair of Levi's and the striped T-shirt I'd acquired in Camarillo.

It felt out of keeping checking in alone to a place where I'd stayed with Jean. Caught between the bitter taste of the present and the glow of the past, I didn't notice the other travellers at the front desk. I picked up my key and walked over to the lift. The clanky metal doors, at odds with the seasoned features of the place, had started to close when a man and a woman squeezed in. I've always been conscious of an erotic ambience in lifts, but until this occasion my views were purely theoretical. The woman, dressed completely in black save for a Persian blue turquoise brooch, was openly giving me what we call in the East End the glad eye. Her glance wasn't offensive but I felt that her husband or companion couldn't have been unaware of the mutual appreciation that was going down. She was stunning. She could have been any age between thirty-five and forty-five, her looks falling between gorgeous and handsome, her dark beauty not out of place around a gypsy fire. The lift moved upwards with arthritic lack of confidence as her huge burnt-toffee eyes levelled into mine.

'Where 'ave you come from?' she asked with a smoky, Portuguese accent.

'Me? I, I've just flown in from London.'

'You look,' she said, smiling a provocative smile as her eyes rested on my tight jeans, the top button left unbuttoned in what I thought of as my own cavalier style, 'from another planet.'

I couldn't think of anything to say to that, so I grinned. She smiled back encouragingly, inviting conversation.

'Where do you come from?' I pushed forth finally.

'From Brazil. Where else?'

Where else, indeed. Brazil, a place of my dreams, hot, sultry, loose-limbed. Life lived in the nowness. I had never met a Brazilian but I knew now why I'd always been wary of going: I was scared I wouldn't have the will to come back.

The lift made it to the third floor where the man got out alone. The mouth grinned – the unmade-up lips were the shade of *latte macchiato*. It took me a second to put it all together; she was unescorted. My face must have gone through the gamut of emotions film actors hope will happen in a close-up, but rarely does. She watched me floundering towards the full implications, inwardly laughing at the changes my Anglo-Saxon reserve was experiencing. The lift stopped and opened. She walked out, paused, twisted her head and looked over her shoulder. She didn't speak, but the words in her eyes sorted the men from the boys. I leapt through the closing doors, my shoes landing with a thump as she moved ahead of me. I followed, mesmerised by the relaxed swing of her hips which hadn't been run-of-the-mill standing still. There was a moment when gumption went out the window and I thought perhaps I had misread the whole scenario. I was reassuring myself – girls only sashay that way if they want men to come on – when she stepped a little to the right allowing me to draw level with her. As I did she draped her arm lightly around my waist. When we stopped in front of her room she slid her hand over my buttock in the way one caresses a young horse. She sighed. I shivered.

'*Vem cá, meu nego.*'

'What does that mean?' I asked hoarsely, my throat momentarily dehydrated.

'All manner of things,' she replied. 'I'm inviting you to draw deep. If you don't, I will do it for you.'

I made it into the room. I was supposed to meet up with Tosi that afternoon but he should understand: he was a Florentine. The shutters were drawn, closing out the midday heat; only the white linen on the wide bed glowed in the near-dark. Slumping on to it, I waited, uncertain of the next move. She stood by the shuttered window, the slope of her back in profile to me. Hot and slow . . . the phrase of my initiator, Nurse Grace, came into my head; I tried to breath deep, low. The lady in black was opening the shutter a fraction, re-hinging it a notch, allowing a shaft of white sunlight to fall across the bed. The stripes of my T-shirt, turquoise and magenta, were suddenly highlighted. She turned, undid her heavy brooch.

Years before when Mike and I still shared the flat in Ebury Street I'd finally met the smudger who took the saucy photos using our pad as a backdrop. Ron was a homely-looking fella, who, like a lot of guys, had taken up photography in the Sixties as a way of meeting glamorous girls. I'd offered him a drink and while his model took off her clothes and added lip gloss to her nipples, I drew him out on his favourite fixation: the quest for the perfect breasts.

'It's big boobs that do it for most fellas. That only means they were taken off the breast too early. I'm not talking about that, son, I'm talking about the discriminating, non-judgemental appreciation of the female form.'

'I'm a leg man, Ron – breasts don't move me how they're supposed to.'

'I know, son, I know, but that's only because you're uneducated. What you don't know you can't grieve about. I'm gonna take care of that, right now. Yer actual inches have no bearing whatsoever on the outcome. You can have the wide back and nothing up front, and still measure forty-two. It's the small back, see. A big measure with a small back. "Wot's your bra size, then?" I ask. Thirty-two double D, that's the answer I'm waiting for. DD, that's the magic cup size, see. Then I know I'm on to a winner.'

'What does it stand for, DD?' I ask.

'It's a standard bra measure, it stands for . . . '

'Delectable double, I should think,' said Mike Caine coming in with the evening paper.

'You are looking at me, but not thinking of me,' she stated, shaking me out of my reverie. 'Both are wrong.'

'You, you don't want me looking at you?' Then, trying to change the subject, I said, 'What brassière size d'you take?'

'I don't, and you shouldn't be looking at me. After the boy comes with the luggage I will be looking at you. Now, undo some more of the buttons on those funny cowboy pants so he puts the bags down quickly and leaves us alone.'

I did, feeling self-conscious under her assertive glance. The bell-man came in and understood the situation immediately. He pinched my thousand lire tip between two fingers, waving it in a loose-wristed gesture in front of his chest, closing the door discreetly, softly.

'You were going to undress for me, weren't you?' she told me.

'Don't I get any help?'

'You weren't going to help me.'

'No.'

'This is all the help you get, then.' She unwrapped her skirt and dropped it to the floor. Stood there in her court shoes.

'I don't like pants or bras,' she said.

I slipped quickly from the bed and pulled off my Levi's. When I looked up, she was sitting facing me, her knees pulled up to her chest. She smiled and eased out of her blouse. I saw what photographer Ron had meant.

'You have beautiful nipples,' I said.

'So do you.'

'Me!'

'I know lots of women who'd give lots for the nipples you have.'

I tumbled on to the bed beside her, groping, trying without much thought or success to run the show. She put a restraining hand on my chest.

'Wait,' she said. 'You English only love to fuck. We Brazilians only love to make love.'

'I thought . . . '

'Yes, I know, you have all kinds of thoughts about what you would like to do. Lots of miss-thoughts about what women expect.'

'I, I . . . '

'You don't have to be macho with me. You don't have to be anything with me. I already know about you. I see you in the elevator: I see a man too good-looking for a man, a boy with the eyes of a girl. I know you, your problems, know how you feel, like a girl sometimes. You ache like a woman but don't know why. Don't know what to do. What is your name, *meu bem?*'

'Terence, my name is Terence.'

'Ah, Terence. It is a Latin name.'

'I didn't . . . '

'A slave who earned his freedom writing lovely things.'

'Did he?'

'Yes.' She rolled me over on to my chest, lifted up my stomach and eased a pillow under me, running a cool hand down my back over my buttocks. Lace in a breeze. It sent a razor of sensations all the way up to my hair-line.

'"I am a man. Nothing human is alien to me." That is something Terence said.'

'That's heavy.'

'You can explore the woman in you with me, if you like. Feel how it is to accommodate, like a *fêmea*. You can only truly appreciate a woman after you know the woman inside you. It will be you and me, our secret, but you can only release if you give yourself to me. No pretence. Place yourself in my hands – fall, die. Die to the macho in you, when I release you. When you come for me it will be like a girl – passive – drained from you. You can then do what you want with me. Anything. Things you've always wanted to do but haven't had the courage to try, frightened to reveal yourself. There is time and space for anything. Anything, but you have to give to me first. We try, *si?*'

'*Si.*'

27

I didn't report to Tosi until the following day. Fellini wouldn't let me return to London.

'I needa you here, Terencino Francobollo,' the great maestro from Rimini wailed.

'Why dis off back to Londra? You 'ave a mistress that cannot wait, hot for your body? Why you must be a *piccione*, everything is 'ere. This is Roma, the Eternal City. You stay. What you need? Piero buy you clothes. I buy you pasta. *Calma, stai qui.* I get to know you. You getta to know me – *Conosci? Va bene?*' He confirmed his English with Piero, who spoke only Italian and French. Tosi – the wonderful Florentine with a little caste to his eye, who saw, nevertheless, like a painter, more beauty than others, and whose face had a soft-edged smile – nodded agreement.

What Fellini actually meant when he said, 'You get to know me' is 'You get to fall in love with me' which is tantamount to what he demands of his actors. It wasn't hard. I caved in.

'I'll stay in Rome, go native. *Va bene.*' Fellini beamed like a benevolent Cardinal. It was the right decision. I was exhausted. After shopping in Via Frattina and combing shoe shops in Piazza di Spagna for a particular shade of cordovan jodhpur boot that Piero wanted, I returned to the Raphael and crumpled into a siesta in the room above where the man-woman roles had been explored. We had drawn and driven one another to places I certainly had never been before. When the dawn finally came and the bells for morning mass trembled through our room I felt transparent.

'Did I bleed you?' she asked me, examining the blood stains on the sheets.

'I'm feeling no pain,' I said. 'I must have hurt you, though.'

'Yes,' she replied, turning the sensation in her mind. 'You hurt me and made me cry.'

'I'm sorry.'

'No, it's all right. I like, like to feel this passion in you, like a killer, violent. You want to kill me. Sometimes I feel I am going to die, but I want. I'm made to be killed that way, and sometimes when you still, a statue in me, I take – my hand of God draws the essence from you. I keep, keep the perfume inside me as long as possible.'

I left her in the bath: I had placed the last morsel of croissant into her mouth, handed her the cup of Indian ink coffee, had run my hand over the perfect, wet breasts. As I made for the door she called, '*E meu bichinho, mais forte.*'

I knew I should never see her again; knew within a day or two I would wish for nothing else.

'The erotic is different to love,' she had said, 'but it isn't outside love. If you can't find love, come to Brazil. Us *mulheres* of the six bloods can use *homens* like you.'

'I could get used to it, now and again.'

'I know, *meu bichinho*, I . . . know.' She grinned the funny open-mouthed grin. I felt I had known her for ever. I have never seen her again.

My life changed radically in Italy during the shooting of Fellini's fifty-minute master work ('His Confessional' a pundit of the maestro's work entitled the short film). I came to understand more of my physical impotence that came and went: the cause was bedded deep in the emotional centre. Knowing this didn't affect the outcome but did make it easier to live with. I had to re-adjust my image of myself. No longer always ready, I was compelled to be more discriminating. It became a factor of my life, never quite allowing me the freedom of choice I'd had before. The least thing could throw me, and a few scrapes it landed me in, too.

On that level Jean became an unknowing spur to my life. She had made possible my moment in the sun. She was the twin soul I felt completed me and who had brought the essential warmth needed for my years in the golden section. My dark star. I couldn't forget her. Couldn't forgive me. At least when I saw that mutual glow on passing faces I knew what they were experiencing. I dreamed of a recurrence of the alchemy that would embolden my leaden life, yet slowly but surely came to the realisation that there were more factors than my own longing at play here. A sadness settled over me as I resigned myself to a life a little in the shadow.

I didn't become morbid; I grinned and bore it like the cockney sparrows that chirped saltily through the Blitz. In truth, I felt like a crab without a shell, but I covered up with the finery of the day and put my energy into my work. It's not bad for an artist, sadness. That's what I told myself in the mornings when I woke up smarting.

The fear I carried with me into every film evaporated during my coming of age with Federico Fellini. It wasn't a large, sombre, cloud-like fear as one experiences in bad dreams, but a sharp, pincer-type fear that reaches out as the cameras roll; the cutting possibility of not being able to deliver all the ideas at the given moment. That moving moment when the film is running through at twenty-four frames a second is fast, but the fear is faster. I'd lived with it as a performer ever since the dreadful time I'd tripped out in front of the footlights at the East Ham Town Hall in Somerset Maugham's *The Sacred Flame* and discovered how wrong it could all go. Performers don't discuss this feeling often: it's part superstition, part belief that even airing their fears will add to them. I thought I'd found a way to live with mine, convinced myself in a masochistic fashion I needed the sensations as a jump start to get in there. Although I didn't actually throw up in the wings before going on, like some I'd worked with, I often came close, and this condition hadn't improved with my entry into screen acting. The first day of shooting I would invariably wake with an ache in my head as though a metal plate had been inserted during the night; it would remain with me until the job was over. I was amazed by some things that Joanne O'Neal, first wife of Ryan and mother of Tatum, told me about Elvis who had experienced the same fear. We agreed on one point, the King and I: it was common to introverts, a barrier that shy people obsessed with performing have to go through. We also shared the view that it was breeching this obstacle that separated us from the extrovert artist to whom it comes naturally to show off, but then we were biased. Joanne told me Elvis would sometimes shake for hours after a performance, 'turning himself back in'.

I'd taken a chance when I confessed to having been fired by Antonioni on *Blow Up*. Fellini had countered by confessing why he was casting the central role so late in the day.

During a visit to London he had been taken to lunch in a

The great Federico.

restaurant club near Albemarle Street frequented by theatrical people: Peter O'Toole happened to be lunching there also. Being an admirer of the Italian film-maker and seeking an original but memorable way to catch the maestro's eye, O'Toole had proceeded to the kitchen where he had charmed the staff into letting him borrow a waiter's jerkin. O'Toole had apparently downed a few before lunch and was on his way to Fellini's table with a napkin over one arm and the director's order of lobster bisque in his hand when he stumbled and laid the hot soup over an innocent fellow-luncher's shoulders. Fellini's all-seeing eyes missed nothing of this charade and he was touched by O'Toole's inebriated efforts as he apologised and tried to make amends by attempting to wipe the bisque from the bystander with 'white frail hands'. The accident stuck in Fellini's mind along with O'Toole's explosive declarations of admiration and desire to work on something together.

When a collaboration was suggested between Fellini, Orson Welles and Luis Buñuel to film a distinguished trio of Edgar Allan Poe short stories, the maestro accepted the offer, the fee and the tale entitled 'Never Bet the Devil Your Head'. He recalled the lobster bisque incident and transposed Poe's original to screenplay form in which the central figure, Toby Dammit (who is always betting his head with the Devil), is a great, but washed-up, classical actor enticed to Rome to star in a Western financed by the Catholic Church with the promise of a Ferrari sports car as a bonus. Fellini then called O'Toole. The actor, by all accounts, was thrilled and accepted. Sometime later, however, Fellini was told by the French production conglomerate he wouldn't be working in tandem with Buñuel and Welles but they were holding him to his deal. Fellini again called the actor and checked his intention and availability.

'Darling, I'm delighted,' O'Toole replied.

Fellini finished his adaptation with screenwriter Zapponi and sent a copy to the actor. A few nights later Fellini's phone rang. It was O'Toole.

'Darling, I'm sorry. I'm stupid. I'm a sod. You're gonna hate me. You're right. I can't do your film. Goodbye.'

'This is how we met, Terencino – *buona fortuna, si?*'

Fellini related this tale to me in that prince of restaurants, El Toula, leaning across our corner table and grasping my cheek between his fingers. 'Not *una problema per il mio Terencino* to play this Tobee, eh? You are a *leone*, a lion. Fearless.'

So. I was aware I was his second choice, a stop gap. It didn't matter. He was the best. He'd brought me to Rome. Kept me here. Took me everywhere with him. I was to become a Fellini actor: a small carpet few English actors had stood on. I found myself waking up in the mornings, giggling.

When I asked a burly Roman electrician who always crewed on Fellini's movies why he liked to work with the maestro so much, he said, '*Non è lavoro*, Signor Terence. *Vacanza*.' It was to be a holiday for me, too, a Roman holiday, the kind I enjoyed most, involved in good work.

Three days before principal shooting began a young woman arrived at the Raphael: she introduced herself as Patrizia, an Italian-speaking Chilean interpreter sent by Fellini. Although she was attractive and bright as a button I felt a bit deflated, realising that Fellini had sought to place someone between himself and me. A lot of the charm of our rapport came from his attempts at English, mine at Italian.

'But we speak fine together. I understand him all right,' I said rather sulkily.

'Listen, he has a mass of stuff to do,' Patrizia pointed out. 'You can't imagine. He doesn't want you to become lonely. Besides, he's lined up some interesting press for you to see and Italian journalists rarely speak English.'

So P. Norelli Bachelet and I did our first interview together. As I recall, it was run-of-the-mill fare, although it struck me that Italians put great store by which and how many women men slept with. During this first press grilling I parried some of the more intimate questions (it does not measure twelve inches) with my new belief that the world was not as fragmented as I'd previously assumed, the core of humanity being inextricably connected. The journalist was oblivious to this, but Patrizia who was translating and therefore party to the exchange became enthused, interjecting comments and questions regarding what literature I'd read and who I'd studied with. I was unfamiliar with most of the names and titles she spoke of, but it was a comical three-way conversation with the journalist picking up the excitement, not understanding a word and leaning forward, pencil poised, saying '*Cosa?*' every few minutes, as though we were discussing some ancient system of multiple orgasm from which he was excluded. Immediately the official appointment ended Patrizia took me off to the Café Greco where she proceeded to open the door into the mansion of self-realisation.

My first shooting day on the film took place in the Aeroporto di Roma. Waiting inside my trailer by International Arrivals, wearing the bizarre make-up that Fellini had devised and sporting the wardrobe that Piero Tosi had chosen (to make me look like a cross between Edgar Allan Poe and Chuck Berry), I was frightened to go out.

Finally came the timid tap on my wagon door and a young assistant escorted me into the building proper. A section of the arrival hall, thick with arriving passengers and welcoming friends, had been dressed by Fellini with his own artists, extras and a series of life-size black and white photographic cut-outs. These had been distributed throughout the airport and could be seen leaning against walls or lying asleep on seats. Curious tourists pausing to observe the goings on would be spotted by Fellini and coralled by charming helpers to feature in the action. I was led to the centre of this mayhem, my bell from Haight-Ashbury – Fellini had insisted I wear it – tinkling like that on a goat brought to slaughter. Peppino Rotundo, Fellini's director of photography, had arranged a host of small lights around the chalk mark that I was guided to, each one fixed to the top of a metal stand. The spot had become a surreal forest. I was duly placed on my mark. It took me a moment to take in the fact that we were about to turn over. '*Stan campana!*' someone yelled. I held up my hand, waited until I caught Fellini's eye, then beckoned him to me. He weaved his way gracefully through the Indian grass of light stands, the expression on his face disconcerted – a puppeteer unexpectedly summoned by one of his creations.

'*Si, Terencino, dimmi, dimmi tutto.*'

'*Scusa* me, maestro. I'm an English actor. I'm here in Rome to make my first Italian film with the great Federico Fellini. This is my first day, first shot. I can't let this moment go by without a word of direction.'

Fellini didn't miss a beat. He leaned his mouth seductively close to my ear; the aroma of hair lotion and eau-de-Cologne wafted across my nostrils.

'This night, last night, you was at a party. Big party, but really an h'orgy. You come late after your show. You drunk. You drink more, anything, but much whisky, lotta whisky. Also smoke hashish, marijuana, sniff cocaine and fuck, much fucking all night. Big woman with big breasts, you fucking her, somebody come fuck you. All night like this. This morning a *macchina* come take you to airport, put you on plane to Rome. But before you get on airplane your chauffeur drop a big tab of LSD into your mouth. Now you here.'

It was the last time I asked my director for direction.

My head was feeling better but the pains in my chest I had had since *Blue* intensified. One evening, coming home from work, gripped in a tortuous Roman traffic jam, I was in considerable physical discomfort. Patrizia, accompanying me in the back seat said, 'You have an ulcer.'

'I don't think so,' I replied. 'It's a 'er, little problem of the heart.'

'No,' she said, 'it's more than that now. It's an ulcer or an ulcerous condition.'

I was taken aback by the air of certainty in her voice and didn't respond.

'It's common in the sign of Cancer, an archetypal weakness. Digestive tract – like the crab, soft underbelly.'

'I'm not a Cancerian. I'm a Leo.' My preoccupation with the pain made my remark sound weedy.

'No, Cancerian. Perhaps born at midday so you experience that full-sun Leonine feeling, but definitely Cancer. Libra rising, I should think. See it across the eyes.'

'How d'you know all this?'

'I'm not only an interpreter. That's a job Fellini created to give me a little pocket money. I'm actually an astrologer – his astrologer, amongst others.'

'But I know I'm a Leo. In Gypsy Petulengro's . . . '

'Look, I don't want to argue. You're in pain. The life you are leading obviously doesn't suit your metabolism, otherwise it wouldn't be complaining. A lot of Cancerians lead a fuller life as vegetarians. I suggest you stop eating meat and fish for a trial period of say, three months. You may feel better. If you don't, what's lost? Any major change in diet is good for the body. You may like it. Why don't you get in touch with your mother? Try and find out what time you were born. A lot of women don't remember. They black it out, too hot a subject. Be prepared to trick her into

Fellini showing us how.

recalling it. Ask, did you have breakfast before the water broke? Was it after dark? When did you arrive at the hospital? That sort of thing.'

I always enjoyed calling home, hearing my mum's cheery voice, listening to the familiar sounds in the background. Sometimes it was the only thing that kept me going on miserable faraway locations.

'Tom,' she'd say, 'your son wants a word with you.'

I'd hear Dad shuffle to the phone, 'Here's your father, have a little chat with him.'

She would put my dad on although he hated telephones, always sounding adrift, uncomfortable, unable to see the person he was talking to. Mum was the opposite – she'd chat away for hours as though you were sitting across from her, completely forgetting the shillings totting up.

'Mum,' I said. 'Do you by any chance remember what time of day I was born?'

'One o'clock,' she said immediately, 'they were playing "Worker's Playtime" on the wireless.'

Patrizia's intuition had been correct. Converted to Greenwich Mean Time and taking into account the curious trio of planets falling on the same degree in Cancer, she calculated my rising sign, thought, in her circles, to denote the inner nature. Mine was cast in Libra, bringing to my hard, tenacious exterior a light, airy, albeit dithery centre. We would sit in my dressing-room, I memorising the long, often poetic dialogue of Toby Dammit, she going over the chart with her ephemeris and slide rule. I was astonished by the finished chart, so vastly different from my early weekly delvings into *Woman's Own* and *Woman*, and not too delighted to discover I wasn't after all like my gregarious, optimistic, leonine mother but closer to the brooding, contemplative, stoic nature of my dad. However, too many characteristics, my own private property, were so clearly foretold on the closely typed pages that I couldn't shrug off the aspects that were less pleasing to me. It wasn't a document that forecast the future. Didn't even attempt to. It laid out the position the heavens were in, relative to me, a matrix frozen at the moment of my birth. I can't pretend I understood all of Patrizia's efforts on my behalf, but the idea that I was intimately connected to something cosmic, had had since birth an array of characteristics like a surgeon's tool-kit with which to learn and master my own destiny, gave me heart at a time when I sorely needed it.

Patrizia often referred to a chum of hers: quoting comments, relating her prowess at yoga and breathing, or describing mouth-watering dishes eaten at her house. Her friend, La Marchesa Vanda Passigli Scaravelli, was extremely close to a venerable gentleman named Jiddu Krishnamurti: Krishnaji or K. to his close associates. Krishnamurti had been discovered when only a teenager by a society known as the Theosophical Society. (Krishnamurti was later to tell me that as a child he had been gormless, without a thought in his head.) Nonetheless, he was taken up by the society who declared that he would become the modern Christ. Krishnamurti was brought to England where they tried unsuccessfully to educate him.

'I only had two interests, clothes and cars,' he said in explanation of this period of his life. In 1923 Krishnaji, then in his late twenties, was taken to the peace and calm of Ojai in California. In Ojai something happened to him which completely changed his life.

'It was as though the ocean was poured into a drop,' he related, in an effort to describe the event. The Theosophical Society declared him the new head of operations. In his acceptance speech of August 1929 at Ommen, Holland, Krishnamurti disbanded the whole order.

'Truth is a pathless land and you cannot approach it by any path whatsoever, by any religion, by any sect . . . ' he told the members. Since then he had travelled the world giving free lectures to anyone who turned up, constantly denying his authority as a saviour or a guru, referring only to himself as the speaker. By the time I was working in Rome he was seventy-three years old.

28

Fellini had written a script, *The Voyage of Mastona*, giving it to me to peruse while we were making *Toby Dammit*. A musician is on a fog-bound plane *en route* to a concert. The tannoy announces that the plane is about to crash when miraculously, the fog clears and a disused military airport is revealed. The plane lands. The frightened, helpless passengers are carted off to a peculiar hotel for the night. Slowly, our hero realises that he has, in fact, died and he is now in a grotesque hinterland, a modern purgatory, from which he cannot escape without a passport. I hadn't read such an inspired script before or since, although Fellini hasn't been able to make this movie.

Patrizia and Vanda arranged for Fellini to meet Krishnamurti to sound out the sage on his view of the after-life. Fellini didn't discuss with me the findings of his talk but he did show me some hair-restorer given to him by Krishnaji. Fellini in turn invited Krishnamurti to see an assemblage of the rushes from *Toby Dammit*. (The Poe story was Fellini's first work for some time and I had the feeling he was using it as a wind-up for his major work, *The Voyage of Mastona*.) According to Patrizia, Krishnamurti had been impressed by the footage. I was invited to Vanda's house for Sunday lunch. Krishnamurti would be there. I was flattered, excited and intrigued.

'What are they like, this Vanda and Krishnamurti?' I kept asking Patrizia. She wouldn't give in to my pesterings.

'When you meet them, you'll see,' was all she would say. 'Don't always try to anticipate everything.'

Sunday arrived. I was driven in Patrizia's minute car to a house on the outskirts of Rome. Patrizia explained that Vanda lived on a farm near Florence where she'd been born, keeping a place in Rome so that Krishnamurti would have somewhere pleasant to stay while he lectured there. Half a dozen other guests had arrived before us. A correspondent from *Time* magazine introduced himself and we chatted a bit. Then I became aware of a small bird-like creature staring at me. As she crossed the floor towards me, however, I noticed her step was unusually purposeful: she appeared grounded in a way I had only come across once before – with my old fencing master, Dragon. On her feet were a pair of rubber flip-flops and I saw that her big toes were splayed widely, almost the same as thumbs. They gripped the sandals as she walked.

'I'm Vanda, nice to see you here,' she said to me. The top of her head reached my chin. The height was misleading; the presence wasn't. The divine eyes that looked up at me from under long lids were so knowing, it was I who felt small.

I grinned, unnerved.

'What are you doing here?' she asked.

'I, er, Patrizia brought me. I was invited.'

'*Si, si*, of course, but it is never an accident somebody finds Krishnaji. What makes you interested in things of this nature?'

'Well, I . . . ' I was about to say I didn't know, but the look was so direct I had the distinct feeling that if I tried to flannel her she would see straight through me.

'I had this girlfriend. She gave me the air.'

'The air? What is this air?'

'She left me. I don't think I'll . . . '

'Probably the best thing that ever happened to you,' snapped Vanda, keeping her eyes locked on to mine. 'Ah,' she said, turning to face the room. 'We have lunch now. We speak again later.'

A man had joined the guests. I'd been facing the only doorway connecting the rest of the bungalow, yet I'd been completely unaware of any entry: he'd appeared like a genie from smoke. I had a moment to observe him as Vanda went over to greet him and there was a hiatus as the other diners wondered how to seat themselves. He wore a raw silk shirt, bottle-green with matching mother of pearl buttons, loose, sand-coloured slacks and a narrow belt which was almost the same shade as the shiny conker-brown slip-ons that encased his narrow feet. Vanda called to me and I found myself seated at the long table opposite the revered gentleman. Krishnamurti didn't speak. Chat was already flowing thick and fast at the other end of the table. He looked at me and smiled as I sat down. I looked into the large, gold eyes which appeared to have infinite depth. He lowered his lids as though to shield himself from the intrusion of my look. I glanced away feeling clumsy.

Mouth-watering food began appearing from Vanda's *cucina*. I'd been having a rough ten days adjusting to the seemingly bland, fleshless diet and was reacting like a Bombay wallah denied curry. The table that Vanda was setting, although vegetarian, was so tasty it didn't cross my mind I was being deprived of anything.

The subject of conversation at the table was a man who had claimed he could walk on water. Apparently, a large glass tank had been erected on a theatre stage and, in front of the packed house, the performer had publicly sank. Krishnamurti was listening. Seeing this, the man from *Time* directed his remarks towards him.

'Do you think he really believed that he could do it? That's the thing that intrigued me.'

Krishnaji pondered. 'He probably did,' he said.

The table fell quiet. The journalist, encouraged by Krishnaji entering the spirit of things added, 'Do you believe there actually are people who can walk on water?'

Again, Krishnamurti considered before framing his answer.

'Well, sir,' he said finally, 'if I answered yes, would you believe me?'

'I would, I would,' assured the foreign correspondent.

'Well, then, yes,' he replied.

This stopped the chat for a bit. In the silence Krishnaji smiled across to me. His thick white hair was brushed neatly across the fine wide forehead. He resumed eating, his attention completely focused on his food. I saw the sleeves of his shirt were clasped at the cuff, and also by a gauntlet button, a size smaller, a few inches above the wrist.

He saw my interest.

'Made at Beale and Inman. Good work, isn't it?'

'It's a nifty shirt,' I said. 'Nice colour. I like dark shirts.'

'Yes,' he said. 'The material comes from India.'

After lunch (the individual pizzas no bigger than the top of a teapot were my favourite), Krishnamurti left the room. A few moments later Vanda introduced me to Alan Naudé, Krishnaji's secretary.

Alan said, 'Krishnaji has asked if you'd like to go for a walk with him.'

'Yes,' I said, 'that would be . . . I'd like to.'

Alan left, no doubt to tell K. his invitation had been accepted.
Vanda asked, 'Are you a vegetarian?'
'I'm giving it a try.' I held up my fingers. 'Ten days today.'
'You should keep it up, make you feel lighter inside.'
'It would be easy if I ate like this every day.'
'Thank you,' said Vanda. 'You should tell Forca in the kitchen.
She does all the work.' I knew this wasn't so, but I said I would.
'Why does it make you lighter, then?' I asked.
'It doesn't make you lighter. It makes you feel lighter.'
'That's what I meant.'
'A diet that is mainly meat clogs the body, prevents the breath
reaching everywhere. There are centres in the body that are only
reached by fine breath; then they vibrate, come to life. Otherwise,
they stay dead – prevent you experiencing life fully.'
'Do you teach breath?' I asked, remembering Dragon's statement
about the rarity of real exponents of breathing.
'I teach piano, yoga and breathing,' she told me.
'Would you teach me breathing?'
'I can only teach breathing with postures, *asanas*.'
'You mean yoga?'
'Yes, the two go together. The yoga that Krishnaji and I do is
not harsh. It is relaxed but precise; it cannot be learned overnight.
If you are in Italy I can teach you.'
'I have to go back to London, but I can come again.'
'If you do, I will teach you.'
'Thank you.'
Vanda shrugged: aristocratic but very Italian.
'You are not unhealthy now, but you're stiff. Blocked. Come
back soon. Start yoga. Learn to breathe properly. It will improve
your life.'
'I could do with that.'
Vanda gripped my arm. The frail hand had a deceptively firm
grip.
'This girl, the one gives you the air, she do you a favour, believe
me. Look into yourself. Make a start while you're young. Plenty of
time to settle down later.'
'Thank you. I'd like to do something, make a fresh start.'
'When you come to Rome, tell Patrizia.'
'OK – and Krishnamurti does this yoga?'
'He does, but don't misunderstand. Yoga is nothing to do with

his teachings. He only started doing yoga when he was fifty. We do it to stay healthy, keep active longer, help body, mind. What he talks of is how you view yourself, the world.'

Guests started to leave, expressing their thanks to Vanda. I detached myself from her, went over to stand near Patrizia.

'He's asked me to go for a walk with him.'

'Who?'

'Krishnamurti.'

'Oh.' Patrizia's brown eyes widened. 'That's an honour.'

K. suddenly appeared. He looked at me and made for the door. I followed. He'd slipped a powder-blue wool shirt over the green one, using it as a sweater. The two colours looked good together – made his complexion glow like amber. He set off at a rate of knots. I expected him to slow down once we cleared the few outlying houses and moved into open country. He didn't. He had the same slightly tilted-back stride as Great Elk, as though his body hung from the sky. Something about the speed of our walk sparked me into a talkative frame of mind and for some reason I began telling him about my father's brother, Bob, who had recently undergone open-heart surgery – a quadruple by-pass. I'd visited him in the Whitechapel Road hospital where he'd shown me his scars and detailed the moment when his surgeon had transferred him from the heart machine back on to his own replenished organ. There was a hiatus when the mechanism was withdrawn but before his heart started to beat. He'd stared death in the face. The surgeon had shouted, 'Breathe, man, breathe!' He'd taken a huge gulp of air and everything had started to pump. Krishnamurti didn't comment. I continued telling him how I'd experimented with hallucinogenics, how I thought they made me view things differently. I couldn't get the words out fast enough. I imagined this was how Catholics behaved at confessional – except the man I was with was no priest.

He stopped abruptly. I halted beside him. He put his hand on my arm and nodded towards a tree standing alone in the near distance.

'Look at the tree,' he said.

I looked: no majesty there. The tree wasn't even big or leafy but a scruffy young sapling having a hard time making it on dry, debris-strewn landscape. I kept looking. He looked too. Then he turned back to me. I turned to him. He smiled. I smiled back. He

Krishnamurti around the time of the Ommen speech.

continued to walk. I joined him and started talking where I'd left off. After about a mile we reached what I assumed was the half-way mark. He turned and started back in the direction we'd come with me still rapping away, thirteen to the dozen. At a certain point he paused and turned to me, placing his hand on my arm. He looked up into the sky.

'Look at the clouds,' he said. I did. There were clouds, no unusual colours, no spectacular sunset, too early. Only clouds. We looked. He turned his face towards mine, smiled a wonderfully kind smile. I grinned back. We continued on. He walked, I talked and walked. When we arrived back at the house I said I'd heard he'd given Fellini some lotion which encouraged hair growth.

'Would you like some?' he offered.

'Well, my dad, he has nice hair, but it's going thin.'

'I'll fetch you some.' He disappeared, returning a few moments later with a small square bottle filled with black liquid. He handed it to me.

'It's not what it says,' he commented, seeing me read the label. 'I put some in a different bottle.'

'Oh, thanks. Does it work?'

He looked at me without expression. 'Yes,' he said.

I realised I'd inadvertently accused him of lying. 'I, er . . . '

'They have cures for lots of things in India,' he said with a smile. 'It comes from India.'

'Can you imagine how it would sell in America? They spend a fortune trying to grow hair,' I said, still looking at the liquorice-coloured potion.

'In America they like to spend money on things that don't work,' he said with a serious face. It was curious to converse with someone who only stated facts. He smiled: I extended my hand, but he stepped forward and placed his arms around my chest and held me to him. For a moment his heart beat against mine. Then he was gone. I stood in the middle of the room, the silkiness of his presence still around me. I felt near to tears, but didn't know why.

On the way back to the Raphael, Patrizia asked me what had occurred during the walk.

'I talked mostly. He only spoke twice: asked me to look at a tree and the clouds.'

Patrizia didn't comment. I had the distinct feeling I'd blown it.

Krishnamurti in Chicago, 1926.

Shortly before the end of my contract, I attended the final lecture given in Rome that visit. Krishnamurti had appeared without warning: one second the podium was bare, the next he was standing behind it – the genie again. There was a moment while the audience, realising he was there, settled in anticipation. Then the clarity of his voice encompassed all present, like the brilliance of a diamond.

'I wonder what you expect of me?' he asked. Of course, I couldn't understand a word. He didn't use any words I failed to comprehend but only when he drew together the threads of what he'd been saying for forty minutes and looked out at us in optimistic expectation did I realise the lecture was over. From the expression on his face I knew he'd arrived at a conclusion that had sailed completely over my head. There was one phrase that kept returning to my mind, although it made no sense to me. I would find myself saying it over to myself, even at times when I should have been thinking of other things. I clung to it as though it was a rope attached to the heavens hanging down to earth.

'When the eagle flies it leaves no mark.'

29

Again it was hard being in London. The pavements I'd stepped as though I'd owned them were now a bitter matrix of memories. Three years: few years in the span of things, but it seemed as though life had begun when they started, ended when they finished.

I had always secretly prided myself on my ability to absorb pain: to have teeth filled without shots, or overcome difficulties without bleating. Nowadays, with emotions exposed to the bone my galvanised iron overcoat was taking water – I was suffering in proportion to my strength. The affair with the limping American was over. Jean was back in town on the arm of a writer who'd scribed a sexually ambivalent play reputedly drawn from his own experiences. I stopped going out. Friends and acquaintances didn't seem able to wait to relish me with details. I retreated into my chambers like a badger to his sett in winter; some days I lit my fire in the morning and stayed close to it all day. By night unable to sleep, I would put on old gear and roam the streets, taking late buses to the East End to buy cups of tea at the stalls I'd frequented as a youth. Having schizophrenic chats with myself, falling asleep fully dressed on the sofa in the early hours: only dressing properly on Sundays to attend my parents' lunch. Although I kept up appearances for my folks and the neighbours, Mum wasn't taken in. When I kissed her hello she would prolong the hug, pressing her face to my chest.

'Oh, Terry,' she would murmur. 'Oh, son.'

Outwardly, I would smile; in my head I would say: I won't let you down, Mum, I'll get myself together. May take a bit of time this time.

Finally, unable to break the bleakness of my existence and having heard someplace that fresh impressions are a source of energy, I had a last lunch with the family before returning to the Eternal City. It was three months to the day since I had last eaten meat.

I'd done it, kept the promise I'd made to myself. On the phone to Mum I requested my favourite leg of lamb. Ethel was delighted: she'd believed I was going to die if I kept up my regime much longer. The lunch was all I could have hoped for: incomparably cooked – no *haute cuisine* pink tints and drops of blood in this joint – with plenty of mint sauce and tatters squeezed around the joint in the baking dish to brown off. I felt back in the fold sitting in the straight-back chair I'd grown up with, round the square, loose-leaf, oak table, bolstered by a family who loved and appreciated me. The eldest son, in the oriental sense of the word.

Later, I gave my brother Chris a lift back to the West End. He was on the loose. I took up his invitation for supper at the Trat on the corner of Romilly Street. As I perused their extensive menu, I recalled the uncomfortable sensation I'd experienced while chewing the muscles of lamb. I realised that I didn't have to rush headlong into eating meat again and ordered a fragrant pasta as though to the vegan born.

I spent days designing a Valentine's card, actually teaching myself calligraphy with my right hand. It was a book, when finished, with rhyming couplets on every page. I delivered the tome myself after dark on the 13th, squeezing it through into the letter box of Jean's house on Montpelier Place.

'God, Stamp, you can be as thick as two planks, sometimes,' Julie Driscoll once exclaimed. Nowadays I think I'm inclined to agree. No Valentine cards fell through my letter box that year. I sold my Roller and fled to Rome.

En route to my first lesson in hollow-limbed *asanas* with Vanda, I detoured to a crafty bar near the Pantheon where, by some alchemy, they'd managed to capture the aroma of roasting beans within the cup. I was nervous, I drank three. I needn't have been. Vanda proved to be a yoga teacher in a million and I learned much else, as well. For, watching her run her house, deal with tradesmen and answer the phone whilst simultaneously demonstrating a shin-to-forehead stretch, or feed her cat a sample of lunch-time spaghetti without once losing the thread of what she was teaching, I began to appreciate beauty in quite a different way.

Brother Chris came to visit me in Italy, envious of the fact that I'd met and been befriended by Fellini. I'd promised to introduce him if he made the jaunt to Rome. Chris showed and so did the maestro – they got on like a house on fire.

The afternoon after the introductory lunch, directed by Fellini at his favourite pasta joint, Chris and I were wandering along Via Frattina, pretending to window shop, eyeing the Italian eyefuls – mouthfuls, as my sib succinctly put it – and suppin' up the ambience in general. Coming towards us through the bustling Friday shoppers I caught sight of Piero Tosi. He appeared to have a friend on each arm: on his right a man taller than Piero, with a forehead so intelligent it went right over his head but, on his left, a woman I hadn't set eyes on for years. I recognised her instantly and my knees went. Piero saw me, grinned and gathered pace. I leaned against the doorway of a shop for support.

I'd first seen Silvana Mangano in *Picture Post*, so alluring and mysterious that I'd searched London for a showing of *Bitter Rice*, eventually stealing away from Plaistow on a 15 bus which dropped me outside the oddly-shaped cinema screening X-certificate continental imports. She was breathtaking in that film and only seventeen at the time. Grown men in the audience groaned when she first appeared and gasped when she revealed unshaved hair under her arms. In deepest Plaistow she remained unknown, which made her my exclusive property. I travelled anywhere to catch the movies she starred in, with a devotion that would have quelled the priests of Diana. By the time I set eyes on her in the flesh she was maturing like the best of the wine. It was hard to tell from that first impression that she had four children and a grandchild.

'*Caro*, Terence,' Tosi said, kissing me affectionately on the cheek and launching into French. He and I had lots to share – wanted so much to chat – that Tosi often overlooked the fact that language was one of the things we didn't have in common. Often, in his enthusiasm to communicate and acknowledging I wasn't Italian, he spoke the only foreign language he knew – French. It was always disconcerting because, with the warmth and support of the people, my Italian had blossomed, whereas I'd made little progress in the more critical atmosphere of France. Anyway, Piero Tosi was banging away in French, understood by both his companions, if not by me. Chris was staring, a horsy grin spreading across his face. In the Stamp face argot it meant: I don't understand nuffink, but I like it, all the same. Across the years and friendly mayhem, Silvana and I touched base.

There are two explanations I've heard regarding the intense familiarity strangers often feel at first encounters: the first involves the theory of reincarnation, where two people who have been together in a past life come together in this one; the other, explained to me by an Ajmer mystic, relates to the journey of the soul. The old gentleman believed that the soul passes through several spheres before reaching the material plane and drawing to itself a physical body and individuality. As the price for such identity must be death, a second journey, to shed those attributes, is required. During the voyage out and in, souls pass like space ships between ports: there are often exchanges. The old Sufi said the empathy that strangers often experienced stemmed from these common exchanges. It struck me as a satisfactory explanation that held great romance. It certainly made sense of the mutual frisson that Silvana and I felt at our first meeting, to say nothing of the devotion I had felt towards her since the time I'd first glimpsed her image.

Silvana came closer to me and placed her hand on my arm. The gesture would have passed for mundane in a country where touch is considered normal, although I experienced the simple contact as though a long-missed comfort were being administered. Much later, when we recalled our memories of this initial meeting, Silvana confessed the gesture was completely out of character for her, as she wasn't usually demonstrative or familiar.

'It was as though my hand moved by itself,' she said. When the hand made contact, she heard herself saying to Tosi and Roberto, her second friend, 'He would be wonderful for the stranger in Pier Paolo's film.'

'Pier Paolo who?' Chris had asked.

'Pasolini,' Silvana told him.

Back at the Raphael where Chris and I were holed up, I kept trying to put into words what it meant for me to finally meet La Mangano face to face. Chris was barely interested. He was enthused by the possibility of my working with Pasolini, whose films I wasn't familiar with, but on whom Chris had encyclopaedic detail.

'*Accattone, Mamma Roma, Oedipus Rex* – to name a few,' he said, gulping down a cup of the hotel's tea. I recalled how Shrimpton had always liked the tea at the Raphael in spite of it being made with bags. I inspected the label hanging by a string from the pot. Yeah, the printed elephant she'd taken to was still there.

'I mean, man, he's a gay Marxist poet/screenwriter/film-maker who's a Roman Catholic and loves his mother.'

'Sounds like a complicated fella to me.'

'Course, but it makes for great movies. You should look at some, in case he wants you.'

'A gay Catholic Marxist? You sure?'

'Listen, Tel, it's Italy. Where else do you have a Fascist Party, a Communist Party and a Religious Party trying to run the show? All official.' Chris paused, considering the ramifications. Pouring himself another cuppa he added, 'You should work more here. It might broaden your outlook.'

'It already has.'

'Yeah. You could get into a lot of trouble here. Everyone is so tasty. To say nothing of the grub. How do you stay trim?'

'I abstain . . . from the pasta. I limit myself to one dish a day. You know the Romans scoff it between the hors d'oeuvres and the main course.'

'Yeah, that's really decadent. I love it.'

'You can say that again. I'm worried about working here a lot, though. Agents in Hollywood say Rome is where white elephants come to die.'

'Well, Clint didn't do too bad out of Spaghetti Westerns, did he?'

'That's true.'

Chris went back to London where he and his partner, Kit Lambert, were launching their new signing, The Crazy World of Arthur Brown, who began his act by setting his head on fire and I began my act with Pasolini and Silvana, playing the role of the stranger in *Theorem*, which almost lived up to my sibling's ideas of decadence.

Here is the story as it was related to me by Pasolini through the producer who spoke English. I recall it vividly because it was the only time that Pasolini told me anything directly apart from the terse direction, 'Open your legs more,' or 'Mile, please,' meaning he wanted me to smile.

A telegram is sent to the house of a wealthy Milanese industrialist announcing the arrival of a house guest from England. The guest duly appears. He makes love to everyone in the household: father, mother, daughter, son and maid, then leaves.

Silvana Mangano with hat.

'This is your part,' Pasolini told me. 'I will need your services for about four weeks.'

'Sounds right up my street,' I said. Services was right. The fee was modest, but a good percentage in participation was offered. As soon as the film became successful, however, Pasolini and his producer, Franco Rossellini, Roberto's nephew, sold the film to a company that had no moral commitment to me: I never saw a lire above my initial fee. Filming in Italy does hold those kinds of hazards even when you have the word of a Catholic Marxist poet and his producer.

I was left to my own devices to bring some credibility to the energetic house guest. When I asked Pasolini about the nature of my character he would only say, with a poetical shrug of his bony shoulders, 'He is a boy.'

I knew the wayward director liked boys, reputedly the rougher the better, but even this gossip didn't furnish me with much to go on. Silvana told me that she and the other artists duly received their lines on the day of shooting but that when she had agreed to play the mother, Pasolini had told her that he saw the guest as having a divine nature, and if a Messiah were here on Earth at the present time the only love a materialistic society such as ours could appreciate would be of a physical nature. So, that was all I had to work with: a boy with a divine nature, obviously able to intuit the secret longings of anyone who came into his life, and endowed with the energy to follow through. It wasn't too far away from our flower-child philosophy of untethered love, but understanding a character is one thing, putting the knowledge into a practical working form is another. The guest had virtually no dialogue. He listened to the members of the household and responded to the given moment. In that sense he was like a character from a silent movie. I started to hone the meaning of a divine nature in much the same way as I'd whittled down the options I'd had as Billy Budd. Pasolini's main concept of religion was Christian, so I figured the prophet he related to was Jesus. As the director's lifestyle and tendencies confined him to a minority group, I thought the advice of Jesus most sympathetic to him would be 'Judge not'. That, I decided, would be my star motivation, the main thought I would keep before me when starting my scenes.

During the first few days of shooting, I noticed that Pasolini kept two cameras on the set: the first manned in the open by

The guest in *Theorem*.

the three-man crew, the other clandestinely operated by Pasolini himself. It didn't take me too long to suss he was trying to grab film on me when I wasn't aware of it. The only way I could fulfil his wishes was to keep myself empty, without any preconceptions at all, to do the whole film the same way I'd played my death scene in *Billy Budd*. That was what I did, playing the part as non-judgementally as I could.

The film was banned by the Church in Italy, which immediately ensured its success elsewhere. Later, they relented and the film broke records in Italian cinemas too. My only worry? What would my mother think when the picture opened in England? It was the first film with frontal nudity and blatant homosexual love-making.

I needn't have worried. After the morning press show at the Curzon to which I invited Mum, she said, 'I didn't really understand it, but it left me with a nice feeling. That copper colour they did your hair didn't look bad, either. What shade they call that?'

In London the scene with me running with a dog received an unexpected laugh. They appreciate such things in Curzon Street.

When I finished shooting I told Mum and Dad they should start looking for a new house. I felt confident I could afford to move them and support the subsequent lifestyle.

'Where do you think we should look?' Mum asked.

'Wherever you like, it's your house. Find something you've dreamed of. Let me know when.'

Tom and Ethel, my mum and dad, had met in the hopfields of Kent. Both families, the Stamps and the Perrotts, had for generations used this annual hop harvest as a working holiday, packing what belongings they needed for the six-week stint into trunks and tea chests and trudging through the early morning to London Bridge Station to board the 'hopping special', or sharing the hire of a lorry with neighbours who picked at the same farm. Both routes passed Blackheath, the open heathland named after victims of the Black Plague who were mass-buried there, and which was, much earlier, thought to be the seat of England. To both my mum and dad the evergreen expanse of heath was the nearest childhood contact they'd had with a natural landscape. Gazing out over the trailboard of the lorry that took them 'down 'opping' and catching a glimpse of the vast common, they felt they were already in the country. They confessed to me they had always looked on Blackheath with a kind of wonder, in awe of families who actually called it home. It didn't come as much of a surprise when they informed me they'd seen a house there that was just the ticket.

The dream home purchased, decorated and furnished, with my folks safely ensconced, I felt free to cast my moorings and set off for the East, my curiosity for things other than showbiz wetted by meeting the exquisite Krishnamurti. Acknowledging I was too coarse, or too dense, to fully appreciate the subjects he spoke of in his lectures, I thought perhaps in India I would meet others who pointed the way from a lower pinnacle, enabling me to ripen a little at a time. Many of the books that I studied warned of leaving things undone when embarking on a quest of this nature. Obligations unsettled, ambitions unfulfilled often delayed the voyager, forcing him to back-track and unravel the knots he'd left behind. As I started the emotional preparations and mental unpacking for the journey East, the thought of my father kept coming up. I had to face the fact that there was an awkwardness between us. I'd always felt that I was my mother's son – brother Christopher Thomas, Dad's favourite. Although I'd spent most of my life trying to please him, seeking his approval, on a one-to-one level there was still something unresolved. I'm sure in his way he was as proud of me as Ethel, but he didn't show it and I wasn't sure. I tried to think if there was anything I could do before I set off. Perhaps I couldn't heal the rift: maybe it wasn't open to healing, but I could try. Lay a bridgehead, perhaps.

I'd often stayed with Silvana and her husband Dino de Laurentiis during the filming of *Theorem* and witnessed the affectionate chaos when Dino returned home on a Friday evening. Everyone greeted him with '*Ciao*,' but Federico, the only son, would rise from the sofa where he'd been sitting with his mother, go to his father and kiss him on the cheek. The first time I saw this I was taken aback. Becoming aware of my response, I saw how typically English and undemonstrative I was: for an Italian it was the most natural thing in the world for a son to kiss his father. I realised I had never kissed my dad, never even thought about it. Surely, I was the unnatural one.

On my next visit home, as soon as my dad opened the front door, I grasped his shoulders the way I'd seen Freddy do it and kissed him on the forehead. He didn't even wince and I felt showered with flowers.

I left London on one of those rare sunny days that make you wonder why you're leaving. As I sat in the black radio cab that had picked me up at the north gate of Albany, my neighbours at Apple were giving what proved to be their last concert from the roof of 3 Savile Row. Number 3. Odd number for the headquarters of a quartet, I mused, as the cabbie and I enjoyed 'Don't Let Me Down' live.

The door of the jet thudded closed. I buckled up.

'Glass of champagne before take-off, sir?' asked a smiling stewardess with eye-catching calves.

'No thank you,' I replied.

It felt out of keeping, alcohol, at the start of my first trip East. I segued into *The Razor's Edge*. Would Larry have accepted? Probably. He didn't make waves, old Larry, but then he was only a figment of Somerset Maugham's imagination. Or was he? He was as real to me as the other boyhood heroes in whose steps I'd tried to follow, maybe more. Yep, in a sense movies had got me into the mess I found myself in. Perhaps movies would pull me out of it.

'India. That's where you should go, young man,' the defrocked priest had advised Ty Powers's Larry in the movie: he'd even abandoned Gene Tierney to follow his quest.

'Just call me angel of the morning, angel. Touch my cheek before you leave me.'

Piped musak on jet carriers. What next?

'In a few moments we shall be making our take-off for Santa Cruz Airport, Bombay. Extinguish all cigarettes, please.'

Jim, the gardener of seedless purple, had bought the farm – killed in a collision with a lone, unchartered balloonist.

The era over almost before it started. Our era. The gold of the section fading fast.

And the dark star? Still there: always present, seldom noticed, like the taste in my mouth.

Sometimes, driving aimlessly, even asleep in dream, I find myself taking the turn off Sunset Boulevard heading south on San Diego freeway, towards LA Airport, on my way to meet the flight that brought her to me. With a start, I realise it's only a play of shadows falling on the mind, and ashes of memory dry my mouth. I feel the chasm open in my chest. It is there, the heart concealed within the heart, an emptiness inside me that mourns, that seeps darkness into my daily existence. I grope towards the ache I've buried alive which constantly smoulders, in the hope of sealing up the ancient state, but it won't forget the moment it glowed and longs to be rekindled. To be warm. To come home. The very own dark star that leads me on, that takes me to far-flung dusty corners. Watching. Listening.

'Has your heart sung to you?' the old dervish asks.

'I'm afraid not,' I reply.

'Have you seen the light in your heart?'

Not wishing to disappoint, not wanting to lie, I mutter, 'Not exactly.'

'But you will,' he assures me with a kindly smile. 'You will.'